AF846762

Research Series on the Chinese Dream and China's Development Path

Project Director
Xie Shouguang, President, Social Sciences Academic Press

Series editors
Li Yang, Vice president, Chinese Academy of Social Sciences, Beijing, China
Li Peilin, Vice president, Chinese Academy of Social Sciences, Beijing, China

Academic Advisors
Cai Fang, Gao Peiyong, Li Lin, Li Qiang, Ma Huaide, Pan Jiahua, Pei Changhong, Qi Ye, Wang Lei, Wang Ming, Zhang Yuyan, Zheng Yongnian, Zhou Hong

Drawing on a large body of empirical studies done over the last two decades, the *Research Series on the Chinese Dream and China's Development Path* seeks to provide its readers with in-depth analyses of the past and present, and forecasts for the future course of China's development. Thanks to the adoption of Socialism with Chinese characteristics, and the implementation of comprehensive reform and opening, China has made tremendous achievements in areas such as political reform, economic development, and social construction, and is making great strides towards the realization of the Chinese dream of national rejuvenation. In addition to presenting a detailed account of many of these achievements, the authors also discuss what lessons other countries can learn from China's experience. This series will be an invaluable companion to every researcher who is trying to gain a deeper understanding of the development model, path and experience unique to China.

More information about this series at http://www.springer.com/series/13571

Xuefeng Li · Xuke Liu

Green Development Model of China's Small and Medium-sized Cities

SSAP

Springer

Xuefeng Li
Urban Development and Environmental Research
Chinese Academy of Social Sciences
Beijing
China

Xuke Liu
Chengdu Academy of Social Sciences
Chengdu, Sichuan
China

ISSN 2363-6866 ISSN 2363-6874 (electronic)
Research Series on the Chinese Dream and China's Development Path
ISBN 978-981-13-0778-2 ISBN 978-981-13-0779-9 (eBook)
https://doi.org/10.1007/978-981-13-0779-9

Jointly published with Social Sciences Academic Press, Beijing, China

The print edition is not for sale in China Mainland. Customers from China Mainland please order the print book from: Social Sciences Academic Press.

Library of Congress Control Number: 2018942917

© Social Sciences Academic Press and Springer Nature Singapore Pte Ltd. 2018
This work is subject to copyright. All rights are reserved by the Publishers, whether the whole or part of the material is concerned, specifically the rights of translation, reprinting, reuse of illustrations, recitation, broadcasting, reproduction on microfilms or in any other physical way, and transmission or information storage and retrieval, electronic adaptation, computer software, or by similar or dissimilar methodology now known or hereafter developed.
The use of general descriptive names, registered names, trademarks, service marks, etc. in this publication does not imply, even in the absence of a specific statement, that such names are exempt from the relevant protective laws and regulations and therefore free for general use.
The publishers, the authors and the editors are safe to assume that the advice and information in this book are believed to be true and accurate at the date of publication. Neither the publishers nor the authors or the editors give a warranty, express or implied, with respect to the material contained herein or for any errors or omissions that may have been made. The publishers remains neutral with regard to jurisdictional claims in published maps and institutional affiliations.

Printed on acid-free paper

This Springer imprint is published by the registered company Springer Nature Singapore Pte Ltd.
The registered company address is: 152 Beach Road, #21-01/04 Gateway East, Singapore 189721, Singapore

Series Preface

Since China's reform and opening began in 1978, the country has come a long way on the path of Socialism with Chinese Characteristics, under the leadership of the Communist Party of China. Over 30 years of reform efforts and sustained spectacular economic growth have turned China into the world's second largest economy, and wrought many profound changes in the Chinese society. These historically significant developments have been garnering increasing attention from scholars, governments, and the general public alike around the world since the 1990s, when the newest wave of China studies began to gather steam. Some of the hottest topics have included the so-called "China miracle," "Chinese phenomenon," "Chinese experience," "Chinese path," and the "Chinese model." Homegrown researchers have soon followed suit. Already hugely productive, this vibrant field is putting out a large number of books each year, with Social Sciences Academic Press alone having published hundreds of titles on a wide range of subjects.

Because most of these books have been written and published in Chinese, however, readership has been limited outside China—even among many who study China—for whom English is still the lingua franca. This language barrier has been an impediment to efforts by academia, business communities, and policy-makers in other countries to form a thorough understanding of contemporary China, of what is distinct about China's past and present may mean not only for her future but also for the future of the world. The need to remove such an impediment is both real and urgent, and the *Research Series on the Chinese Dream and China's Development Path* is my answer to the call.

This series features some of the most notable achievements from the last 20 years by scholars in China in a variety of research topics related to reform and opening. They include both theoretical explorations and empirical studies, and cover economy, society, politics, law, culture, and ecology, the six areas in which reform and opening policies have had the deepest impact and farthest-reaching consequences for the country. Authors for the series have also tried to articulate their visions of the "Chinese Dream" and how the country can realize it in these fields and beyond.

All of the editors and authors for the *Research Series on the Chinese Dream and China's Development Path* are both longtime students of reform and opening and recognized authorities in their respective academic fields. Their credentials and expertise lend credibility to these books, each of which having been subject to a rigorous peer-review process for inclusion in the series. As part of the Reform and Development Program under the State Administration of Press, Publication, Radio, Film and Television of the People's Republic of China, the series is published by Springer, a Germany-based academic publisher of international repute, and distributed overseas. I am confident that it will help fill a lacuna in studies of China in the era of reform and opening.

Xie Shouguang

Acknowledgements

After a relatively short gestation period, the *Research Series on the Chinese Dream and China's Development Path* has started to bear fruits. We have, first and foremost, the books' authors and editors to thank for making this possible. And it was the hard work by many people at Social Sciences Academic Press and Springer, the two collaborating publishers, that made it a reality. We are deeply grateful to all of them.

Mr. Xie Shouguang, president of Social Sciences Academic Press (SSAP), is the mastermind behind the project. In addition to defining the key missions to be accomplished by it and setting down the basic parameters for the project's execution, as the work has unfolded, Mr. Xie has provided critical input pertaining to its every aspect and at every step of the way. Thanks to the deft coordination by Ms. Li Yanling, all the constantly moving parts of the project, especially those on the SSAP side, are securely held together, and as well synchronized as is feasible for a project of this scale. Ms. Gao Jing, unfailingly diligent and meticulous, makes sure every aspect of each Chinese manuscript meets the highest standards for both publishers, something of critical importance to all subsequent steps in the publishing process. That high quality if also at times stylistically as well as technically challenging scholarly writing in Chinese has turned into decent, readable English that readers see on these pages is large, thanks to Ms. Liang Fan, who oversees translator recruitment and translation quality control.

Ten other members of the SSAP staff have been intimately involved, primarily in the capacity of in-house editor, in the preparation of the Chinese manuscripts. It is time-consuming work that requires attention to details, and each of them has done this, and is continuing to do this with superb skills. They are, in alphabetical order: Mr. Cai Jihui, Ms. Liu Xiaojun, Mr. Ren Wenwu, Ms. Shi Xiaolin, Ms. Song Yuehua, Mr. Tong Genxing, Ms. Wu Dan, Ms. Yao Dongmei, Ms. Yun Wei, and Ms. Zhou Qiong. In addition, Xie Shouguang and Li Yanling have also taken part in this work.

Mr. Ren Wenwu is the SSAP in-house editor for the current volume.

Our appreciation is also owed to Ms. Li Yan, Mr. Chai Ning, Ms. Wang Lei, and Ms. Xu Yi from Springer's Beijing Representative Office. Their strong support for the SSAP team in various aspects of the project helped to make the latter's work that much easier than it would have otherwise been.

We thank Ms. Xiang Na for translating this book and Ms. Zhang Danfeng for her work as the polisher. The translation and draft polish process benefited greatly from the consistent and professional coordination service by Global Tone Communication Technology Co., Ltd. We thank everyone involved for their hard work.

Last, but certainly not least, it must be mentioned that funding for this project comes from the Ministry of Finance of the People's Republic of China. Our profound gratitude, if we can be forgiven for a bit of apophasis, goes without saying.

Social Sciences Academic Press
Springer

Contents

About the Authors

Xuefeng Li born in 1977, is Associate Research Fellow and Professor at Institute for Urban and Environmental Studies, Chinese Academy of Social Sciences. His primary area of research is urban economics.

Xuke Liu is Assistant Research Fellow and Professor at Chengdu Academy of Social Sciences. His studies focus on development economics.

Part I
Overview

Chapter 1
Green Development: The Choice of Our Times

1 Definition and Implications of Green Development

As a new pattern of development today, green development promotes harmony between human beings and nature, and green economy, a new economic model and the economic choice geared towards ecological progress, places high value on protecting the climate and environment on the one hand, and improving economic efficiency and growth on the other. As Hu Angang points out, green development emphasizes the marriage of economic growth and environmental protection, thus resulting in a more socially beneficial and sustainable approach to development that truly has the needs of the people at the core. According to John Knott, green development is essentially a return to a climatically, geographically, and culturally appropriate way of architecture and building, in combination with new technologies. It requires people to use energy and other resources more wisely, and in the meantime, to protect and help restore the natural ecosystem and the ecological process insomuch as to achieve a symbiosis and synergy between human beings and nature. At the heart of green development is an emphasis on the integration and coordination between economic growth, environmental protection and sustainable use of resources. The concept of green development carries two layers of meaning. First, the economy needs to go green, which means economic growth should never be pursued at the expense of the environment, but be conducive to environment and resource sustainability. Second, greening must be economical in that environment protection efforts should help boost the economy and become a new way to fuel economic growth. The idea of a "resource-saving society and environment-friendly society" as China has proposed is a reflection of these principles of green development. For cities, green development means the coordination between economy, society, resources and environment. While ensuring the steady, sustainable economic growth in cities, efforts must be directed towards minimizing the negative impact of economic activities on resources and environment, and improving public welfare as well as living standards. In the terms "green development", "green" suggests "sus-

© Social Sciences Academic Press and Springer Nature Singapore Pte Ltd. 2018
X. Li and X. Liu, *Green Development Model of China's Small and Medium-sized Cities*, Research Series on the Chinese Dream and China's Development Path,
https://doi.org/10.1007/978-981-13-0779-9_1

tainability" or "sustainable development". In 1987, when presenting the report "Our Common Future" on behalf of the World Commission on Environment and Development, Gro Harlem Brundtland, former Prime Minister of Norway, put forward the concept of sustainable development, arguing that "sustainable development is development that meets the needs of the present without compromising the ability of future generations to meet their own needs". This concept encompasses two key principles: one is the responsibility of one generation for the next and the other is the interdependence of the social, economic and ecological systems. Hence, green development may be understood at least in the following different ways: (1) the social, economic and environmental systems must be well balanced; (2) energy is limited on a global scale; (3) cities' builders, decision-makers, administrators and occupiers should work together and share responsibilities; (4) people should respect nature while safeguarding the interests of humanity; (5) intergeneration equity must be maintained; (6) efficient energy utilization needs to be combined with flexible design and recyclable materials; (7) city residents need to be protected from the threat of pollution.

Industrialization and urbanization are now advancing in depth in China. As the place where industrialization is taking place and where a region's growth pole lies, cities are the engine that drive economic growth.[1] In 2010, 287 cities at and above the prefectural level, which together cover 6.5% of the country's land, had 29% of the national population and contributed 61% to the national GDP. Numerous rural workers flowed into cities that held greater appeal in economic efficiency, employment opportunities, infrastructure, public services, living standards, etc. By the end of 2011, China's urbanization rate exceeded 50% for the first time in history, meaning more people were now living in cities and towns.[2] However, China's economy has yet to move away from the old pattern characterized by high resource consumption, high waste emissions, undue expansion and low efficiency. Cities, as densely populated economic centers, consume a great deal of energy and other resources on a daily basis, and generate enormous amounts of wastes, pollutants and greenhouse gases,[3] which inevitably undermines environmental quality. In 2010, the 287 cities at prefecture level and above accounted for 31.2% of China's residential water consumption and 52% of its power consumption. Among them, the 31 provincial capitals (including municipalities directly under the central government), with only 9.8% of the total population, contributed 16.1, 17.4 and 14.9% respectively of the nation's industrial SO_2 emission, waste water and chemical oxygen demand (COD).

[1]Economist Intelligence Unit, Siemens. Green City Index [R]. http://www.siemens.com/entry/cc/en/greencityindex.html,2011.

[2]Pan Jianhua, Wei Houkai, et al., Annual Report on Urban Development of China—Green Prosperity in the Era of Cities, M, Beijing, Social Sciences Academic Press, 2012.

[3]Zheng Siqi, Rui Wang, Edward L. Glaeser and Matthew E. Kahn. The Greenness of China: Household Carbon Emissions and Urban Development [J]. Journal of Economic Geography, 2010, 10(6):1–32.

In order to address the grim resource and environmental challenges amidst rapid urbanization, China's cities must shift toward a greener development path. Boosting the green economy and developing the green development index as guidelines for action are, therefore, urgently necessary and crucial for our future.[4]

2 Theoretical Underpinning for Green Development

The relationship between human beings and nature is a very essential subject for serious study of traditional Chinese culture. It echoes in some way the modern idea of ecological progress. Classical Marxist theories also contain insight into the conservation of nature and ecology.

With an emphasis on harmony between human beings and nature, ancient thinkers deemed humans a part of nature and the love and protection of, and respect for, nature a cardinal principle. Laozi (philosopher in the Spring and Autumn Period, founder of Taoism) believed that "from the Taoist point of view, there are no such distinctions as high and low", and that "Tao is great; Heaven is great; Earth is great; and Man is also great. There are four greats in our domain, and Man is one part of it", which reflects the idea of human beings and nature as equals. Zen, based on the Buddhist idea of equality between all living creatures, advocated that "all living beings can become Buddhas", which means everything in the universe has the right to exist and prosper.

Confucians were among the first to be awakened to the importance of conservation. They made it clear that, "thick woods attract birds and animals" and "birds will flock to roost in a lush growth of trees that cast a heavy shade", while "birds and animals will desert a rugged and barren hill". Mencius believed that nature would flourish under protection but demise when exposed to undue exploitation. He noted "with proper care and nourishment of nature, there is nothing which will not grow; without nourishment, there is nothing which will not decay away".

The *Zhuangzi* explains the workings of nature—"The Perfect Music first had its response in the affairs of men, and was conformed to the principles of Heaven; it indicated the action of the five virtues, and corresponded to the spontaneity (apparent in nature). After this, it showed the blended distinctions of the four seasons, and the grand harmony of all things;—the succession of those seasons one after another, and the production of things in their proper order". Xunzi maintains "nature is governed but by the law of its own—neither does it exist for the integrity of Yao (a saint in ancient China) nor does it perish for the tyranny of Jie (an infamous tyrant in Xia Dynasty)". Taoism highlighted "the law of the Tao is its being what it is", with emphasis on respecting laws, applying nature's laws in people's daily life and, on the basis of that, achieving the harmony between people and between individuals and

[4]Li Xiaoxi and Pan Jiancheng, Establishment of China Green Development Index—Brief introduction of "Comparison at Provincial Level of the 2010 Annual Report of China Green Development Index", Review of Economic Research, 2011 (2):36–54.

society. This is exactly what Laozi promoted, as he put it, "Man takes his law from the Earth; the Earth takes its law from Heaven; Heaven takes its law from the Tao. The law of the Tao is its being what it is".

Marxism maintains that "man himself is a product of nature, which has developed in and along with its environment", so natural environment itself is an indispensable condition for human existence and development. Marx examined the conversion of substances and energy between human beings and nature and advocated a virtuous cycle of development that would promote natural balance. He commented on the environmental issues back then, saying "So far as their (excretions) utilization is concerned, there is an enormous waste of them in the capitalist economy. In London, for instance, they find no better use for the excretion of four and a half million human beings than to contaminate the Thames with it at heavy expense". Engels went one step further, believing men should exercise proper restraint in exploiting nature. He warned that "let us not, however, flatter ourselves overmuch on account of our human victories over nature. For each such victory nature takes its revenge on us… The people who, in Mesopotamia, Greece, Asia Minor and elsewhere, destroyed the forests to obtain cultivable land, never dreamed that by removing along with the forests the collecting centers and reservoirs of moisture they were laying the basis for the present forlorn state of those countries…that we, with flesh, blood and brain, belong to nature, and exist in its midst, and that all our mastery of it consists in the fact that we have the advantage over all other creatures of being able to learn its laws and apply them correctly."

In summary, both traditional Chinese culture and classic Marxist works provide a significant ideological and theoretical base for ecological progress.

3 The Urgency of Green Development

With mounting pressure on resources and environment as well as increasingly grim ecological consequences of industrialization, countries around the globe began to rethink their policies in the 1960s. Several epoch-making publications including *Silent Spring*, *The Limits of Growth* and *Declaration on Human Environment* served to awaken people's ecological awareness. In 1987, the report Our Common Future released by the World Commission on Environment and Development (WCED) defined the concept of sustainable development for the first time in history. In 1992, the Rio Declaration on Environment and Development was signed at the Earth Summit. It included the idea that would later become a global consensus—"development today must not threaten the needs of present and future generations". There is an increasing awareness among the people of the importance of concerted efforts of humanity to protect the earth's ecological system. Ecological and environmental issues have now drawn unprecedented attention, and to tackle them, the international society has worked closely together. The United Nations Framework Convention on Climate Change (UNFCCC), Kyoto Protocol, Montreal Protocol, Bali Road Map and international cooperation under these instruments are leading the human society into a brand new era of ecological progress. The annual United Nations Climate Change Conference, which had been held in Copenhagen, Cancun, Durban, Doha and Warsaw and would be in Lima in near future, has become one of the most important multi-lateral negotiation mechanisms and the trend setter in sustainable development. Within China, there is a universal consensus on gearing economic and social development towards resource efficiency and ecological progress. This is not only due to the huge pressures on resources and environment but also because of the need to survive global competition.

China faces grim resource and environmental challenges, which the 18th CPC National Congress report encapsulates as "increasing resource constraints, severe environmental pollution and a deteriorating ecosystem". With a huge population but a weak economic foundation and very limited resource per capita, China took only decades (that is, since the founding of the People's Republic of China in 1949, especially after the adoption of the policy of reform and opening up) to complete the industrialization that had taken Western countries one or two hundred years. Despite rapid growth of productivity, the process also brought severe resource and environmental issues. In recent years, China has remained a big mineral and energy importer that increasingly depends on foreign trade. Limited space in many cities caused a considerable amount of agricultural and ecological land to be converted to urban uses. Many resource-intensive cities, mired in social and economic difficulties, are in urgent need of economic transformation. In 2012, China's COD emissions totaled 24.237 million metric tons, and ammonia nitrogen emissions 2.536 million metric tons, both ranking first in the world. Zhai Qing, Vice Minister of Environment Protection, believes that water environment would see fundamental changes only if China cut its water pollutant emissions by 30–50%. *The 2013 Air Quality Report Covering Key Regions like Beijing-Tianjin-Hebei Region, Yangtze River Delta, and Pearl River Delta, as well as Provincial Capital Cities and Municipalities Directly under the Central Government* published by the Ministry of Environment Protection (MEP) finds that among the 74 cities monitored throughout 2013, only 3 cities—Haikou, Zhoushan and Lhasa—had the annual mean concentration of pollutants generally under the minimum thresholds (meeting the Class II standards), and all other cities were above these thresholds, with Beijing-Tianjin-Hebei region most polluted. A series of safety incidents (such as contaminated soil and rice) draw extensive attention towards soil pollution. *The 2013 Investigation Report on China's Soil Pollutions* jointly published by the MEP and Ministry of Land and Resources (MLR) indicates such problems as severe soil pollution in some regions, worrying quality of farmland and striking soil problems in deserted industrial and mining land. Environmental complaints, appeals, disputes and protests have been on the rise in recent years in different parts of the country. In those places which reported a high number of such incidents in a short period of time, hundreds or even tens of thousands of people were involved, showing growing public discontent about deteriorating environment. However, government authorities are very often ill-prepared for such incidents and sometimes would resort to the wrong solution. Meng Wei, president of the Chinese Research Academy of Environmental Sciences and academician of the Chinese Academy of Engineering, argues that China is now a heavily polluted country plagued by old and new problems of pollution, the complexity and severity of which are unprecedented in the world's history. China is now experiencing environmental issues that had sprouted and developed in one or two hundred years in developed countries, and many of the issues are mixed, compounded and having a lot to do with the economic structure. Overall, the pressure from a deteriorating environment is mounting.[5]

Green development is also driven by the need to boost a country's international competitiveness and influence. Since the 2008 financial crisis, environment has become an increasingly significant issue in international dialogues. On the one hand, developed countries which are more capital-abundant and technologically advanced have tried to use green trade barriers as a tool to gain the upper hand in the global competition. Regardless of their historic responsibility for climate changes and the imperative needs of the developing world for socioeconomic advance, the advanced economies would ask the less advanced to assume the same amount of responsibility during international climate negotiations. When trade disputes with China arise, they would restrict the sales of Chinese products on their markets, claiming the production was energy-intensive and caused excessive greenhouse gas emissions. If we in China could not leverage technology to cut energy consumptions and mitigate the environmental impact of our social and economic activities, we will finally get ourselves in a disadvantageous position in negotiations and can do little about trade barriers. Apart from these, the grim environmental challenges have also compromised China's reputation on the international arena and discouraged the inflow of international capital and talent. With shrinking resources and rising costs, China's position as the world's factory is being challenged by Southeast Asian as well as African countries. Environmental pollutions are deterring foreigners from working in China. The problem is getting so serious that quite a few international companies have to offer "smog subsidies" to keep their expat employees in Beijing and Shanghai.

Thus improving the environment is an urgent priority for us as it determines whether our development is sustainable and whether we can compete internationally under new circumstances. Just as Xi Jinping has stressed, "we should be fully aware of the urgency and difficulty of protecting the environment and reducing pollution as well as the significance and necessity of improving the environment."

---

[5]Gu Ruizhen, Wu Jingjing and Luo Sha, *Xi Jinping: Building A Beautiful China with Ecological Progress—the 7th Discussion on How to Fully Understand and Implement the Essentials of Xi Jinping's Keynote Speeches,* http://www.wenming.cn/xj_pd/ssrd/201307/t20130722_1359815.shtml.

Chapter 2
Green Urban Development—Goals and Requirements

Green urban development does not only mean actions to protect ecological environment, but also efforts to base these actions on optimal principles aimed at enhancing urban functions, to instill the idea that productivity is inseparable from ecological environment and in this sense protecting and improving ecological environment is a way to protect and improve productivity, to incorporate ecological progress into every aspect of and the whole process of economic, political, cultural and social developments, and to build new-type cities that are ecologically harmonious, people-oriented, multi-functional and with their own unique characteristics.

1 Objective I—Ecologically Harmonious Green Cities

Under the principles of promoting ecological progress, a new type of city should have its development principles centered around ecological units. Like a living creature, the city should have a more ecofriendly process of metabolism in accordance with the natural course of urban development, increase the green and open spaces within and become a "freely breathing" existence. Urban development and its spatial design ought to be more about meeting the combined requirements of human beings, economy and ecological environment, than expansions and increases of components in a mathematical sense.

Urban planning and development should follow the following basic ecological principles: first, the principle of co-existing and counteracting, which means all spatial components of a city should be well coordinated together; secondly, the principle of best fitting functions, which means its spatial scale and structural design should aim for the optimal utilization of urban resources; thirdly, the recycling principle, meaning urban development should take into account the renewal and reuse of urban space and other resources; fourthly, the symbiotic principle, meaning the interdependence and mutual benefits between urban zones utilized for various purposes.

© Social Sciences Academic Press and Springer Nature Singapore Pte Ltd. 2018
X. Li and X. Liu, *Green Development Model of China's Small and Medium-sized Cities*, Research Series on the Chinese Dream and China's Development Path,
https://doi.org/10.1007/978-981-13-0779-9_2

In the era of promoting ecological progress, the key to reconciling the relationship between urban development and natural environment is a shift away from "changing nature" toward "developing a close affinity with nature", respecting nature and fitting in nature, with emphasis on ecological progress. Cities are supposed to grow naturally in the soil of their geological locations, maintaining a balanced relation with natural environment, both ecologically and morphologically, instead of intruding upon its natural surroundings. The men-made cities and the great nature are interdependent, and together, they constitute the ecological system of primal environment and secondary environment.

Primary conditions and constructing environment are different for cities, so the features and standards of green urban development also vary. However, generally speaking, green cities ought to meet two criteria—sound ecological environment and scientific spatial design, for which the specific requirements are shown in Table 1.

An essential part of green urban development is to establish a multi-layer, all-encompassing landscape engineering system, with special efforts directed at developing a green spatial system that consists of "green centers", "green shafts", "green corridors", "green belts" and "green overpasses" and increasing public vegetated area per capita. With limited stock of land for urban development, it is of unique significance to encourage vertical planting and increase rooftop gardening. The green roof policy in Germany serves as a good example for China.

Green Roof Policy in Germany

Germany is one of the countries boasting the most well-developed, most effective green roof technologies in the world. Initially, the green roof gardens in Germany was merely an environmental subject under discussion. By middle 1980s when environmental organizations were first incorporated into local governments, the subject of promoting rooftop gardens was brought up on the agenda.

When the construction of rooftop gardens was gradually included into local construction norms, there were still many government officials having difficulty understanding it. They were concerned that whether developers would be willing to build green roofs and that the increased construction costs might push them away to build in other cities. However, it turned out that roof gardens were not as costly as expected and also the benefit of good reputation that came with them saw roof gardens well-received by developers. With the continued expansion of environmental organizations and the increasing environmental awareness among the public, rooftop gardens were increasingly popular.

In some cities and states of Germany, local governments have realized the benefits of rooftop garden and started subsidizing its construction—15 euros per square meter. In Germany, the construction cost of a rooftop garden larger than 500 m^2 can easily be under 15 euros per square meters, which normally takes the form of open, perennial green rooftop gardens within a specific area.

Table 1 Ecologically harmonious green cities

1st level objective	2nd level objective	3rd level objective	Specific requirements
Ecologically harmonious green cities	Sound ecological environment	Topography	Keep the original topographical features and the primary geomorphological features as much as possible
		Vegetation	Reserve the original vegetation and protect primary vegetation areas
		Water	Protect natural water bodies, build water-conserving cities and protect wetland
		Atmosphere	Strict control of air pollution and ensure a blue, clean sky
		Noise	Quiet residential areas separated by greenbelts
	Scientific spatial design	Spatial design	An affinity with mountains and water by keeping them in their natural conditions
		Corridor and greening	A multi-layer greening system with the combination of green centers, green corridors and green belts, with a touch of green in every space and green design for building elevations and the fifth façade
		Capacity	Restrict capacity by restricting physical layout including the constructing capacity of every land block, section and belt, with combination of high density in parts and low density on the whole
		Vegetation areas in parks	A high proportion of urban parks, eco-parks, and tourist recreation areas, with the city blended in parks and featuring easy access
		Traffic and municipal administration	Rapid transport system underground, with shared pipeline, in vertical cities

2 Objective II—People-Oriented, Harmonious Cities

Urban development in the era of industrial civilization often puts great importance on grandiose standards, resulting in grandiose buildings that are improperly massive but without any regard to human needs; urban design, from a micro-perspective, pays excessive attention to details, which results in limited vision. Due to the disagreement between macro and micro designs, urban planning in that era inevitably features some spatial incongruities such as urban layout defined by roads, inconvenient functional zoning, and excessive enormous high-rises that are completely out of tune with their surroundings.

In the era of promoting ecological progress, the development of new type cities means advocating urban planning defined by communities, street blocks and neighborhood. In particular, the mixed-function communities defined by walking distance unit instead of driving distance unit is a valuable model for us. The effectiveness of such communities speaks to the fact that community building standards is in agreement with human-based criteria and these criteria should be the basic gauge measuring if a city is habitable. The development of people-oriented, harmonious cities must follow the most fundamental principle, that is, to put great importance on and meet the "human-based criteria". The essence of the above theory is that urban planning and development should be more focused on human needs, taking into account human criteria, human needs, emotions and feelings, with the design of various facilities matching proportionally to the size of human body and meeting the needs of human existence, collective behavior, traveling, resting, entertaining as well as psychological needs, and should enhance the union of human living space with the nature and aim to construct a most habitable environment full of unique characteristics.

Human needs are diverse, varied in different phases and confined by level of productivity, material accumulation, environmental capacity and level of social development. Currently, the first level objective of building people-oriented, harmonious cities means exemplary living environment and intensive utilization of space, which, to be more specific, is to improve urban living comfort, provide sufficient employment, remove the development barriers between urban and rural areas and reduce the municipal operation costs. Table 2 gives a list of basic objectives of people-oriented, harmonious cities and their corresponding specific requirements.

For a long time in history, most Chinese cities have focused on economic growth with little attention to social development, and emphasized industrial development with little regard to people's living standards, resulting in many prevalent problems like huge debts incurred by construction of residential areas, low proportion of land utilized for residential purpose and improper construction principles for residential areas. Drawing on advanced foreign experience in combination with actual conditions of Chinese cities, it is evident that construction of residential areas must be positioned as a higher priority in building people-oriented, harmonious cities.

Table 2 People-oriented, harmonious cities

1st level objective	2nd level objective	3rd level objective	Specific requirements
People-oriented, harmonious cities	Living comfort	Living standards	Safety, comfort, and pleasure
		Environment quality	Healthy, pollution-free and little noises
		Green awareness	Sustainable living style and consumption
		Spatial planning standards	Reflecting human-based criteria, objecting to grandiose construction standards
		Spiritual criteria	Emancipation of mind, restore of humanity
	Full employment	Jobs	Multi-dimensional and multi-layer
		Quality	Short distance between home and workplace or easy access to a good transport system, relatively high wages
	Removal of urban and rural barriers	Spatial design	Close urban and rural ties, spatial continuity and agreeable landscapes
		Rural areas	New-type modern villages surrounding cities, with unique characteristics and living comfort no less than urban living environment
		Rural employment	Urban agriculture and eco-tourism
	Reduction of municipal operation costs	Intensive utilization of space	Compact, organic and mixed spatial arrangement
		Maintenance and administration	Digital administration, easy maintenance of municipal facilities and encouraging community autonomy
		Urban renovation	Effective combination of the new and the old, reflecting historical continuity

Basic Requirements for Construction of Residential Areas

First, to ensure sufficient land supply for residential area construction. Land for residential areas must be allotted strictly in accordance with national standards, and its proportion much be increased gradually in line with social and economic development.

Secondly, to set a proper construction intensity for residential areas. The construction of residential areas should be mainly within the low to medium intensity range, in combination with a sound open spatial system and a good transportation system, forming a habitable living atmosphere and proper spatial arrangement standards. The construction standards for a harmonious city should be based on human needs: to create a pleasant living space and environment by proper land allotment and boundary control, to increase public space like vegetated areas and improve accessibility of transport hubs, to establish a transport system and spatial arrangement favorable to walking activities, to advocate individuality and uniqueness of neighborhood, land blocks and buildings, and to create a pleasant, conspicuously distinctive public environment.

Thirdly, special efforts directed toward developing hybrid communities and achieving the unity of various social classes. A mix of diverse housing types in the same land lot, including proper proportions of economically affordable housing, public rental housing and low-rent housing, which will unite people from different social classes and interest groups, prevent social polarization and achieve community harmony. In addition, efforts should be directed towards developing commercial facilities amid residential areas, emphasizing construction of supporting infrastructure and reducing residents' travelling needs for daily consumption.

Fourthly, to expand the distance between municipal roads and between neighborhood roads, keep neighborhood roads at proper width, build all-day vehicle-free promenade that consists of green corridors and arcades, set up dedicated bikeways, encourage green travelling means such as walking and bicycling.

3 Objective III—Multi-functional Organic Cities

Urban development in the context of industrial civilization puts great emphasis on the pursuit of rationality. Whether it is Sir Ebenezer Howard's garden cities featuring simplicity and order or the various visions of future cities, at the heart of these ideas is the rationalist construction of a new global order for the world's cities. However, amid the globalization trend, cities vary across regions and cultures; they differ greatly in historical and current conditions as well as level of development. They are diverse, rather than homogeneous, even under the growing influence of the information age, with each section of any city having its own functions, internal structure and spatial formation. Therefore, neither the glass and concrete jungle nor the rational city zoning works at a time when ecological progress is being stressed like never before. Efforts must be directed towards "creating an integrated, multi-functional environment", one that is an organic continuity in which different departments and elements of a city are brought together based on the principle of diversity. This open, comprehensive urban system—a mixture of ambiguity, eclecticism, complexity and contradiction—is best exemplified by an organic city. The pursuit of diversity and disorder in the era of promoting ecological progress is essentially a celebration of differences and tolerance, reflecting functional layering, structural openness and flexibility, through which harmony is achieved out of disorder.

Green development and ecological progress is a majestic goal and the pursuit of this goal will be a long process that requires continuous efforts. During this process, especially important for small and medium-sized cities is to coordinate the relation between urbanization and industrialization—both the main drivers behind urban development. Industrialization provides strong momentum for urbanization and urbanization will in return enhance the extend and level of industrialization; both are equally important and indispensable. This, as an essential embodiment of scientific development concept, is the cognitive basis for a correct view of the relationship between urbanization and industrialization. The construction of multi-functional organic cities is the underlying strategy based on the drivers of urban development, and the idea of diverse functions is a significant part of new-type cities in the era of promoting ecological progress, both pointing the same objective. Instead of emphasizing industrialization alone as we did in the past, the idea of multiple functions for cities mean, on top of promoting industrialization, efforts should be directed towards developing cultural, educational, scientific and technological and social functions, enhancing core competing capabilities and providing various possibilities and plenty of room for further evolution of cities' functions.

Relative independence and a complete set of adequate functions for cities are increasingly emphasized in modern urban development. The development of organic cities must underscore the relative independence of different functions, meaning an organic city should be a comprehensive municipal compound of geographic zones, different from the single-purpose industrial parks or the single-function satellite cities (e.g. commuter towns) in the early stage of urbanization. Organic cities not only provide sound dwellings, living and entertaining facilities, but also sufficient employment opportunities, and only in this way can cities have self-balancing and self-improving capabilities to realize sustainable development.

Based on the above theory, it can be concluded that in the process of becoming multi-functional organic cities, small and medium-sized cities must focus on strengthening their sustainable competitiveness and seeking various routes for sustainable urban development. Therefore, multi-functional, organic cities should set the objectives and meet the specific requirements as listed in Table 3.

Table 3 Multi-functional, organic cities

1st level objective	2nd level objective	3rd level objective	Specific requirements
Multi-functional, organic cities	Strong industrial functions	Dominating industry	New and high technologies
		Industry clusters	Industry clusters full of competitiveness
		Tertiary industry	Expand to both high-end and low-end sectors, provide employment and focus on production-oriented service industries
		Agriculture	Shift to green, sunrise industries such as metropolitan agriculture, tourist agriculture and eco-tourism
	Cultural and educational functions that advocate equality and competition	Social equality	Encourage mixed residential complexes, indiscriminative provision of services, end hierarchical segregation and build new-type neighborhood relation
		Competition and support	Encourage entrepreneurship and tolerance for failure, and set up a complete social relief, disaster prevention and mitigation system
		Education	Develop world-class education and vocational education
		Cultural industry	Establish cultural industrial base, develop distinctive cultural industry clusters, and provide cultural and sport facilities that are accessible by the public
	Strong function of amassing production factors	Talent	Create the image of front-runner cities, attract capable persons, offer training opportunities to unskilled laborers and increase the stock of human capital
		Industries	Attract new and high tech companies, develop industry clusters and seek new industrial growth areas

(continued)

Table 3 (continued)

1st level objective	2nd level objective	3rd level objective	Specific requirements
	Highly effective administrative functions	Government functions	Improve the efficiency of government administration and build a service-oriented government
	Easy internal and external access	Internal and external connection	Highly efficient and easy-to-access transportation system

4 Objective IV—Cities with Unique Characteristics and Charms

Eliel Saarinen, a renown Finnish architect, once said that "let me see your city and I can tell you what the residents pursue in culture". In the era of promoting ecological progress, it is required that efforts be devoted to the design and implementation of every detail in every corner to build a unique, appealing city with a distinctive image full of strong regional features and striking ethnic expressions and also to the nurturing and promotion of the city's own spirit, which will be a representation of the city's refined taste and choice of humanistic values.

In the pursuit of ecological progress, the emphasis is first on the paramount importance of eco-environment and then the people-oriented principle. It is also stressed that efforts should be directed to build uniquely appealing cities with their own characteristics while keeping and promoting regional traditions, regional culture and geographic environment.

Historical continuity is essential for a city to keep its lasting charm. Thus, in the era of promoting ecological progress, the modern world must be taken from a historic perspective, and cities viewed as museums where various cultures converge and accrues. Rather than one-sided pursuit of a retro style, the stress on the contextualism in cities' spatial structure should reflect the desire of modern and future societies to reinstate traditions and humanity. While transforming old cities, it is as important to preserve historical and cultural heritages as to optimize their spatial structure.

The pursuit of unique characteristics for a city in essence points to the question that the city and its residents constantly ponder over—"who am I?", without leading to any indicative answer, which happens to fall in line with the requirement of contextualism. The methodology of contextualism is to keep such a train of thoughts over the above question in the city's spatial structuring and to present the answer in various spatial components including streets, squares, signs and buildings, constituting a spatial reflection of the answer to that question. Therefore, what contextualism requires is by no means simply conserving historical heritages, but covers a wider range of issues related to a city's culture, spirit, image building and development, so much so that its residents and visitors can clearly discern its unique spirit and quality by assessing these spatial symbols and thus interpret the indirect answer to the question of "who am I".

There are three aspects to work on in order to build cities with unique characteristics and charms, including: to explore deeply and preserve historical inheritances, to grasp precisely the spirit of the city and to design the city's image following a scientific methodology. Table 4 shows the specific requirements for achieving this goal.

Table 4 Cities with unique characteristics and charms

1st level objective	2nd level objective	3rd level objective	Specific requirements
Cities with unique characteristics and charms	Historical inheritances	Cultural preservation	Restoration and conservation of tangible cultural heritages (cultural relics), and preservation and inheritance of intangible cultural heritages
		Presentation of culture	Construction of history museums
		Propagation of culture	Education of traditions for local residents, distribution of knowledge on regional history and culture through public media
	City image	Spatial landscape	Rhythmic spacing and undulating skyline
		Spatial sequence	Instead of simply using traffic lines as structural axis, the main axis penetrates through a series of buildings, with a transition zone between the city's new and old parts that are in orderly sequence
		Downtown area	Strikingly distinctive downtown area and major hubs, as well as landmark buildings reflective of the city's image

(continued)

Table 4 (continued)

1st level objective	2nd level objective	3rd level objective	Specific requirements
		Roads	An easily discernable road network, a public transportation system that suits people's needs, an all-day land traffic setting for both pedestrians and cyclers
		Signage system	Street design elements and signage (e.g. signs, sculptures, ornaments and advertisements) that are unified in style, full of cultural expressions and reflect the refined taste of the city
		Entries and exits	Design of municipal landmarks that fully demonstrate the city's image
	City spirit	Fully open space	The most valuable land should be designed into fully open areas without any surrounding walls and barriers; the green urban land system and recreation spaces should be open to the public; avoiding any open space that is improperly huge
		Semi-open space	The design of neighborhood units should focus on semi-open space and a display of a friendly atmosphere

Chapter 3
Key Areas of Green Development for Small and Medium-sized Cities

For small and medium-sized cities, achieving green urban development and ecological progress requires integrated planning with a focus on making breakthroughs in areas such as continuous industrial upgrade, developing green transportation, improving community construction and promoting a new type of urbanization.

1 Boosting Continuous Industrial Upgrade

Continuous industrial upgrade is the primary driver behind urban development, the essential material base for ecological progress and the unavoidable requirement in building a resource-conserving and environmental friendly society.

Against the backdrop of ecological progress, industrial development in medium and small-size cities should be based on at least two premises: first, relatively low resource consumption, light pollution and minimized impact on local or surrounding resources and environment; secondly, relatively high running efficiency. Given the actual conditions of these cities, there are two more noteworthy points: the first is to respect the existing development foundation and give full play to local competitive advantages, and the second is to make meticulous choice of economic growth model and pillar industries from the perspective of boosting a city's sustaining competitiveness.

The strategy of industrial upgrading is mainly aimed at gradually establishing a circular ecologically sustainable industry system that is pivoted on highly efficient resource utilization and recycling, that features low consumption, low emission and high efficiency, and that is in accord with the idea of sustainable and scientific development, and finally achieving the shift of growth model away from high consumption and high pollution towards resource conservation and environmental friendliness.

To actively promote green industrial development in small and medium-sized cities, the major tasks include: (1) to actively develop ecologically sustainable metropolitan agriculture, i.e. to develop agricultural parks, boutique agriculture and

© Social Sciences Academic Press and Springer Nature Singapore Pte Ltd. 2018

X. Li and X. Liu, *Green Development Model of China's Small and Medium-sized Cities*, Research Series on the Chinese Dream and China's Development Path,
https://doi.org/10.1007/978-981-13-0779-9_3

agricultural tourism, to build multifunctional, high quality, modern metropolitan agricultural sci-tech parks with the integration of characteristic, boutique production, scientific research, agricultural education, entertainment and tourism, and to steer agriculture towards a modernized model of "eco-agriculture" that is based on science and technology, is friendly to environment, resource-intensive and with the incorporation of tourism. (2) to build new and high-tech industries and high-end manufacturing bases, i.e. with the aim of green industries, green enterprises, green products and green technologies, efforts should be directed towards nurturing bellwethers of ecologically sustainable new and high-tech industrial parks, greatly strengthening the capabilities of research, design and innovation, and achieving scale economy of new and high-tech industries that features high value added, high technology, low energy consumption and low pollution. (3) to accelerate the development of modern services industry, i.e. to base its development on the functions and features of modern cities, promote new types of business, advocate green consumption ideas, build shopping malls and a services network that suits well people's daily needs, etc.

As industrial development is the base for enhancing a city's competitiveness, the core of building up persistent competitiveness is to take precaution against economic risks and promote continuous industrial upgrade. So how can we constantly strengthen a city's competitiveness and ensure its sustainable development through industrial upgrading? Lessons learnt from the development history of many cities show that a diversified economic system is an essential way to maintain a stable economy while continuous industrial upgrade is at the heart of ensuring persistent competitiveness.

Singular industrial structure versus diversified economic system: Japan's Tsukuba versus America's Irvine

Tsukuba in Japan is a world famous scientific research center comparable to the Silicon Valley in California, America. It is home to nearly 140 scientific research institutes owned by the nation or large organizations, including RIKEN (Institute of Physical and Chemical Research), KEK (High Energy Accelerator Research Organization), JATAFF institute (Japan Association for Agriculture, Forestry and Fisheries), National Institute for Environmental Studies, etc. It has attracted 30% of Japan's research organizations and 40% of researchers. However, with the downturn of virtual economy in the 20th century, Tsukuba has been mired in a plight.

Irvine city was developed on the basis of Irvine Farmland. With a balanced development strategy, the city has struck a perfect balance between municipal development, environment, level of living comfort, etc. The city boasts a diversified industrial structure dominated by high technologies that make it less susceptible to risks. In the meantime, its sustainable development is also supported by convenient transportation, market-oriented operational mechanisms, a complete educational and commercial system, competitive wages and sufficient employment opportunities, etc.

In conclusion, a diversified industrial structure with strong mainstay industries can help enhance a city's ability to withstand risks.

Continuous industrial upgrade is essential: the development history of Hsinchu, Taiwan

The Hsinchu Science Park, one of the most successful science parks ever built in Asia, consists of several scenic villages, boasting stretching, undulant mountains and pleasant landscapes. But deep in these mountains situated a group of companies with the most advanced technologies in Taiwan. The Hsinchu Science Park has unfathomable influences on the high-tech industry of Taiwan; most of local technological barons are originated from Hsinchu. Many tycoons in Taiwan lined their pockets first in Hsinchu, including Zhang Zhongmou (CEO of Taiwan Semiconductor Manufacturing Co., Ltd.), Stan Shih (founder of Acer Group), Cao Xingcheng (Chairman of the Board for United Microelectronics Corporation), Gao Cixuan (founder of D-Link Corporation), etc., who have created their own as well as Taiwan's economic legendary. In the PC era when 286, 386, 486 and 586 computers thrived one after another, Taiwan used to be the world's largest manufacturing base for computer cases, displayers, keyboards and mainboards.

Taiwan now is no longer the only top player on the PC market; many regions and countries have joined the feast. Meanwhile, the production value of PC and related equipment has plunged, with some big companies like IBM shedding their PC business completely. With PC business slumping continuously, Taiwan, once the OEM base, is losing a large quantity of orders. The past nearly 60 years have seen Taiwan striving for economic growth without paying attention to education on humanities. It is an industrial and commercial society dominated by utilitarianism that takes aim at economic profits and an official career. One of the main challenges faced by Taiwan's sci-tech companies in their way to industrial upgrade is lack of outstanding talents for industrial engineering and such talents can be the trump card for them to emerge from the life-and-death competitions with the world's tier-1 companies. Only a few of Taiwan's universities have set up the major of industrial design and engineering, which are not very popular among students. Years have gone by without establishing a human resource supply chain that can support the industry's development. Meanwhile, design is not merely an issue of appearance, but also reflects the comprehensive aesthetic taste derived from social conditions including culture, level of economic development, knowledge and art. This is what constrains the upgrading of Taiwan's high-tech industry.

Conclusion: Efforts should be directed towards developing technologically advanced manufacturing industry, providing favorable conditions for local enterprises to enhance R&D and innovation, guiding capable enterprises to gradually establish their own brands, and gradually getting rid of the growth model that is solely dependent on cost control.

In the process of industrial upgrade, the role of government is particularly essential in the following areas:

(1) To improve government efficacy, e.g. to offer more transparent, information-based government administration, enhance operational efficiency and reduce the time spent by enterprises in dealing with government.
(2) To prepare properly and implement strictly industrial development plans and complete the entry and exit mechanisms for enterprises, e.g. to establish a comprehensive assessment system for new projects and select new investors strictly following the standards of "two lows and three highs" (low energy consumption, low power consumption, high technology, high value added and high contribution rate to tax revenues), to give full play to the aggregation effect of bellwether enterprises, introduce a group of small and medium-sized companies with great potentials and whose functions will supplement and support those big ones, forming a complete industrial chain.
(3) To reduce commercial costs and create an environment encouraging and advocating entrepreneurship, e.g. to offer low-cost office buildings, necessary preferential taxes and other essential public services to enterprises and individuals with great potentials.

2 Great Efforts Towards Green Transportation

The transportation system is the arteries of a city, which directly determines how efficiently the city runs. For small and medium-sized cities, the development of green transportation is absolutely necessary to avoid serious traffic jams that are common in big cities as well as the embarrassing situation of "wide roads but few traffic".

The development of green transportation means to establish a proactive, ecologically sustainable, well-performing green transportation system for guiding and balancing the generation, composition and operation of a city's needs for highly efficient transportation, to strive for a composition of transportation needs for elevated quality and aggregated scale, to provide smooth, safe, comfortable and clean transportation services and to successfully build an ecologically sustainable transportation system featuring people-oriented services, computer-based operation, and rapid transit.

First, green guidelines based on transportation needs. As mentioned earlier, green transportation requires quality elevation and scale aggregation of such needs. Here, "quality elevation" means to prevent inefficient or low efficiency transportation needs and stimulate effective or highly efficient needs. "Scale aggregation" means to guide the generation of transportation needs so that their spatial distribution will follow certain patterns in scale, which will serve well in organizing and providing green public transportation. When it comes to transportation planning, it should provide guidelines of transportation network at a macro level in line with urban development plans, steering the distribution patterns of urban population and industries in a way that will generate proper distribution of transportation needs well suited to the formation of green transportation network. Based on the green principle, transportation plans should provide such macro level guidelines in favor of urban development, elevate the quality of urban transportation needs, promote the development of highly educated, localized population, guide urban industries to achieve upgrading to high-end ones and help achieve balance between urban employment, residence and services. Following the green principle, new cities should construct communities and facilities in a pattern that fits the public transportation network, with compact neighborhood design. Throughout the whole process of urban development, a one-vote veto rule should apply to approvals relevant to transportation, which means no approval should be granted to those projects (e.g. construction of residential areas) that do not meet the requirements of transportation planning or fail to pass the traffic impact assessment.

Secondly, green organization for the provision of transportation services. Green transportation refers to the provision of "smooth, safe, comfortable and clean" transportation services. "Smooth" means to ensure the best transport means easily accessible by residents so that by travelling on the public transportation means they can complete any point-to-point trip within a certain amount of time, (e.g. 30 min for trips between two urban locations or an hour between urban and rural locations). "Safe" means to minimize the number of traffic accidents. "Comfortable" means to provide relaxing, sound transport conditions. "Clean" means to reduce pollutions from the transportation system. Efforts should also be directed towards planning, organization and management for construction of transport facilities and provision of transport means, with the aim to achieve extensively accessible, orderly, safe, comfortable green transportation with low energy consumption and low pollution.

Thirdly, green management of traffic flows, i.e. effective temporal and spatial arrangement of transportation needs to maximize traffic performance, minimize operational costs, maximize energy saving and emission reduction and minimize traffic pollution. It is necessary to utilize modern digital and information technologies to realize green control over urban traffic flows, provide computerized facilitation for traffic flows, and establish an all-round transportation information system which mainly includes five major subsystems: urban express way monitoring information system, vehicle speed information system, optimized traffic signal control system, intersection surveillance system and integrated traffic management system.

Fourthly, to build an extensively accessible and resource-intensive urban road network. The urban road network construction should be extensively accessible as well as resource-intensive. The road network should extend as far as the city spreads, with road construction ahead of urban development and ensuring certain scales of length and coverage. The road network planning should incorporate a chessboard grid layout without any T-junctions or dead ends and guarantee all vehicles can drive freely around the whole city. The road construction should follow the planning based on the expectation of the actual scale of transportation needs. A road network of overly low density will not be able to ensure traffic-flow efficiency of human and goods, causing traffic jams. So the urban road network construction should meet certain standards and set up the lower threshold of construction density to satisfy the current and future transportation needs. On the other hand, the road network construction should never go beyond what is actually required. An overly dense road network will expropriate more land than needed and cause waste of resources. In particular, wide roads within CBD areas put excess distance between business operations, create sporadic distribution of services providers and split up the services market, which hampers the development of commerce and services sectors. So a proper upper threshold of road network density is also necessary.

Fifthly, to prioritize the development of public transportation. At the heart of green transportation is to prioritize and utilize public transportation, adopting low rate fares and enhancing public transportation services between political centers, business centers and major residential areas as well as public transportation between urban and rural areas. Wherever possible, municipal government should strive to expand the public transportation services to every village. Efforts should be directed towards strengthening the connection between the city and its surrounding cities as well as the major cities at a higher level of jurisdiction, with the aim to achieve an integrated public transportation system with these cities.

Sixthly, non-motorized transportation planning based on people's needs. Walking and bicycling are the primary as well as the ultimate ways for residents to travel around, and also the most environment friendly and healthy. Encouraging these two means of transportation is a significant objective of the green transportation strategy. To do so, it is necessary to set up pedestrian and bicycle lanes that suit people's needs. From a functional perspective, bicycle lanes and pedestrian only streets should be built into three types—with business function, recreational function and transportation function. The first type should be along rivers or encircling mountains or radiating from the city's central squares (e.g. with one or two dedicated lanes for bicyclers and pedestrians). Main business districts should have the second type, usually a 300–500 m long street dedicated for bicyclers and pedestrians and not allowing any motor vehicles except firefighting trucks. For the third type, given the resource intensive principle in utilizing land, all urban roads should have a lane for mixed use by bicyclers, pedestrians and vehicles.

The implementing tactics in the small and medium-sized cities' green transportation strategy include:

(1) A process progression tactic, e.g. transportation planning comes before urban development; public transportation routes are planned before community construction; public transportation in residential areas is available before residents

move in; impact assessment on transportation is completed before construction of major projects and communities; etc.

(2) A temporal progression tactic—including demonstration comes first before promotion, new districts come first before old ones, etc.

(3) Tactic of investing in and financing transport infrastructure, including government-led investment and financing for large public transportation supporting facilities in city main roads and central areas, as well as investment and financing for transport infrastructure in residential areas and factory areas led by developers, etc.

(4) The fiscal policy for managing public transportation, including low rate fare but high quality services of public transportation, fiscal subsidies tied to the operating performance of public transportation operations, innovation of transportation management system, etc.

3 Accelerating the Improvement Process of Communities

In the urban development of small and medium-sized cities, community construction is always a weak link, and due to lack of rational, effective urban planning, there have been many chronic problems accumulated in the process, e.g. too many isolated buildings, few communities built in a unified style, striking presence of villages inside cities, low construction standards, high energy consumption, chaotic styles, lack of communal facilities, lack of public services, etc.

To expedite the improvement of community construction in small and medium-sized cities, it should focus mainly on the following areas:

(1) To push forward the transformation of community buildings, which is the first and foremost step in improving community construction. Existing buildings in villages inside cities should be transformed following the same standards that are adopted by nearby urban function zones, which can then serve as a spatial platform for achieving economic and social advancement within the jurisdiction, regulate social and legal orders and promote urban industrial upgrade. The transformation of these buildings should adopt two different models—one is a renovating model for those of better quality and with shorter history, and a unified rebuilding model for those of poor quality and with long history.

(2) To set up a complete water treatment system, i.e. to invest in construction and renovation of underground urban pipeline system, accelerate the improvement of drainage pipelines in villages inside cities, step up the efforts in new underground pipeline constructions as well as the efforts in preventing reckless and excessive waste water discharge, renovate and improve municipal drainage pipeline network, gradually clear up all problems and completely achieve split-flow of rainwater and sewage. Funds required for these projects should be raised through multiple sources like government, shareholding companies and urban villagers. Design and construction should adopt modern standards, which means not only

the two types of pipelines should be laid out separately in two networks, but also there should be supporting facilities for the sewage pipe network and set up an "oil separation tank" for the main pollutants, which can precipitate greasy dirt and prevent clogging.

(3) To build a community energy saving system. In small and medium-sized cities, the first link in their energy conservation system is extensive utilization of solar power. There are currently two ways of doing it in these cities: converting the solar power by the use of solar collectors to power solar water heaters, solar cookers, etc. or converting solar power into electricity to be stored in solar cells for lighting. The second link is to install a full-coverage natural gas pipeline system in all communities, which will require a big investment from multiple entities like government, villagers and other market entities.

Rizhao city (Shandong Province): a typical example for extensive utilization of solar power

On the coast of China's Yellow Sea in Shandong Province, Rizhao city gained its name for being the city to have the sun shine upon when the sun first rises from east. Its air quality and close-shore water quality both meet the nation's first-rate standards, thanks to extensive utilization of solar power in this city. In the city, 99% households use solar powered water heaters, and in the rural areas, the percentage is 30% and growing. At least 6,000 households use solar cooker for cooking meals. Over 60,000 greenhouses have a heating system powered by solar panels. The street lamps and traffic lights in the downtown area are also powered by solar panels.

(4) To build an eco-friendly garbage disposal system. A significant link in improving the community garbage disposal systems in small and medium-sized cities is to encourage sorting, recycling and reutilization of household garbage. The garbage sorting work should be focused on kitchen garbage, with a full set of thorough, detailed plans based on extensively collected data and meticulous investigation results. When it comes to recycling and utilization, the planning should include regenerative feed additives projects and compost making projects utilizing kitchen garbage. As to transportation, dedicated vehicles should be used for transporting kitchen garbage alone. Improving the collecting and transporting system that supports household garbage sorting is another significant link in bettering the community garbage disposal system. It is necessary to completely get rid of the current collecting and transporting system consisting of make-shift garbage bins, garbage sheds (spots) and platform stations for garbage transfer, to promote a highly efficient system that uses closed-style garbage collection bins, small-size motor vehicles for transportation and garbage trucks with detachable carriage for garbage transfer, with the whole process done in an enclosed

way, and to achieve separate transportation of sorted household garbage. Small and medium-sized cities should establish renewable resources recycling systems that are based on urban community recycling stations, focused on terminal markets, and aimed at processing and reutilization in specific spots as well as in the entire area. Guidance and regulation should be in place for the existing wandering-around guerrilla style collection and recycling businesses. Renewable resource recycling stations with unified signage should be set up extensively in all communities.

(5) To build community greening and beautifying system, which is the most important step in improving community construction in small and medium-sized cities. Three dimensional greening should be promoted, covering five aspects: community parks, roads, building surfaces, roof tops, and lawn turfs. The beautifying system covers lighting project, pipeline and wires realignment project and advertising objects. The lighting project should strike a perfect balance between energy conservation and beautifying the city, using energy saving lamps and striving to avoid energy losses and light pollution from a technical angle. The pipelines and wires realignment project should aim for ensuring all pipelines and wires installed underground or in the vicinity of walls across the city (including the villages inside cities), and bring an end to the "spider web" like wires hanging over the top of villages inside cities.

(6) Innovation of community democracy and management systems—to achieve this, communities in small and medium-sized cities should focus on the following aspects: division of responsibilities between community work stations and neighborhood committees, with the former acting as a grassroots working unit for the government set up through appointments of the higher level government, and the latter acting as a grassroots autonomous organization set up through election. This autonomous neighborhood committee should be a democratic administration, and the members of the committee should strictly follow laws and regulations, maintain and increase the value of collective properties year by year, and carry out orderly administrative work in terms of the committee's seal, financial accounts, employment, division of work, etc. Efforts should be directed towards setting up a coordinative organization for Party building work within the community, seeking and absorbing capable Party members into the CPC's community branches from various community organizations such as property management companies, property owners' committee and intermediary agencies, and focusing on addressing the major issues within the community. Also, it is necessary to step up efforts in creating a new community work landscape featuring government guidance, social participation, residents' self-management and market operation. On one hand, community autonomy should eventually reinforce community administration and on the other, community administration should guide community autonomy.

(7) To push forward the development of community culture and health services. Promoting community culture has four aspects: to popularize primary education, revive the mass culture, introduce refined arts and build cultural brands. Efforts should be directed towards promoting healthy lifestyle among commu-

nity residents, actively carrying out various health promotional activities based on the satisfaction of health needs among the community residents and aimed at improving people's civility and health, and enhancing the harmony between human beings and the environment.

(8) To further promote community construction theme activities. Municipal governments should attach great importance to community construction, take it as an important part of their social administration and public services in the new era, and regard it as the main pivot of grassroots construction work. The planning of these theme activities should take full consideration of local economic and social conditions, channel as much human resource, materials, funds and efforts as possible to communities and aim to benefit community residents and the city as a whole.

4 Focusing Efforts on Promoting a New Type of Urbanization

In recent years, the urbanization process of small and medium-sized cities mainly has the following issues: brain drain due to lack of industrial support; widening urban and rural gap during the accelerated urbanization process; no guarantee for the interests of farmers whose land has been expropriated, which causes increasingly acute conflicts; excessive use of land resource, etc.

Against the backdrop of ecological progress, small and medium-sized cities need to address the following issues in their efforts to boost a new type of urbanization:

(1) To take a path with both urbanization and industrial development going hand in hand. In the following decade, small and medium-sized cities would become the main players in China's urbanization process, which means a huge flow of rural residents into these cities. Comparatively, small and medium-sized cities have great growth potential, without the prevailing issues commonly seen in big cities such as horrible traffic jams and environmental issues, and urbanization in these cities will have relatively lower costs. However, the main constraint in these cities is lack of employment opportunities, that is, with inadequate industrial development, many rural residents that migrate to the cities cannot secure a job or maintain stable earnings. Despite the heat of property markets in small and medium-sized cities, most buyers are in fact migrant workers returned from big cities to purchase properties at home. Except during the Chinese New Year or other major holidays, a lot of apartments are vacant or only the elders and kids live in them. Therefore, the further elevation of urbanization quality in small and medium-sized cities requires that great importance should be attached to industrial development, with two processes going ahead hand in hand. To achieve this, the key step is the cultivation and development of industries. Considering the available technologies, human resources and industrial foundation, each city should have a clear assessment of its own industrial base,

regional advantages and resource advantages, stick to ecologically sustainable, technology-led advancement, emphasize the important role of labor-intensive industries and local processing industry with regional characteristics, promote the development of industrial chains with their own unique features, enhance the capacity of industries to absorb labor and increase local incomes, facilitate spatial development in cities with overall planning, push forward industrial agglomeration, boost development of industrial parks, and realize economies of scale and economies of agglomeration.

(2) Good management of urban resources, providing better instruments for industrialization and urbanization. A new type of urbanization requires hard efforts to improve urban environment, spatial expansion and aesthetic refinement that combine to increase the value of the city itself. Good management of urban resources and improvement of living environment are necessary measures to improve residents' living standards, which reflect the needs of all residents and the people-oriented principle. They are also the prerequisites for improving the city's image and reputation and enhancing its attractiveness, the main means to raise urban development funds and increase livelihood expenditures, and the requirements for industrial transformation and upgrade as well as for the development of emerging industries. Urban management must be pivoted around effective use of spatial resources and optimization of ecological and cultural resources. To be more specific, this means, (a) to build business districts with high density in selected locations and increase the value of land in surrounding areas; (b) to relocate and transform villages inside cities, achieve urbanization of rural land, expand urban development space and elevate land value; (c) to optimize the combination of ecological and cultural resources, fully utilize the natural conditions, establish more open public ecological zones in the vicinity of mountains and water, build public cultural facilities such as museums, libraries and gyms, and refine the city's culture; (d) to build new urban districts when necessary, boost the development of these new districts through relocation of government bodies, and expand urban development space. It is noteworthy that sound management of a city is important but cannot be relied on as the main driver behind urban development. Real estate industry cannot be the mainstay of economic growth, sales of land cannot be the main source of government revenues, and the increase of land value and price level of housing properties cannot be the benchmark for the level of urban development.

(3) Overall planning for urban and rural development. Instead of rural and urban development in an isolated way, a new type of urbanization requires overall planning of rural and urban land utilization, rural and urban industrial development as well as rural and urban people's livelihood. Regional eco-system is an integrated organ, thus ecologically sustainable urban development is by no means an isolated course. The overall planning of rural and urban development should cover the following aspects: First, to attach great importance to top-level design, carry out proper planning before any action, including an overall rural and urban development plan, an overall land utilization plan, a detailed regulation plan for rural and urban fringe zone, and a comprehensive transport

hub network, to complete as soon as possible the *Recent Construction Plan*, the *Plan of Municipality Urban Systems*, village stationing plan and overall development plan of villages and towns, to achieve as soon as possible 100% coverage of binding detailed plans, 100% filing on records, and integrated planning of rural and urban development, which will define the basic framework of overall planning of ecologically sustainable rural and urban development and social, economic development. Secondly, to make overall plans for rural and urban industrial development, i.e. to apply the strategy of industrialization in agricultural development, support the development of leading companies boosting agricultural processing and expand the distribution of agricultural products; to focus on metropolitan agriculture and automated agriculture, promote experimental agriculture, encourage the union of agriculture and tourism and increase technological application and value added in agricultural products. Thirdly, to promote cities to support rural areas as well as industry to support agriculture, which means providing stimulus for agriculture and animal husbandry through special subsidies such as technology, agricultural equipment and demonstration bases. Fourthly, to make overall plans of social undertakings such the livelihood of the elderly in rural and urban areas, make continuous efforts to improve the social security system mainly consisting of five types of insurances (endowment insurance, medical insurance, unemployment insurance, work related injury insurance and maternity insurance), set up special funds to support the realization of full coverage pension system in rural areas and gradually increase their pension levels.

(4) To establish a reasonable interest sharing system during the urbanization process. Doubtlessly, urbanization is a process of gradual economic growth and social wealth accumulation, and also a process where the value of urban resources gradually rises. Then here comes the question—how should the accumulated wealth be split? How can all involving parties share the increased value of urban resources? It is a question of social equality, and a key issue whose solution will affect the sustainability of urbanization. At the heart of this interest sharing system is granting urban residency to rural people who have moved to cities and relocating farmers whose land has been expropriated. In the first issue, the work force of migrant workers from rural areas plays a significant role in China's urbanization, thus, respecting them, ensuring their rights and interests, and promote the equal status between rural and urban residents are key contents of the new type urbanization. Efforts should be focused on their employment by providing necessary trainings and other supports, protecting their rights and interests, requiring employers to sign work agreements, pay the due amounts as required by the social security system and pay migrant workers' remunerations on time. It is also necessary to have an overall plan for the relocation and education of children of migrant workers, which will help retain a stable work force to support development. In the second issue, we must pay close attention to the essential interests of those farmers living close to the city who have lost their basic means of production and thus have nothing to live on. To be more specific, the solution of this issue should follow the "government-led

and livelihood-first" principle as well as the "coordinated long term and short term planning" principle, incorporate a full set of methods on providing training and social security for rural residents whose land has been expropriated, and adopt various benefiting measures such as unified housing development, local settlement, equity and dividends, overall retirement planning, free training and prioritized employment, which, if well played, will constitute a perfect solution to the challenging issues arising from demolition and relocation.

(5) Intensive utilization of construction land. Compared with big cities and mega cities, small and medium-sized cities have more spare land resources. However, this is by no means any reason for reckless land use. In China where tight supply of land resource is a constant reality, intensive utilization of land is a highlighted point in the urbanization process, which requires, first, to reasonably enhance the density and intensity of urban development, i.e. to strictly follow the *Code for Classification of Urban Land Use and Planning Standards of Development Land* (GB50137-2011), define proper scale and structure of urban construction land on the basis of rational population forecast and economic development expectations, implement a density-based rewarding policy if necessary, encourage frugal use of land for industrial development and put forward clear investment intensity requirements for new enterprises. Secondly, to sort out the relationship between new and old urban districts. While accelerating the construction of new urban districts, efforts should also be focused on transforming and reviving the existing urban districts, i.e. to carry out reforms based on actual conditions and drawing on America's *Tradable Development Right*, and achieve innovation of land ownership and development right structure in both new and old urban districts, which can serve as a way to transform and compensate the existing urban districts as well as to control street blocks with historic meaning. Thirdly, reasonable definition of urban boundary. The administration of urban fringe areas should be more focused on defining land that cannot be used for construction by establishing actually binding ecological red lines that set out farmlands, forests and ecological reserve zones, which is aimed at protecting essential natural resources and open space, and save the treasure for future generations.

Chapter 4
A Strategy of Green Development Model

Ecological progress in small and medium-sized cities will not be achieved in one stroke. The current green development strategy should incorporate several tactics including: major breakthroughs in key areas, highlighted characteristics, institutional development, technological innovation and a competitive environment for the fastest and best accomplishment.

1 Major Breakthroughs in Key Areas

To achieve ecological progress is a systematic project; small and medium-sized cities, which needs a long process to accumulate strengths, can hardly attend to every aspect of this task in the short run. Therefore, they must review their own conditions and accordingly select some key areas where their efforts should be focused on making breakthroughs.

The selection of these key areas and directions should be based on a comprehensive assessment of each city's own level of development and major challenges it faces. Some cities have a large urban population but are economically underdeveloped, with no distinct pillar or mainstay industries either with fledging industrial parks or no industrial parks in scale, or having large-scale pillar industries that features low technological development, weak competitiveness of their products and low value added. For these cities, the main goal should be industrial upgrade focused on ecology, technology and employment capacity, restructuring the city's industries and enhancing overall competitiveness. Some small and medium-sized cities, which are more well developed and economically stronger, with a big proportion of high and new tech industry in their economies, especially those that are already inflicted by the "metropolitan syndromes" such as traffic jams (e.g. Kunshan city), should direct their efforts towards green transportation in the near future, including: systematic planning in four aspects—demand, supply, management and optimized road networks; great efforts should also be made to develop public transport and scientific design of

© Social Sciences Academic Press and Springer Nature Singapore Pte Ltd. 2018

X. Li and X. Liu, *Green Development Model of China's Small and Medium-sized Cities*, Research Series on the Chinese Dream and China's Development Path,
https://doi.org/10.1007/978-981-13-0779-9_4

non-motorized transport system. In cities with longer urban development history, where the old districts and old communities have become a serious constraint over further improvement of urban functionalities and urban living standards, the emphasis should be placed on construction of new districts and in the meantime, community construction that is closely related to the fundamental interests of residents should be at the heart of recent efforts for achieving ecological progress, with the aim to make breakthroughs in building renovation, water treatment system, garbage disposal system, greening and landscaping system, etc.

2 Highlighted Characteristics

There is no one template for cities to achieve ecological progress. A city only comes alive when it expresses individuality, and the so-called "modernization" is not piles of steel and cement, but reflected through the ecological prints, humanistic symbols and the glow of sciences that are inherent in these modern buildings and spaces.

There are several aspects to work on to highlight a city's characteristics, including:

(1) To fully draw on local natural conditions and ecological advantages for building a unique urban ecological system with striking ecological features. As an old Chinese saying goes "people who live in mountains should live on what mountains have to offer and these live by sea should live off the sea", the same principle applies for urban development. Coastal cities should have their efforts focused on coastal features, make full use of coastlines and beaches, and highlight the inclusiveness and openness of coastal views. Cities situated along rivers should focus on developing features based on the river, make the most of its ecological value and set aside sufficient public space along both river banks, with an overall plan of major public facilities in these spaces. Cities in the forest areas should draw on local vegetation, sound air quality and abundant botanic and zoic resources, adopt a spatial plan of multiple urban centers, increase the development density and intensity in some parts, minimize the pressure incurred by urban development on forests, liven up the forestry areas with metropolitan vigor, calm down the hustle and bustle of cities with the serenity of forests, create a complementary ecological pattern in which "the city prospers in woods and the woods thrive in the city".

(2) To dive deep into a city's cultural history, highlight its cultural characteristics and reflect them in its economic and social development. Every city has its own unique history of development, which, like a piece in a big puzzle, is an epitome of certain development stage in human history. As contextualists advocate, a city must address the question of "who am I" along the way of development, which does not simply mean the protection of its historical heritages, but involves a wide range of questions regarding its culture, spirit, image building and development. Therefore, urban culture and spirit must be blended into urban planning, landscaping, architectural design, development and construction, with emphasis

on its individuality and characteristics, which is a prerequisite for elevating a city's traits and achieving ecological progress.

(3) To develop advantageous feature industries, each with its own prominent features. Based on local resources and existing conditions, urban development should be focused on uniquely advantageous industries, establish a value-added industry chain, enhance product brands, and form industry clusters with their own characteristics and carrying heft regionally, domestically or even globally, e.g. laptop computer production in Kunshan city, architectural ceramics in Foshan city, etc.

3 Institutional Development

The protection of environment is inevitably dependent on institutions.[1] Only the most strictly implemented institutions and the most rigorous rule of law can provide solid guarantee for ecological progress.[2] For small and medium-sized cities, they must come to realize that institutional development must come first before the achievement of ecological progress, otherwise, the pursuit of ecological progress will turn out to be just empty talk.

Institutional development must be carried out in the following aspects:

(1) To fully implement the strictest protection system of farmland, water resource management system and environmental protection system: the allotted land for cultivation should be off limits for anyone, regardless of what is the purpose; promote the laws and regulations for protecting resources and environment to a great extent, such as Environmental Protection Law, Marine Environment Protection Law, Law on the Prevention and Control of Atmospheric Pollutions, Law on the Prevention and Control of Environmental Pollution by Solid Wastes, Water Law of the People's Republic of China, etc., and impose legally based punishment on any breach of such laws and regulations.

(2) To firmly carry out the national standards on land and water resources utilization and formulate investment intensity standards and pollution discharge standards based on local conditions. It is necessary to carry out serious inspection for any activity that falls short of these standards and if any, to ordain correction within certain period. Those who fail to rectify their operations should be shut down or dismantled within a certain period. New companies should meet these standards on investment intensity and pollutions, and if fail to meet, should be denied approval.

---

[1]Hu Jintao, Firmly March on the Path of Socialism with Chinese Characteristics and Strive to Complete the Building of a Moderately Prosperous Society in All Respects, the report made to the 18th CPC National Congress on 8 November, 2012.

[2]Xi Jinping, the speech made on the 6th Group Study of the Central Political Bureau on 24 May 2013.

(3) To improve the evaluation system of economic and social development, tone down the importance of GDP in the evaluation, and include indicators reflective of resource consumption, environmental damage and ecological benefits. Accordingly, a punitive and rewarding system should be in place, the power of veto should be part of all key ecological and environmental indicators (any individual or organization that fails to meet the requirements of all key indicators should not be given the green light), and an accountability ascertaining system should be in place for any major ecological or environmental accident.

4 Technological Innovation

Technological advancement is an important supporting pillar for achieving ecological progress. The contradiction between "limited resources and environment bearing capacity" and "unlimited urban development" has put human beings in a dilemma—struggling to strike a balance between environment and urban development—for which the key is technological advancement.

In order to achieve ecological progress, small and medium-sized cities should focus on the following aspects to boost technological innovation:

(1) Technological innovation plans and programs with specific details of stimulating policies, such as to encourage applications for technological patents and provide rewards for successful ones, to appropriate designated funds, to enhance the support for technological innovation, to back up local efforts on practical technologies, and establish a rewarding mechanism for major technological innovations.
(2) To reinforce the self-sufficiency of regional and characteristic industrial technologies in combination with local environmental features and industrial development features, introduce technologies based on local economic needs and social development, provide technological support for the development of regional and characteristic industries (economy), and promote industrial upgrade. Take cities in northwestern China as examples. With insufficient water resources on one hand and abundant sunlight on the other hand, these cities should support water saving technologies and solar power utilization technologies in different industries.
(3) To amplify the leading, exemplary role of demonstrative projects on technological innovation, focus on innovative enterprises and sci-tech demonstrative projects, make big efforts to push ahead new and high technologies to transform traditional and feature industries in different regions, gradually improve the innovating capability of the whole industry, and boost economic transformation and further innovation.
(4) To actively promote the improvement of regional innovating capabilities, gradually establish a complete mechanism and social environment favorable to innovation and entrepreneurship, and improve the technological innovation sys-

tem and the science and technology service system, oriented by the market, with enterprises playing a major role and the perfect marriage of industries, academies, research bodies and technological promotion organizations.

5 A Competitive Environment for the Fastest and Best Accomplishment

The proper and accurate measurement of ecological progress of a city involves a comprehensive assessment by many parameters. Currently, though there is yet to be an authoritative evaluation system that can provide a comprehensive assessment of the levels of ecological progress, the experimental and demonstrative projects and a competing system for fastest and best achievements organized by relevant government departments can to some extent reflect a city's ecological progress from different perspectives.

For fastest and best achievements, small and medium-sized cities can mainly focus on building themselves into a national model city for environment protection, national garden city/national ecological garden city, and/or a national pilot zone for demonstration of ecological progress. To achieve this, efforts should be mainly directly towards the following aspects:

(1) To become a national model city for environmental protection. The evaluation and accreditation of such national level model cities cover various aspects such as society, economy, environment, urban development, hygiene, gardens, etc. In 1997, China's first group of cities accredited as national model cities for environment protection includes six cities—Zhangjiagang, Shenzhen, Dalian, Zhuhai, Xiamen and Weihai. By 2012, this number has grown to 92.

(2) To become a garden city or ecological garden city at national level. The selection of such cities is carried out by the Ministry of Housing and Urban-Rural Development of the People's Republic of China (MOHURD) in accordance with Standards of National Garden Cities, which assess candidate cities from eight criteria including comprehensive administration, greening work, construction management and control, ecological environment, energy efficiency and emission reduction, municipal facilities, living environment and social security. For any city to win the accreditation of national garden city, it must meet all requirements of the basic parameters, and to win the accreditation of national ecological garden city, it must meet all requirements of the basic and additional parameters, for the latter is a notch higher than the former and is more demanding on the improvement of a city's ecological functions, on the protection of bio-species diversity, natural resources and cultural resources, on the guarantee of ecological safety, sustainable urban development, living standards as well as the harmony between human beings and nature. Starting from 1992, MOHURD would publish annually the names of national garden cities accredited each year. However, so far, there only has been a list of pilot cities for the title of "national ecolog-

ical garden city", including Qingdao, Yangzhou, Nanjing, Hangzhou, Weihai, Suzhou, Shaoxing, Guilin, Changshu, Kunshan, Jincheng and Zhangjiagang.

(3) To become a pilot demonstrative zone of ecological progress at national level. In July 2014, six ministries including National Development and Reform Commission (NDRC) and the Ministry of Finance (MOF) jointly issued the *Notice on Establishing the First Batch of Pilot Demonstrative Zones of Ecological Progress*, which included 55 regions including Miyun County of Beijing. These demonstrative zones will target at removing the major constraints on protecting regional ecological environment, and take steps to experiment and explore, thus to gain experience, set examples and lead the way to ecological progress.

Part II
Special Reports

Chapter 5
Land Consolidation and Development of Small and Medium-sized Cities

1 The Status Quo of Land Consolidation in China

1.1 Definition and Content of Land Consolidation

Land consolidation has been extensively practiced worldwide with a long history. In Germany, land consolidation can go as far back as 1953 when the former Federal Republic of Germany issued its first Land Consolidation Act, which was revised and enriched twice in 1976 and in 1982 respectively. It is mainly focused on the consolidation and rearrangement of land patches, transformation of rural areas, development of construction land and land consolidation for large construction projects, consolidation of forestland and farmland for special crops, updating land related documentations, etc. Other countries like France, the Netherlands, Italy, Portugal, Canada, Australia, Japan and South Korea also carried out similar land consolidating activities, though under different names, e.g. Land Consolidation, Land Readjustment, Land Re-plotting, Land Pooling, etc.

The past has shown that China has made continuous effort exploring and its land consolidation work has gradually come into being. Even before any explicit statement about the concept of land consolidation, China already started such practices, including national land development and rectification, land reclamation, transformation of old downtown, etc. Along with the probing and progressing of land consolidation practice, a land consolidation concept that is well-suited to China's current economic and social development needs has gradually taken shape, that is, certain measures and means must be adopted, as required by land utilization schemes and overall land utilization planning in certain regions, to adjust the relationship between land utilization and society and economy, improve land utilization structure, make scientific planning and reasonable layouts, achieve comprehensive development and utilization, improve the utilization efficiency and productivity of land resources, increase the quantity of utilizable land, and ensure a virtuous cycle between economy, society and environment.

© Social Sciences Academic Press and Springer Nature Singapore Pte Ltd. 2018

X. Li and X. Liu, *Green Development Model of China's Small and Medium-sized Cities*, Research Series on the Chinese Dream and China's Development Path,
https://doi.org/10.1007/978-981-13-0779-9_5

Put simply, land consolidation refers to the measures and the process of adjusting land utilization means to achieve land utilization goals. Based on the specific target areas, it can be categorized into rural land consolidation and urban land consolidation. Rural land consolidation takes place in rural areas, mainly including adjustment of land structure, consolidating sporadic land patches, consolidation of residential land as well as land utilized by township and village enterprises, land levelling, soil improvement, reclamation of waste land, improvement of ecological environment, comprehensive construction of supporting facilities such as roads, ditches, etc. Urban land consolidation targets urban areas for higher urban land utilization efficiency and rational layout, mainly by pooling together land within a certain region and consolidating or reshuffling land patches, and at the same time, building or transforming infrastructure such as roads, increasing land usage for public purposes such as greening work, and consequently improving the land utilization conditions and environment within that region.

1.2 Status Quo of Land Consolidation in China

1.2.1 Object: Mainly Targeted at Rural Land

Land consolidation started with rural land and at the moment, China is still focusing on rural land consolidation. The 41th Article of the *Land Administration Law of the People's Republic of China* revised in 2004 explicitly puts forward that "the State encourages land consolidation. People's governments of counties and townships (towns) shall organize rural collective economic organizations to carry out comprehensive consolidation of fields, water surface, roads, woods and villages according to the general plans for the utilization of land to raise the quality of cultivated land and increase areas for effective cultivation and improve the agricultural production conditions and ecological environment. Local people's governments at all levels shall adopt measures to ameliorate medium-and low-yielding land and consolidate idle and scattered and abandoned land." From this, it is obvious that China's land consolidation work is mainly in rural areas.

Urban land consolidation is also an integral part of land consolidation work. However, China made a late start on this and thus is still in a probing stage. In recent years, the rapid progression of industrialization and urbanization in China has given rise to a big appetite for land. But due to reasons like the more challenging nature of urban land consolidation, widely sporadic land patches and insufficient land resource, land supply resulted from urban land consolidation is limited, while land supply resulted from rural land consolidation is relatively significant. In particular, the consolidation of rural land surrounding cities has become a main source of land for reserve and supply.

1.2.2 Objective: Land Consolidation Is More Focused on Economic Benefits

The objectives of land consolidation are diverse, including economic, social and environmental goals. The comprehensive benefits of land consolidation mean the union of economic benefits, social benefits and environmental benefits. All land consolidation work should pursue the natural union of economic, social and environmental benefits. However, China is more focused on the economic benefits of its current land consolidation work instead of its social and environmental benefits. In China's current political and economic systems, economic benefits come as a priority in the land consolidation work. Doubtlessly, such work requires capital investment, which is provided by investors mainly because they are in pursuit of direct or indirect economic benefits resulted from land consolidation. Therefore, economic benefits naturally become the primary objective of land consolidation activity in China.

Generally speaking, economic benefits are measured by the comparison between input and output. The economic benefits of land consolidation refer to the difference between the economic benefits of land before and after the consolidation, minus the input. For agricultural land, the economic benefits from land consolidation can be more usable farmland, improved quality of farmland and increased agricultural output. However, rural land consolidation alone will bring very limited economic benefits. So right now, a lot of land consolidation work is set to draw on the policy of "linking the increase in land used for urban construction with the decrease in land used for rural construction", reclaim some rural construction land as farmland through land consolidation, reduce the rural land for construction purpose in exchange for an increase in urban land for construction purpose, and as a result, harvest significant economic benefits from the increment of urban construction land.

During China's urbanization process, there is a sharp contrast between tight land supply for urban construction and idled construction land in rural areas. In order to tackle this imbalance, government rolled out the policy of "linking the increase in land used for urban construction with the decrease in land used for rural construction". In 2004, the *Decision of the State Council on Furthering the Reform and Intensifying the Land Administration* (GF [2004] No. 28) stated that "consolidation of rural land for construction purpose is encouraged, and the increase of urban land for construction should be linked with the decrease of rural land for construction." In 2005, the Ministry of Land and Resources granted approval to some cities to try out this policy, and in 2008, it issued the *Measures for the Administration of the Trial Work of Linking the Increase in Land Used for Urban Construction with the Decrease in Land Used for Rural Construction* (GTZF [2008] No. 138). Though this policy has to some extent mitigated the imbalance between urban and rural construction land, some land consolidation work, driven by the pursuit of economic benefits, has overlooked or ignored social and environmental benefits. For instance, in some areas, the so-called "increase-decrease linkage" took the form of "increase first and decrease afterwards", struggling to ensure the quantity and quality of the corresponding decreased rural construction land. It is not rare that sometimes there is only increase without any decrease, or the increased urban construction land is of higher quality than the decreased rural construction land, or the increase is much more than the decrease in quantity.

1.2.3 Mode: Government-Led Land Consolidation Featuring Inadequate Institutions and Various Forms

The history of land consolidation around the world shows that this process can be led by either the government or landowners, or based on planning. In China's current land consolidation and reserve system, land consolidation is often led by government and pushed ahead by administrative stimulus. Mostly, it is relevant government departments or organizations designated by government who are the main forces in land consolidation, which features a single source of funds, low level of professionalism and marketization, let alone any industrialization of land consolidation.

Laws, regulations, policies and institutions in regard to land consolidation in China are still in a fledging period. Provisions about land consolidation and reclamation are mostly concentrated in the *Land Administration Law* and the *Regulations on Land Reclamation*, without forming into a separate law. The 2004 revised *Land Administration Law of P.R.C* has more provisions on land consolidation and reclamation than its previous version, but is still confined to "encouraging land consolidation" and principle for preparing the overall plan of land utilization (which include keeping a balance between farmland occupied and farmland developed and reclaimed). It is far from playing an effective guiding role as required. Furthermore, there are only a few policies that land consolidation work can be based on, including the *Decision of the State Council on Furthering the Reform and Intensifying the Land Administration* (GF [2004] No. 28), the *Measures for the Administration of the Trial Work of Linking the Increase in Land Used for Urban Construction with the Decrease in Land Used for Rural Construction* (GTZF [2008] No. 138), etc.

In China, the practices of land consolidation nationwide have developed into several different modes. In urban areas, the main modes include: "vacating the cage to change birds" (which means to get rid of the obsolete and introduce a new way of utilization), functional adjustment, all-around transformation, overall planning of urban and rural areas, and road expansion. In rural areas, the main modes include construction of new-type village, scale economy of agriculture, linking the increase in land used for urban construction with the decrease in land used for rural construction, etc. These different modes of land consolidation are not isolated, and in some cases, a mix of different modes is seen in one area.

2 Land Utilization Conditions and Trends in Small and Medium-sized Cities

2.1 *Land Utilization Conditions*

According to the classification criteria of city scale in the *Green Book of Small and Medium-sized Cities 2013*, cities with less than 500,000 permanent downtown residents are small cities, those with 500,000 to 1 million are medium-sized cities, those with 1 million to 3 million are large cities, those with 3 million to 10 million are mega cities and those with above 10 million permanent downtown residents are giant cities. Based on this classification, small and medium-sized cities are those whose population of permanent downtown residents is below 1 million. By the end of 2012, China has 657 administrative cities, including 4 municipalities directly under the central government, 15 sub-provincial level cities, 270 prefectural-level cities and 368 county-level administrative cities. Due to lack of unified authoritative statistics on permanent downtown residents, while classifying cities based on the population scale, for cities at or above the prefectural level, total population within the municipal districts is used as the criterion, and for county-level cities, the criterion is a calculated result using the formula total population *[the population within the municipal districts of cities whose populations are below 1 million/these cities' total population]. Among the 657 administrative cities in China, there are three giant cities each with a population of over 10 million, 18 mega cities each with a population of 3–10 million, 106 large cities each with a population of 1–3 million, and 530 small and medium-sized cities whose populations are below 1 million. Although small and medium-sized cities should also include the central towns that are jurisdictionally at or above county level but are not administrative cities. Without sufficient statistic data, this research only covers the data of administrative cities.

2.1.1 Low Land Utilization Rates in Small and Medium-sized Cities

By the end of 2012, there are 530 small and medium-sized cities among China's administrative cities, accounting for 80.7% of the total number of administrative cities. The combined population of their municipal districts is 144.7 million, accounting for 32.2% of the total population within the municipal districts of all administrative cities. Combined, these small and medium-sized cities cover an established area of 19,830 km^2, accounting for 43.3% of total established area of all administrative cities, much higher than the corresponding population proportion. In comparison, for large, mega and giant cities, the population proportions are 38.8, 19.3 and 9.7% respectively, which are higher than their proportions of established urban area—32.3, 17.4 and 7.0% respectively (see Table 1). Therefore, population density in small and medium-sized cities is distinctly lower than in large, mega and giant cities, and their land utilization intensity also conspicuously lower than their bigger counterparts.

Table 1 Population, land and economy of China's administrative cities (2012)

Population size	No. of cities	Proportion (%)	Total population (10,000 persons)	Proportion (%)	Established area (km^2)	Proportion (%)	Regional GDP (RMB100 million)	Proportion (%)
>10 million	3	0.5	4364	9.7	3199	7	46,322	12.7
3–10 million	18	2.7	8667	19.3	7959	17.4	94,927	26.1
1–3 million	106	16.1	17,413	38.8	14,775	32.3	132,060	36.3
<1 million	530	80.7	14,470	32.2	19,830	43.3	90,722	24.9
Total	657	100	44,914	100	45,763	100	364,032	100

Source Compiled and calculated based on *China City Statistical Yearbook 2013*

2.1.2 Low Rates of Land Utilization Efficiency in Small and Medium-sized Cities

In 2012, the regional GDP of small and medium-sized cities among China's administrative cities added up to RMB9.0722 trillion, accounting for 24.9% of the combined GDP of all administrative cities, far lower than the proportion established urban area (43.3%) and also lower than the proportion by population (32.2%). This indicates relatively poor economic development, low productivity per capita, low productivity per unit area of land and low land utilization efficiency in small and medium-sized cities. In contrast, the GDP proportions of large, mega and giant cities in the combined GDP of all administrative cities are 36.3, 26.1 and 12.7% respectively, all much higher than the proportion by established urban area (32.3, 17.4 and 7.0% respectively). It is obvious that the productivity per unit area of land in small and medium-sized cities is distinctly lower than in large, mega and giant cities, so is their land utilization efficiency.

2.2 *Development Trends in Small and Medium-sized Cities*

2.2.1 Policy Preference Has Provided Opportunities for Higher-Pace Growth in Small and Medium-sized Cities

Both academic scholars and government leadership in China have a consensus on urbanization, that is, it must take a path leading to balanced development of large, medium-sized and small cities. As early as in 2001, China put forward in its 10th Five-Year Plan that "we must seize the opportunity to carry out the urbanization strategy", and also "while focusing on development of small cities and small towns, efforts should be direct towards the growth of small and medium-sized cities, improving the functions of regional central cities, giving full play to the leading role of big cities, reinforcing the planning, construction and overall administration in different types of cities, taking a path that fits well into China's own circumstances and heading for coordinated development of large, small and medium-sized cities as well as small cities and small towns". The later urbanization process saw rapid burgeoning growth of big cities but flat, annually incremental development of small and medium-sized cities. Compared with big cities, small and medium-sized cities lag behind in terms of development, resulting in the structural imbalance of Chinese cities when it comes to scale. To develop small and medium-sized cities can on one hand avoid the "metropolitan syndromes" incurred by overly dense population in big cities and on the other hand, can avoid the "rural defects" of too scattered rural industrialization and small cities and small towns. In addition, it can also contribute to the local urbanization and household relocation of rural migrant workers. Without clustered industries and sufficient population, land utilization efficiency in small and medium-sized cities is low, with a great potential yet to be tapped into. Therefore, the recent years have seen China's urbanization policies more leaned towards the development of small and medium-sized cities.

In 2011, China's 12th Five-Year Plan stated the necessity to "form a strategic urbanization landscape", "adopt the principles of overall planning, reasonable lay-out, improving functions and the big leading the small, follow the natural course of urban development, rely on big cities, focus on small and medium-sized cities, gradually form a cluster of cities with far-reaching radiating influences, and promote the coordinated development of large, medium-sized, and small cities and small towns". In 2012, the report to the 18th National Congress of the CPC stated that "we should make scientific plans for the scale and layout of urban agglomerations; and we should make small and medium-sized cities and small towns better able to develop industries, provide public services, create jobs, and attract population". In 2013, the Third Plenary Session of the 18th CPC Central Committee adopted the *Decision of the Central Committee of the Communist Party of China on Some Major Issues Concerning Comprehensively Continuing the Reform*, which also emphasized that "we will stick to the path of a new-type urbanization with Chinese characteristics, push forward people-oriented urbanization, promote the coordinated development of megacities, medium-sized cities, small cities and small towns, promote the integrated development of industries and cities, and advance urbanization and the building of new rural areas in a coordinated manner". It also raised the need to "introduce new population management methods, accelerate the reform of household registration system, completely lift restrictions on new residence registration in administrative townships and small cities, relax restrictions on new residence registration in medium-sized cities in an orderly manner, lay down appropriate conditions for new residence registration in large cities, and strictly control the population size of megacities." Additionally, it also encouraged helping the eligible population to move away from agriculture and become urban residents. In March 2014, the CPC Central Committee and the State Council jointly issued the National Guidelines for Developing a New Type of Urbanization (2014–2020), which more explicitly stated the need to "speed up the development of small and medium-sized cities", "to take this task as the main direction for optimizing the city scale composition, provide stronger guidance for arrangement of industries and public service resources, improve the quality and increase the quantity", and "to improve the standards for city designation, apply strict inspection and approving procedures, designate counties as cities in an orderly manner if they meet the requirements of becoming an administrative city, and develop qualified counties and major towns into small and medium-sized cities". To sum up, the small and medium-sized cities in China will have a feast of new opportunities.

2.2.2 Population Migration Has Provided Momentum for Faster Development of Small and Medium-sized Cities

New additions of China's urban population are partly attributable to migrant population from rural areas, thus the flow of rural migrant workers plays a big role in the nation's urbanization. Sample surveys carried out by the National Bureau of Statistics (NBS) indicate that in 2013, the nation had a total of 268.94 million rural migrant workers, among which 61.8% or 166.1 million were non-local and 38.2% or 102.84 million were local rural migrant workers. The latter refers to rural migrant workers working within the jurisdiction of the town where their registered permanent residence belongs, while the former means rural migrant workers who work in other places other than the town of their registered permanent residence.

Since 2011, the proportion of local rural migrant workers in the nation's total rural migrant workers has increased, for three years in a row so far, with an average annual increase of 4.65 million between 2010 and 2013. Given that these workers work in the region where their registered permanent residence belongs, such increase in both total number and in proportion will contribute to the development of small and medium-sized cities as well as small towns.

The flow of non-local rural migrant workers can be further split up into intra-provincial flows and cross-provincial flows. The *2013 National Monitoring and Investigation Report on Rural Migrant Workers* issued by the NBS indicates that cross-provincial flows are mainly towards large and medium-sized cities while intra-provincial flows are mainly into small cities and small towns (see Table 2). So intra-provincial flow of rural migrant workers will contribute more to the development of small and medium-sized cities as well as small towns. From 2008 to 2013, the proportion of intra-provincial migrant workers in the total population of rural migrant workers has been on rise, and starting from 2011, this proportion exceeded the proportion of cross-provincial migrant workers. By 2013, there were 88.71 million rural workers migrating within their home province and 77.39 million cross provinces, accounting for 53.4 and 46.6% respectively in the total population of non-local rural migrant workers, which has provided a strong labor base supporting the development of small and medium-sized cities.

From the flow of rural migrant workers, the increases of both the proportion of local rural migrant workers and the proportion of intra-provincial rural migrant workers will help the development of small and medium-sized cities in China.

Table 2 The number and composition of non-local rural migrant workers by type of city (2013), unit: 10,000 persons, %

Indicator	Total	Cities directly under the central government	Provincial capital cities	Cities at prefectural level (incl. sub-provincial level cities)	Small cities and small towns	Other
Non-local rural migrant workers	16,610	1410	3657	5553	5921	69
Among which: cross-provincial	7739	1115	1749	3064	1742	69
Intra-provincial	8871	295	1908	2489	4179	0
Composition	100	8.5	22	33.4	35.7	0.4
Among which: cross provincial	100	14.4	22.6	39.6	22.5	0.9
Intra-provincial	100	3.3	21.5	28.1	47.1	0

Source The *2013 National Monitoring and Investigation Report on Rural Migrant Workers* issued by the NBS

2.3 *Key Points of Land Consolidation in the Process of Developing Small and Medium-sized Cities*

2.3.1 To Prioritize the Role of Urban Land Consolidation in the Development of Small and Medium-sized Cities

In China, "land urbanization" has outpaced population urbanization, which features extensive utilization of construction land with low efficiency. From 1996 to 2012, the average annual increase of construction land across the nation was 7.24 million *mu* (15 *mu* = 1 ha), among which the average increase of urban construction land was 3.57 million mu. From 2000 to 2011, the established urban area increased by 76.4%, much higher than the urban population growth rate of 50.5%. During the same period, rural population decreased by 133 million while land used for rural residency increased by 30.45 million mu.[1] Compared with large cities, land utilization in small

[1]Source: National Guidelines for Developing a New Type of Urbanization (2014–2020) jointly issued by the CPC Central Committee and the State Council.

and medium-sized cities is more extensive and lower in utilization efficiency. The further development of small and medium-sized cities will inevitably give rise to more demand for land. To satisfy this demand, the first step is to provide more land through urban land consolidation, rather than blindly increasing construction land through rural land consolidation. Although the former is much more challenging than the latter, the further outward expanding land utilization model will eventually cause waste of land resource given low intensity and low efficiency of existing land utilization in small and medium-sized cities.

First of all, it is necessary to raise the awareness of intensive and economical land utilization. Generally speaking, the relation between human activity and land in small and medium-sized cities is not as tense as in large cities, hence there is little awareness of the necessity for intensive land utilization. Some cities expand in a radiating manner, devote too much effort to wide roads and big square, and set up excessively large new downtown districts, development districts and industrial parks. To improve land utilization efficiency, the first step is to have the awareness of intensive and economical utilization of land, and avoid becoming too keen on obtaining lots of land in large scale.

Secondly, it is necessary to create an institutional environment in favor of prioritizing urban land consolidation. In order to improve land utilization efficiency, the urban land consolidation within the established urban area should come before acquiring additional land for urban construction. This requires an institutional environment that ensures the priority of urban land consolidation, that is, to formulate and implement relevant policies and regulations to guide involving parties to prioritize urban land consolidation. Examples of such policies and regulations include: strict control of the scale of newly added land for urban construction, raising the proportion of land stock use in urban construction, prioritizing urban land consolidation in examination and approval procedures, project initiation, and market entry and trading, etc.

Thirdly, urban land consolidation should be carried out along with transformation of old districts, villages inside cities and rundown urban areas. It is undeniable that urban land consolidation is a challenging task, but opportunities arising during the transformation of old districts, villages inside cities and rundown urban areas will make it easier. Unified planning, relocation and construction of infrastructure will guarantee the interests of the original land beneficiaries, improve living environment, promote intensive utilization of land resource and enhance the social and environmental benefits from land consolidation. Also, land consolidation will liquidize the stock of urban land and increase effective supply of urban land.

At last, it is necessary to encourage owners of waste or idled industrial and commercial land to undertake land consolidation on their own. Along with urban development and industrial restructuring, the locations of some existing industrial and commercial land are no longer fit for the originally intended purposes, especially for the industrial companies within central urban areas. However, the ownership of such land remains unchanged. If government's land consolidation and reserve organization intends to acquire the land, the original owners of such idled land are often very reluctant to cooperate, or even resist for issues like compensations. The rollout of preferential policies encouraging these owners to carry out the work of land consolidation on their own can reduce initial input and make it much easier. Specific policies allow companies to adjust the attribute of land in accordance with existing overall urban planning, e.g. converting industrial land into residential land, so the companies can become the level-one developer of consolidated land and trade it on market, etc.

2.3.2 To Attach Great Importance to the Social and Environmental Benefits of Land Consolidation and Underline the Livability of Small and Medium-sized Cities

A conspicuous sign of irrational spatial distribution and scale composition of cities in China is that the scale of a city does not match the bearing capacity of its resources and environment. Some large cities are under lots of pressure from a massive population, which exacerbates the conflict with their overall bearing capacity, while small and medium-sized cities do not have enough industrial clusters and population to tap their great potential. Compared with large, mega and giant cities, small and medium-sized cities enjoy an advantage in environmental bearing capacity and are more livable. To fully draw on this comparative advantage, small and medium-sized cities must stop focusing merely on economic benefits and ignoring social and environmental benefits in their land consolidation work. From a long term perspective, poor social and environmental benefits will eventually have an adverse impact on the economic benefits of land consolidation or even put economic benefits at risk. Therefore, small and medium-sized cities must pay attention to social and environmental benefits of their land consolidation work.

First, to enhance assessment of environmental impact of the planning. With years of exploration and improvement, China's grown fairly skilled at assessing the environmental impact of construction projects, with a set of administrative systems and operational model widely recognized and accepted by all walks of the society. However, in comparison, the environmental impact assessment for planning work started much later —China's *Regulation on Environmental Impact Assessment of Planning* (State Council Issue No. 559) was not rolled out until August 2009. Reinforcing the environmental impact assessment of planning can make planning more scientific, prevent environmental pollution and ecological damage at the source, promote all-round, coordinated and sustainable economic, social and environmental development, and also provide a basis for land consolidation work.

Secondly, to increase the participation of interested parties in land consolidation. Currently in China, the main participators in land consolidation are usually related government departments or government-assigned organizations. However, land consolidation brings broad social and environmental benefits and can have profound impact on urban development, residents and industrial and commercial companies. To bring out more social and environmental benefits, it is necessary to admit the rights of all interested parties, increase their participation and mobilize their enthusiasm.

Thirdly, to accelerate the land consolidation of industrial and commercial waste land. Along with China's industrial transformation and upgrading, management, reform and relocation of polluting companies for environmental protection, some industrial and commercial land in some established urban districts have been abandoned, without a complete eradication of pollutions, which cause mayhem to the health of the residents in surrounding areas and environment. In the overall planning of a city's land consolidation work, local land administration and environmental protection authority should have a thorough investigation of the pollutions in its abandoned industrial and commercial land, set up files, take appropriate measures and pick up the consolidation work, with the aim to reduce the risk of adverse impact on residents' health and environment.

2.3.3 To Plan in Whole and Combine Land Consolidation with Industrial Development, Transportation and Infrastructure Construction

Land consolidation work in small and medium-sized cities should fit well into their development planning. Urban development planning is a key prerequisite for preparing land consolidation plan in which land consolidation should be in combination with industrial development, transportation and infrastructure construction.

The National Guidelines for Developing a New Type of Urbanization (*2014–2020*) mentioned that "the layout of China's urban clusters is not completely reasonable, the internal division of labor within city clusters is not well coordinated and the efficiency resulted from cluster effect is low", and thus "it is necessary to regard it as the main direction of optimizing city scale composition to accelerate the development of small and medium-sized cities", for which the main measures include, "to provide more guidance for arrangement of industries and public service resources", "to encourage and direct industrial projects into small and medium-sized cities as well as county seats where local resources and environment can accommodate more and there is still great potential for further development, and rely on advantageous resources to develop feature industries and lay a solid industrial foundation", "to step up construction of municipal infrastructure and public service facilities, favor small and medium-sized cities as well as county seats in allocation of public resources like education and medical services, support the establishment of higher education institutions and vocational collages in small and medium-sized cities, encourage outstanding educational and medical institutions to set up branches in small and medium-sized cities, and enhance the appeal resulted from the clustering effect", "to improve comprehensive transportation passageways and inter-regional main transportation network, reinforce transportation connection between city clusters, step up the planning and construction of integrated transportation system among city clusters, improve the transportation network in and out of small and medium-sized cities as well as small towns, and give full play to the supporting and guiding role of a comprehensive transportation network on urbanization landscape".

The development plan for small and medium-sized cities contained in the *National Guidelines for Developing a New Type of Urbanization* (*2014–2020*) provides a direction for the land consolidation work in China's small and medium-sized cities.

When it comes to a specific city in a specific region, land consolidation work requires detailed overall planning based on the position of this city in the regional city cluster, local natural resource, geographic conditions and land utilization status quo, so that land consolidation can be well coordinated with industrial development, transportation and infrastructure construction in a way the former contributes to the latter and vice versa.

Chapter 6
Efficiency Improvement and Institutional Innovation for Urban Land Utilization

With the fast advancement of urbanization and industrialization in China, the "hard (inherent) constraint" of land resource has become increasingly prominent. Against this backdrop, it is inevitably necessary for small and medium-sized cities to innovate their urban development theories and reform the land utilization systems in order to improve the land utilization efficiency.

1 It Is an Urgent Task to Achieve Intensive Land Utilization

In the mid-and late 1990s—only over a decade after China's policy of reform and opening up, Shenzhen was already under the palpable constraint of land resource. And now over three decades after the policy, the inherent land resource constraint on urban development has become a grueling reality most Chinese cities have to grapple with.

Since its reform and opening up to the world, China has seen rapid advancement of urbanization. The urbanization rate of population has risen from 17.9% in 1978 to 53.7% in 2013, at a staggering pace that is rarely seen in world history. However, the scale of land utilized for urban development has been on an even steeper growth trajectory. Between 2001 and 2010, the established urban area across China and the land for construction purpose increased by 5.97 and 6.04% on average year on year while the average annual growth of urban population was merely 3.78%. In particular, during the 10th Five-Year Plan period, the average annual growth rates of established urban area and scale of land utilized for construction purpose reached 7.7 and 7.5% respectively, much higher than the 4.13% average annual growth of urban population. From 1990 to 2000, the total established urban area in China increased 78.3% from 12,200 to 21,800 km^2 while the urban population grew 53.5% from 297 million to 456 million. By 2010, the established urban areas added up to 40,500 km^2, up by 85.5% in a decade, and the urban population burgeoned to 666 million, up by 46%. These figures indicate that the increase of land for urban development has outpaced

© Social Sciences Academic Press and Springer Nature Singapore Pte Ltd. 2018
X. Li and X. Liu, *Green Development Model of China's Small and Medium-sized Cities*, Research Series on the Chinese Dream and China's Development Path,
https://doi.org/10.1007/978-981-13-0779-9_6

the urban population growth, and entering the new millennium, the speed gap is further expanding, which means a worsening "land enclosure" phenomenon during the course of urban development.

On one hand, the reckless expansion of land for urban development has eroded land for agriculture and eco-systems and constituted a severe threat to food safety and ecological safety. On the other hand, the urban areas are rimmed with land utilization issues due to improper structure and low intensity. For instance, the State Council issued the *Notice of the State Council on Promoting the Land Saving and Intensive Use* in 2008, which requires "following the principles of gradual advancement in a systematic way, economical utilization of land, intensive-style development and rational layout, determining a city's strategic position, functional objectives and development scale in a scientific manner, and enhancing the its comprehensive capacity to sustain long-term development". But in reality, some cities have recklessly expanded the scale of land acquired for urban development regardless of water and ecological constraints, which increased land use without enhancing their comprehensive capacity to endure and sustain further development. *The Indicators for Controlling Construction Land Usage for Industrial Projects* revised in 2008 states that the building density of any industrial project should be no less than 30%, and the land used for building office buildings and living and servicing facilities should be no more than 7% of the total coverage of the project. It is strictly forbidden to build supporting facilities not for production purpose within the project area, e.g. sets of residential housing, experts' building, hotels, guesthouses and training centers. In principle, there should be no green landscape within industrial enterprises' premises. However, cities at various levels have made a big fuss about green field and brown field projects for diverse types of industrial parks and have been constantly expanding their designed areas, with some stretching out for even hundreds of square kilometers. Some cities have even gone so far to build "garden-like" plants, taking up an excessive scale of land for industrial development and featuring rather low land utilization efficiency, which is pretty common among these cities.

In recent years, the "ghost towns" frequently reported in the public media are an epitome of extensive and reckless land use during the course of China's urbanization. The most well-known "ghost town" is Kangbashi in Ordos (Inner Mongolia), where there was supposed to be a population of 300,000 in 2010 while government's statistics indicates the actual number of residents is less than 1/10 of what was expected. Chenggong in Yunnan Province, situated in close proximity to its provincial capital Kunming, can be regarded as the largest "ghost town" in Asia. Since its initial development in 2003, it was expected to accommodate nearly 6.5 million residents. However, the town, despite of its constructed roads, residential apartments, shopping malls and kindergartens, is almost abandoned.

In fact, there is a considerable number of small and medium-sized cities that have trouble attracting and retaining sufficient population, and some small and medium-sized cities are very keen on development of new urban districts and elevation of urban land value through urbanization activities. However, without the support of prospering industries, there won't be enough employment opportunities for migrant workers from rural areas and the sustainable development of such new urban districts will inevitably become a question. It is also note-worthy that urban development runs its own natural course and a city can only have a certain amount of "kinetic energy". So if the development of a new urban district is at the expense of an existing one, then it means massive waste of urban land resource along this way.

2 To Establish a Sound Evaluation System for Urban Land Utilization Efficiency

The evaluation of urban land utilization efficiency must be considered on two levels: the first one is national and regional standards and their optimization and implementation, which is the bottom-line assessment; the second is assessment of benefits and impacts of urban land utilization, which is a comprehensive evaluation.

2.1 *National Standards, Regional Standards and Optimization and Implementation*

National and regional standards are mainly found in the *Code for Classification of Urban Land Use and Planning of Urban Development Land*, various indexes for controlling land use in engineering construction projects as well as industrial projects, scale and building density of land for real estate development, etc. The main issues involved in the preparation and implementation of these standards include:

(1) Update of these standards lags behind the changing urban economy and society. The 1990 standards were not updated until 2012. With the *Law of the People's Republic of China on Urban and Rural Planning* enacted in 2007 and the *Notice of the State Council on Promoting the Land Saving and Intensive Use* in 2008, it was not until 1 January 2012 that the latest *Code for Classification of Urban Land Use and Planning Standards of Development Land* took effect. Many indicators have long fallen short of what is required by urban development. Take the proportion of residential land for example. Urban planning and development ideas have for a long time put too much emphasis on production but little on living, which resulted in relatively low proportion of residential land in urban areas—a chronic issue that calls for rectification. The prescribed threshold for residential land proportion in 1990 was only 20%. The current soar of real estate prices in Chinese cities is largely attributable to the low proportion of residential land and insufficient land supply for residential purpose.

(2) "Soft constraints" feature strongly in these standards. Most cities, with the engraved mindset that "the law can hardly be enforced if the offenders are many", dismiss violations as an insignificant matter. Reports from People's Daily Online in June 2006 showed that land use investigations carried out during the period September 2004–June 2006 indicated the rate of land use violations to be at

least around 60% or even higher above 90% in some cities, of which the most severe violations were all linked with government. In recent years, China has adopted remote sensing and monitoring technology, which has to some extent contained the violations of land use laws and regulations. But such violations are still rampant.

(3) China is a massive country with great regional variations in terms of climate conditions, level of economic development, developing conventions and routes. When it comes to regulation, national standards can hardly encompass everything that is needed in different regions while regional standards tend to be strongly selective and poorly implemented.

In comparison with its previous version, the latest GB 50137—2011 *Code for Classification of Urban Land Use and Planning Standards of Development Land* (hereafter referred to as "the GB 50137—2011 Code") includes climatic regionalization for buildings, based on which land use indicators are adjusted accordingly. In the meantime, it has raised the upper limit and lower limit for the proportion of residential land, from 32 and 20% to 40 and 25% respectively. The upper limit of land use for industrial development is reduced from 30% to 25% while the lower limit remains leveled at 15%. The above-mentioned adjustments reflect the requirements of social and economic development and also to some extent the regional differences in China.

The problem is even the GB 50137—2011 Code lacks a complete understanding of the variations resulted from difference development levels and development stages of urban economies and societies. In September 2014, research conducted by *China Business News* over the major cities in the Pearl River Delta, Fujian Delta, Jiangsu-Shanghai region and Beijing-Tianjin-Tangshan region showed that the higher the proportion of services sector in a city's economy is, the higher the real estate prices will be. Why? Mainly because cities with different industrial structures are variedly developed, but the same set of standards is applied to all of them, requiring the same proportional structure of urban land use. Generally speaking, the secondary sector usually contributes more to tax revenues than the services sector, hence local governments are prone to allocate more construction land for development of the secondary sector. In another word, it is a result of "rational choice" by city-level governments that the proportion of land use for industrial development reaches or even exceeds its upper limit. Consequently, it leads to insufficient supply of land for residential purpose and rising housing prices. This issue is particularly prominent in cities that are well-developed economically and with a higher proportion of service sector in their economies.

2.2 *Comprehensive Assessment of Urban Land Utilization Efficiency*

The most common indicators of urban land utilization efficiency include investment intensity per unit area of land, tax revenue contribution per unit area of land, regional GDP (total industrial output value) per unit area of land and population density, among which the first and second indicators are widely adopted by many development zones and municipal governments as the proactive management indexes for land development and utilization—that is, setting up threshold values of investment intensity and tax revenue contributions for new market entrants. Population density is used as a comprehensive measuring index for how much land can take. The above-mentioned indicators reflect to some extent the intensity of economic activities and the size of population that land can accommodate, but they fall short in terms of providing effective assessment of land utilization structure and sustainability. Therefore, it is a must that new indicators are introduced for comprehensive and all-round evaluation of urban land utilization efficiency.

Innovation of modern urban planning and development ideas has profound impact on the evaluation of urban land use efficiency. Economic output and benefits are no longer the highest or the only measurement. The weights of environmental and livability indexes have been constantly on the rise. When it comes to specific indicators, the goal is no longer "the higher the better or the lower the better", but comprehensive consideration of diversity requirements with emphasis on "moderateness". For instance, for the per capita land use for construction purpose, an overly high number indicates waste of land resource and an excessively low figure means an adverse impact on production and living standards.

The comprehensive evaluation of urban land use efficiency must take the perspective of sustainable development and focus on three aspects—intensity, benefit and structure of land development and utilization. Generally speaking, a "moderate" intensity is preferred, the more benefits the better, and as for structure, it should on one hand conform to national or regional standards and on the other hand incorporate necessary adjustments based on actual conditions of each city (Table 1).

3 Innovating Urban Planning and Development Ideas

Globally, with the fast progression of industrialization and urbanization, there was a surge of systematic reflections over traditional urban planning ideas and urban layout frameworks. The "post-modern" ideological trend has opened up a new way for urban development in the post-industrialization era. The urban planning of post-modern cities has gradually shifted away from regarding industrial development and economic growth as the primary or the only objective, and put much more emphasis on individual needs of urban residents. The simple functional zoning has

Table 1 Indicators for comprehensive evaluation of urban land use efficiency

	Indicators
Intensity of land development and utilization	Population density, building density, plot area ratio, investment per unit area of land, waste water discharge per unit area of land, energy consumption per unit area of land, fresh water consumption per unit area of land, waste gas discharge per unit area of land
Benefits of land development and utilization	GDP per unit area of land, value added of secondary and tertiary industries per unit area of land, tax revenue contribution per unit area of land, number of the employed per unit area of land, total retail sales of consumer goods per unit area of land, average wage of the employed
Structure of land development and utilization	The proportion of residential land, the proportion of land used for public administration and public services facilities, the proportion of land used for industrial development, the proportion of land used for roads and transportation facilities, the proportion of land used for greening and public squares

been replaced by integrated development, and on top of that, great importance is attached to sound ecological environment, unique urban contextual inheritances and their impact on improving land utilization efficiency.

3.1 *Organic Theory in Urban Planning and Urban Development*

Urban development puts great emphasis on the pursuit of rationality. Whether it is Sir Ebenezer Howard's garden cities featuring simplicity and order or the various visions of future cities, at the heart of these ideas is the rationalist construction of a new global order for the world's cities. However, amid the globalization trend, cities vary across regions and cultures; they differ greatly in historical and current conditions as well as level of development. The networks of urban spatial structures are diverse, rather than homogeneous, even under the growing influence of the information age, with each section of any city having its own functions, internal structure and spatial formation. Therefore, neither the glass and concrete jungle nor the rational city zoning works at a time when ecological progress is being stressed like never before. Post-modernists expressly criticize the modern urban zoning practice and believe it is a fantasy constructed on the basis of rational planning ideas on mechanical functions and orders that are merely logic thinking but void of any sentimental elements. Therefore, efforts must be directed towards "creating an integrated, multi-functional environment", one that is an organic continuity in which different departments and elements of a city are brought together based on the principle of diversity. This open, comprehensive urban system—a mixture of ambiguity, eclecticism, complexity and contradiction—is best exemplified by an organic city. The pursuit of diversity and disorder in the era of promoting ecological progress is essentially a celebration of differences and tolerance, reflecting functional layering, structural openness and flexibility, through which harmony is achieved out of disorder.

3.2 Ecological Concept in Urban Planning and Urban Development

Post-modern physical cities are based on the concept of ecological units. Urban spatial expansion or spatial design should be in conformity with the combined requirements of human beings, economy and the nature, rather than in pursuit of expansion or component increases in the mathematical sense. The principle of co-existing and counteracting means all spatial components of a city should be well coordinated together. The principle of best fitting functions calls for the most appropriate design of spatial scale and the best utilization of urban spatial resource. The recycling principle implies that urban development should take into account the renewal and reuse of urban space. The symbiotic principle refers to the interdependence and mutual benefits between urban zones utilized for various purposes. Like a living creature, a post-modern city should have a more ecofriendly process of metabolic process in accordance with the natural course of urban development, increase the green and open spaces within and become a "freely breathing" existence.

3.3 Contextualism in Urban Planning and Urban Development

Post-modernism views the world from a historic perspective, taking cities as museums where various cultures converge and accrue. Historical continuity must be maintained if a city wants to keep its lasting charm. Rather than one-sided pursuit of a retro style, the stress of post-modernism is on the contextualism in a city's spatial structure that truly reflects the desire of modern and future societies to reinstate traditions and humanity. While transforming old urban districts, it is as important to preserve historical and cultural heritages as to optimize urban spatial structure. The essence of contextualism points to the ultimate question that a city and its residents should ask—"who am I?", without offering any indicative answer. The methodology of contextualism is to keep such a train of thoughts over this particular question in the city's spatial structure and to present the answer in various spatial components including streets, squares, signs and buildings, which constitutes a spatial reflection of the answer to the question. Therefore, what contextualism requires is by no means simply conserving historical heritages, but covers a wider range of issues related to a city's culture, spirit, image building and development, so much so that its residents and visitors can clearly discern its unique spirit and quality by reading these spatial symbols, and thus indirectly answer the question of "who am I".

3.4 *Humanism in Urban Planning and Urban Development*

Modernistic planning of urban development often puts great importance on grandiose standards, resulting in grandiose buildings that are improperly massive but without any regard to human needs; urban design, from a micro-perspective, pays excessive attention to details, which results in limited vision. Due to the disagreement between macro and micro designs, urban planning in that era inevitably features some spatial incongruities such as urban layout defined by roads, inconvenient functional zoning, and excessive enormous high-rises that are completely out of tune with their surroundings. Post-modernism advocates urban planning defined by communities, street blocks and neighborhood. In particular, the mixed-function communities defined by walking distance unit instead of driving distance unit is a valuable model for us. The effectiveness of such communities speaks to the fact that community building standards is in agreement with human-based criteria and therefore these criteria should be the basic gauge measuring if a city is habitable. The most fundamental principle of "humanism" in urban spatial planning and development is to put great importance on the "human-based criteria" and abide by them. The essence of the above theory is that urban planning and development should be more focused on human needs, taking into account human criteria, human needs, emotions and feelings, with the design of various facilities matching proportionally to the size of human body and meeting the needs of human existence, collective behavior, traveling, resting, entertaining as well as psychological needs, and should enhance the union of human living space with the nature and aim to construct a most habitable environment full of unique characteristics. With the exclusion of extreme ideas in humanism, this doctrine is in fact in line with the requirement of "putting people first" in the scientific outlook on development.

The combination of organic theory, ecological concept, contextualism and humanism offers a new way for urban planning and development, and in the meantime, provides theoretical basis for scientific evaluation of urban land use efficiency and institutional innovation aimed at intensive and economical land utilization.

4 Innovating Urban Land Utilization System

Based on the problems in land utilization in small and medium-sized cities, the author of this book believes innovation should be focused on the following five aspects.

4.1 To Promote Compact Development and Mixed Use of Land

By the trends in building and developing modern cities, most cities in European countries attach great importance to effective use of limited urban space by adopting compact design. Even in the vast territory of America, the compact style design of cities is gaining popularity. Following the example of European countries, two thirds of states in US have chosen "smart growth". Portland City was the first to take this path, and now with 50% population growth, its land only grew by 2%, and it has become one of the most attractive cities in the US. With increasingly conspicuous conflict between a large population and limited land per capita as well as increasingly tight land resource, most cities in China are bound to adopt the compact style for urban design.

Planning and control are necessary for compact development model and mixed uses of land, but the time sequence of planning can be in conflict with recent construction projects. To display a compact, organic and mixed spatial layout, small and medium-sized cities can try to improve the incompact spatial setting using related methods of "smart growth", including: first, to improve building density when circumstances allow and building height is under control, and achieve higher near-line ratio for buildings along streets; secondly, to reduce the setback of buildings appropriately and encourage walking within communities; thirdly, to build centers that include areas for businesses, civil use, culture and entertainment; fourthly, to emphasize the diversity of functions of buildings, e.g. shopping mall and other business operations on the ground floor and offices and residential apartments on higher floors; fifthly, to avoid having car parking lots in places that are in adjacent to streets, etc.

4.2 To Learn from the Smart Growth Model and Explore for a New System of Land-Use Rights

Tradable Development Right (TDR) played an important role in America's movement of reviving old urban districts and protecting open space. Through TSR, American farmers can continue farming in their original land after economic compensation and historical heritages in old cities can be preserved and at the same time benefit their owners.

The key to TDR is to recognize the separation of land use right and ownership. Currently China doesn't have the concept of land use right but land is owned by state. Government approval is required for the change of use for construction land or converting agricultural land to land for non-agricultural purposes in any city. Many small and medium-sized cities are faced with a grueling task of transforming old districts and preserving ecologically controlled zones. From a practical point of view, no matter how the national land system evolves, it is necessary to take it as a way to compensate for and control historical street blocks and ecological zones, and experiment it in certain regions.

In this sense, some practices in America are worth learning from. For instance, we can establish ecological zones such as farmland and forests that should be under control and set them up as development-right transfer regions. Based on the land size collectively owned by villages, the land can be translated into certain proportional units of the corresponding development right. All surrounding areas for construction and development purposes should be incorporated into these regions' development rights. If developers want to develop these areas, they must purchase development rights from the transfer regions. This way, the land rent losses in these ecologically controlled zones are in fact apportioned into the cost of construction and development in surrounding areas. Doubtlessly, such practice requires government supervision, a fair-play trading platform and efforts to strictly prevent illegitimate land leasing for non-agricultural development by villagers in these ecologically controlled zones. The development of green ring belt in Beijing is a good demonstration of such practice with sound achievements, which speaks to the potential of rolling it out as a policy and the value of putting it into practice.

4.3 To Innovate the "City Boundary Management" System

Strict control and administration over a city's boundary is meaningful for small and medium-sized cities. Currently in China, city boundary administration usually involves definition of city boundary by setting up a wide green belt along the ring-shape expressways around the city, establishing the administrative boundary for urban-rural joint areas, defining the boundary of established urban areas for urban planning in the overall plan of land utilization, etc. The prevailing issue in such arrangement is the role of planned economy was overplayed and problematic implementation.

It is indeed necessary to reform our current methodology of defining urban boundary—that is, the boundary of established urban area in the overall urban planning is now usually defined one-sidedly by accredited planners and government, which merely provides an ambiguous estimate of urban land scale and various projects. It is not only random but also lack of legal significance. Both urban residents and developers are unaware of such boundary. Government does not provide clear guidance through its investments in public facilities. Therefore, this boundary, except in statistic work, serves no purpose in urban development.

The success of Urban Growth Boundary (UGB) scheme in US has set a good example that is worth learning from. However, due to fundamental problems in terms of development stage, land system and political system, it can hardly apply in China. So far given the attitudes of developers, residents and government, China won't see the full support of UGB as in the US, however, it should take UGB as one potential direction for institutional reforms and make efforts in this regard. The urban boundary administration should pay more attention to the demarcation of land forbidden for construction purposes. Legally binding boundaries should be set up for basic farmland, forests and ecological protection zones in order to protect essential natural resources and open space and preserve sufficient natural treasures for future generations.

For small and medium-sized cities, institutional innovation is a key content of bold exploration in urban boundary administration. In practice, they must first unwaveringly protect green belts and leave enough room for the implementation of future policies, and secondly, take initiative to learn from America's UGB scheme and establish their own versions of UGB based on their own conditions.

4.4 To Learn from the Theory of Organic Cities and Embark on the Path of Integrated Industrial and Urban Development

One of the trends amid modern urban development is the weakening of functional zoning, that is, instead of emphasizing on urban divisions, urban layout tends to seek intermixture and synthesis, which is the so-called "organic theory". Before 2000, China built a large number of industrial parks in order to push ahead the industrialization process. These industrial parks, located far from downtown areas, are for the singular purpose of industrial operations, resulting in the situation of complete separation of residence and work place and consequently weigh heavily on the transportation system and the sustainable development of these parks. Similarly, "satellite cities" sprouted out around mega cities to assuage the pressure on these central cities. These "satellite cities" are typically commuter towns with little commercial and industrial activity and fail to play a good role in mitigating the pressure on those central cities. The prevailing result is with the lingering-on problems in central cities, the traffic jams between "satellite cities" and their central cities turn into a new problem and the living standards of urban residents are hardly improved. After 2000, China came to realize the importance of addressing this problem and thus stressed that it is equally important to provide residents sound dwelling, living and entertaining facilities as well as sufficient employment opportunities. The development of new modern cities is increasingly focused on their relative independence and completeness of urban functions.

For a long time, the key issue small and medium-sized cities are faced with is failure to attract enough population during the urbanization process. No matter how big they expand in terms of land, they find it hard to retain permanent residents mainly due to lack of opportunities for employment and potential career development. Therefore, for small and medium-sized cities to play a main role in China's urbanization, it is necessary to provide favorable policies in areas like reform of permanent residency register (Hukou) system, social security, etc., and more importantly, to encourage industrial development based on local conditions, focus on integrated urban and industrial development and provide jobs for new migrant workers.

4.5 To Formulate and Implement Plot Ratio Based Incentive Policies

The New York Zoning Resolution issued in 1916 mainly covers contents like building heights, setback limits, the compatibility of different land usages, etc. Under this resolution, the New York City was divided into several districts with different height limits, each with certain endowed development rights and prescribed further setbacks for buildings to allow sufficient sunlight in neighboring blocks. With constant social advancement, in order to minimize input of public funds but to build maximum public space, government hopes that private developers can provide some space as public space or build some public facilities. Against this backdrop, the plot ratio based incentive policies were rolled out. Such Incentive Zoning System was quickly copied by other cities. At the heart of such incentive zoning system is the trade-off between Community Improvements and plot ratio for developers. The higher plot ratio contributes to more intensive and compact development, at the expense of including some community improvement projects by developers in their construction projects, e.g. extra open space, affordable housing for low-income earners, special purpose buildings, public art programs, etc. The essence of such incentive zoning system is to relax the original zoning limit (such as plot ratio limit) on the condition that developers contribute to public benefits.

The original intent of setting plot ratio for development projects is to internalize external effects and the plot-ratio based incentive policy was invented based on this intent. As an economic policy, it has to provide economic incentives to stoke up the construction enthusiasm of developers. The implementation of this policy has several phases: at the initial stage, it improved the public environment of the society. Then, with deeper understanding of the policy among developers, the incentive of more economic benefits drove them to use this policy for the satisfaction of their own interests by building a small number of public facilities to gain higher plot ratio. As a result, despite the increase of a limited amount of public space and public facilities, highly intensive construction projects have eventually undermined a great deal of public interests. In this sense, government's original intent of internalizing external effects fails to materialize. However, this type of flexible zoning policy is a positive and meaningful attempt that leads to new adjustments of this policy and the release of more reasonable, effective policies for the better realization of social benefits.

Although currently China has specific regulations on the density of high rise buildings, with plot ratio generally within the range of 0.7–2, which is not strictly implemented in practice. In view of construction lessons learnt from other cities at home and abroad, plot ratio based incentive policies can be implemented in some prosperous or densely populated regions. When calculating plot ratio or coverage area incentives or favorable policies should be provided to developers who play an active role in contributing to urban open and public space. Lessons learnt from developed countries indicate that plot-ratio related incentive policy in the initial construction phase will greatly stimulate the enthusiasm of developers and thus help shorten the construction cycle. However, in the long term, it is still necessary to implement appropriate regional regulations to keep specialized spaces under control. At the moment, small and medium-sized cities are in the stage of rapid growth, efforts should be directed towards formulating and implementing plot-ratio related incentive policies as soon as possible to encourage developers and in the meantime regulating development by controlling building height in densely constructed areas.

5 Improving Urban Land Use Intensity and Promoting the Transition of Urbanization

China is now in the middle of a rapid urbanization process, with an increasing number of cities in growing scales that are playing increasingly important roles and with more and more rural labor force surplus migrating into urban areas. Meanwhile, with the advancement of urbanization, the demand for land from all walks of life is exploding, which has resulted in the conversion of massive agricultural land (including farmland) into land for urban development, hence the increasingly conflictive relationship between people and land.

Solving the land use issue during the urbanization process plays a significant role in the smooth progression of urbanization. At a time when land use issues are increasingly acute, China is destined to go down the road of strict implementation of the land conserving and intensive utilization system, improving land utilization efficiency, especially urban land use intensity, providing guidance for economic restructuring and industrial restructuring, and promoting the transition of urbanization.

5.1 Status Quo of Urban Land Utilization and Definition of Intensive Land Use

(i) **Status quo of urban land utilization**

China entered a period of exceptionally fast economic growth in 2003, with annual GDP growth rate at above 10% for five consecutive years and then hovering above 7.5% for the following few years. From 2003 to 2013, China's annual GDP growth averaged at 10.2%. Along with rapid economic growth and advancement of urbanization, land demand, especially demand for land for construction purposes, from all walks of life has been constantly on rise, which can be been easily seen by the size of land approved for construction purposes.

Statistics show that during the period from 2003 to 2013, the land approved for construction purposes (including construction projects in rural areas) added up to 54,580 km^2, which is 2.47 times the total area of land for urban development by the end of 2000, or 8.6 times the size of Shanghai city or 3.2 times the size of Beijing city. Meanwhile, it is a prevailing practice to convert farmland to construction land, which accounts for 43% of the land approved for construction projects. This is why

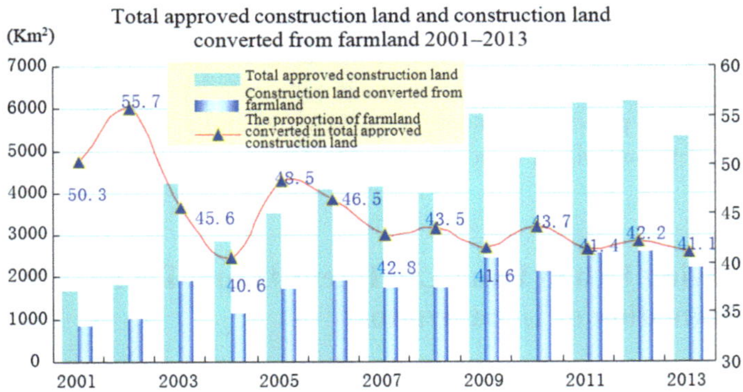

Fig. 1 Total approved construction land and construction land converted from farmland 2001–2013

China's total area of farmland has been dropping for several years in a row, and the government is increasingly under pressure to protect the 1.8 billion *mu* (a unit of land, 15 *mu* equals to 1 ha). From 2001 to 2013, the total accumulated area of construction land converted from farmland reached 24,000 km^2 (see Fig. 1).

There was also a sharp increase of urban construction land. China had 22,114 km^2 of total urban construction land in 2000, which rapidly grew to 45,751 km^2 by the end of 2012, with an average increase of 1,970 km^2 each year. Such sharp increase in construction land is increasingly contradictory to the nation's reality of large population, limited land and farmland shortage. According to the report on the survey of land use changes across the nation, China had 1.945 billion *mu* of farmland in 1998 (1.56 *mu* per capita), which, after consecutive decreases, dropped to 1.8257 billion *mu* in 2008 (1.37 *mu* per capita), with annual reduction averaged at over 13 million *mu*.

Land is one of the most important basic natural resources that are indispensable for human beings to survive and prosper, and also an essential instrument in industrialization and modernization. In sharp contrast with tight land supply, extensive urban land utilization with low efficiency is prevalent, and waste of land resource is a grievous reality in China. Statistics show that inefficient use of urban land added up to 5,000 km^2, accounting for 11% of the total established urban area; there is 10–15% of idled land and 40% of inefficiently used land in rural areas, which constitute great potential for further development. Currently, the average plot ratio of industrial land in China is only 0.3-0.6, and the urban land per capita is 145 km^2, far exceeding the national threshold.

In order to achieve sustainable land utilization and provide sufficient land resource for the current and future needs of social and economic development in a critical stage of industrialization and urbanization, China must meet the demand for construction land in the course of economic development and in the meantime conserve certain quantity of farmland for food security. This requires China to protect farmland, promote economical and intensive land use and adopt a new land utilization model that minimizes land used for construction projects, optimizes land utilization efficiency and fits China's actual conditions, which is a fundamental guideline that China should stick to in the long run and the inevitable choice in China's new-type urbanization process.

(ii) **Definition of intensive urban land utilization**

As our society advances ahead and our understanding deepens, the understanding of intensive land utilization has been constantly evolving.

The concept of intensive urban land utilization is inherited from the theory of intensive rural land use that initially derives from the research on agricultural land in the theory of rent by David Ricardo, a renowned classical British economist. Intensive rural land use refers to "an agricultural production model that requires intensive input of means of production and labor as well as employment of advanced technologies and management theories to maximize the return on a certain area of land". Later, the concept of intensive land use was also introduced into research on urban land development, which formed the concept of intensive urban land utilization, that is, the process of keep improving land utilization efficiency (production per unit area of land) through various methods such as technological advancement, increasing investment in the existing inventory of land, improving the allocation methods of production factors, etc.

At a seminar held in 2005, the Ministry of Land and Resources (MLR) explicitly put forward that the definition of economical and intensive land use contains three main aspects: first, economical use of land, which means all construction projects must try their best to use land in an economical way; secondly, intensive use of land, which means every project must enhance productivity (measured by input-output ratio) per unit area of land used and improve the intensity of land utilization; thirdly, higher efficiency of land allocation and utilization, which means consolidation, replacement and reserve of resource to make reasonable arrangements about how much land is made available and how quickly it is made available, optimize the structure and distribution of land for construction purposes, unlock the full potential of land resource, and improve the allocation and utilization efficiency of land.

In 2012, the Ministry of Land and Resources (MLR) released the *Opinions on Promoting the Development of an Economical and Intensive Land Use System*, bringing forward a framework of "planned management and control, planned regulation, standard control, market-oriented allocation, policy incentives, monitoring and supervision, evaluation and feedback, shared responsibility", with focuses on the contents of eight systems, including: a management and control system of land utilization overall plan, a system of planned regulation, a control system of construction land use standards, a market-oriented system of land resource allocation, a system of policies encouraging economical and intensive land use, a land use monitoring and supervising system, a land use evaluation system, and a system of shared responsibilities for economical and intensive land use.

On 22 May 2014, MLR rolled out the *Provisions on the Economical and Intensive Use of Land*, aimed at fully implementing the most stringent protection system of farmland and the most stringent economical and intensive land use system, enhancing the capability of land to sustain economic and social development, and stepping up the effort towards ecological progress. The *Provisions* provide a complete, all-round elaborations over economical and intensive land use from six aspects including guidance for scale, layout optimization, standard control, market-oriented allocation, efficient utilization, supervision and evaluation. It is the first ministerial enactment in China that is dedicated to regulating and guiding economical and intensive land use activity.

With gradually deepened understanding, the public has come to realize that economical and intensive land use is not only about increasing output from a unit area of land, but also about reasonable land use structure and layout, improving ecological environment, etc. Additionally, the measuring parameters of land output include economic benefits as well as social and ecological benefits. Therefore, the definition of economical and intensive land use is further extended to a process in which various means are adopted to constantly improve land utilization efficiency and economic benefits, as well as to achieve sound economic, social and ecological benefits.

To sum up, the author believes that economical and intensive land use should be defined on three levels—macro, meso and micro levels. On the micro-level, it means improvement of input-output ratio for a unit area of land. On the meso-level, it puts more emphasis on rationalizing and optimizing land use functions and structure. On macro-level, it refers to improvement of overall benefits from the perspective of a city, which hence requires the city to have proper size, rational strategic positioning, coordinated industrial structure, etc.

Since the release of the first *Catalogue of Restricted Uses of Land* and the *Catalogue of Prohibited Uses of Land* in 1999, China has rolled out a series of policies and regulations on economical and intensive land use, with a considerable number of achievements, e.g. a basic economical and intensive land use system has been established, a framework of "planned management & control, planned regulation, standard control, market-oriented allocation, policy incentives, monitoring and supervision, evaluation and feedback, shared responsibility" has been formed, and land use efficiency has been improved. Especially after the *Notice of the State Council on Promoting the Land Saving and Intensive Use* and the Third Plenary Session of the 17th CPC Central Committee proposed to insist on "the most stringent intensive land use system" in 2008, China has continuously stepped up efforts in implementing and publicizing the economical and intensive land use system. As a result, this concept is gradually taking root across the country, and the nation's overall intensity of land use has improved.

5.2 *Relationship Between Intensive Urban Land Utilization and Urbanization*

China is a country with a large population but relatively limited land, especially farmland. Given this reality and the current rapid advancement of industrialization

Table 2 Comparison of per capita land used for construction in different types of residential areas

Types of residential area	Mega cities	Large cities	Medium-sized cities	Small cities	Administrative towns	Villages
Per capita land used for construction purposes (square meter per capita)	74.6	88	107.9	142.7	149	55

and urbanization, the mismatch between supply and demand of land for development is increasingly marked. On the one hand, land demand has ballooned while the resource of farmland has drastically decreased during the process of urbanization. On the other hand, land use for urban development keeps in an extensive and low efficiency style. To change the contradictory relation between urbanization and protection of farmland, China must reform its urbanization model and facilitate economical and intensive land use.

In the relation between urbanization and intensive urban land use, on one hand, urbanization is overall a positive force in promoting economical and intensive land use, however, urbanization in an extensive growth model will result in faster growth of land demand than population growth and hence cause waste of land resource. On the other hand, enforcing an economical and intensive land use system will help the transition of urbanization from an extensive growth model to an intensive growth model.

(i) **Urbanization as an overall positive force in promoting economical and intensive land use**

The essence of urbanization is to have related population and industries concentrated in limited space of cities through the economies of urban agglomeration, and to have industrial clusters and population clusters. Through such economies of agglomeration, the economies of scale can play a stronger role in cutting costs and bringing up output efficiency. The major three urban agglomerations in China—namely, the Beijing-Tianjin-Hebei area, the Yangtze River Delta and the Pearl River Delta, which in combination accounts for 2.8% of China's total territory, has concentrated 18% of the nation's population and generated 36% of its GDP, which is a typical example of intensive land use resulted from the economies of agglomeration during the course of urbanization.

Judging by the per capita land for urban development in different types of residential areas, the higher the population density is, the smaller per capita land area is for urban development. Since per capita land use in urban residential areas is far less than in rural residential areas, the simple decrease of rural population and increase of urban population during the urbanization process can result in saving massive areas of land. Table 1 in Chap. 1 shows per capita land use in large and mega cities is around half of that in villages (Table 2).

In an economic sense, the output ratio of urban land can be several times the output ratio of rural land, or even several dozen or several hundred times in some cases, therefore, the intensity of urban land use is far higher than that of rural land use. Given the high input and high output nature of urban land, land use efficiency and intensity level in urban areas are much higher than in rural areas. Intensive utilization of land is a basic feature of urban land. Meanwhile, urbanization requires reasonable allocation of urban land resource, that is, a process of making reasonable use of land, resources, capital and technology so as to tap the full potential of urban land from a temporal as well as spatial perspectives and achieving the optimized and comprehensive benefits of urban land use. All in all, urbanization itself is a process of improving land use efficiency and intensity level.

(i) **Enforcing an economical and intensive land use system can contribute to the transition of urbanization model**

Poor economic base, weak start, and rapid growth mark the process of urbanization in China. The past over three decades have seen China's urbanization rate take a giant leap from 17.9 to 53.7%. Now in hindsight, in a growth model that is driven by extensive consumption of resources such as land, China has now ended up with structural imbalance of urban and rural land use, irrational scale and structure, extensiveness and low efficiency of construction land use, population urbanization outpaced by land urbanization. All these have resulted in massive waste of farmland resource, resources and environment overuse. Research findings show that China's construction land use scale per 100 million yuan GDP is 2.3, 8 and 4.8 times of the land use scale of America, Japan and South Korea respectively in the first decade of the 21st century.

The first and foremost issue that developing a new type urbanization needs to solve is land. China's 2nd National Land Survey statistics indicate that, compared with statistics from the first survey, construction land use scale has increased from 29.18 million ha to 3.5 million ha, up by 5.819 million ha, among which 4.595 million ha are for urban construction projects and 1.225 million ha for those in rural areas. Per capita construction land use in both urban and rural areas of China are higher than their national thresholds and corresponding world averages. In the meantime, total area of good-quality farmland across China has drastically reduced, along with the per capita farmland, which is less than half of the world average. There is a considerable amount of farmland that are with high or medium level of pollutions and thus no longer suitable for cultivation. Severe shortage of land per capita, continuously deterioration of soil quality, low efficiency of land use, as well as idled and wasted land resource combine to exacerbate the tense relation between land resource and human activity.

China must reform its growth model towards an intensive style in order to gratify the increasingly demand for land from its continuously growing economy, ensure a certain quantity of farmland for food security, protect ecological environment, and achieve sustainable development of land. To help achieving this objective, it is required to enhance economical and intensive land use, tap the full potential of existing construction land and mobilize the current inventory of construction land. The plan of "a new type of urbanization" requires simultaneous development of population and land urbanization as well as a harmonious relation between people and the city they live in. The key priority here is economical and intensive land use—an inevitable choice in the course of developing a new type of urbanization, which can in turn contribute to the transition of urbanization growth model.

5.3 *Major Issues in Implementing Intensive Urban Land Utilization*

Since the idea of establishing an economical and intensive land use system was put forward, there have been various active explorations into an intensive style new type industrialization and urbanization across China, which have improved land use intensity as well as promoted relocation, agglomeration, transformation and upgrading of industries. However, there are many problems during its urbanization process, e.g. scattered distribution of industrial clusters, indistinctive features, relatively small in scale, weak capability to agglomerate, etc., which have increased rigidity of demand for land resource, exacerbated the conflict between land supply and demand, and complicated the dilemma between development and protecting farmland.

(i) **Improper urban planning, extensive land use and irrational land use structure**

Land use planning is an essential instrument of government to guide and control land use, which is proactive, restrictive and instructive. Urban land use structure directly reflects the proportional relations of land use among various entities, and is a key factor determining the land use results.

Due to lack of long-term plans or improper planning, China's urban development has long deviated from the realities of its own economic strength and conditions. The pursuit of size and comprehensiveness is common, resulting in massive waste of land resource. In recent years, China has seen rapid expansion of land for various construction projects, taking up 200,000–350,000 ha of farmland each year on average, with rampant extensive uses and land wastes. Low efficiency of urban land use is also evident, currently with 5% of urban land idled. Within the designated scope of land for urban development, there is about 266,700 ha of idled land or farmland approved for construction but yet to be converted.

Right now, China's extensive land use model has not been changed fundamentally. Statistics show that over 40% of urban land use features low efficiency, as much as 10–15% of residential housing in rural areas are vacant, and there are 5000 km^2 of land inefficiently used for urban industrial construction, mining and warehousing. Against this backdrop, government should make overall land use plan with specific provisions of scale, layout, structure and detailed arrangement of land for construction, set an upper limit of total area of land used for construction, and strictly apply the restrictive indicators and the provision of regulation by region in the overall land use plan.

In the land use structure within Chinese cities, the following issues are universal: disproportional land use for the secondary and tertiary industries, relatively higher proportions of land used for industrial development and residential housing, relatively lower proportions of land used for commercial services, transportation and greening. Especially in recent years, land used for industrial development has grown rapidly at low costs, and there is plenty of land acquired for industrial development but then left idled. Irrational structure of urban land use has led to many conspicuous problems such as housing shortage in old urban districts, traffic jams, lack of room for further development for enterprises in central downtown districts, and deteriorating residential and ecological environment, and hence, the overall benefits of urban land use have been compromised.

(ii) **Urban expansion has eroded too much farmland**

Along with higher levels of urbanization comes increase of cities and towns and expansion of urban areas, which thus means reduction of farmland. Some cities and towns are reckless in seeking further geological expansion, with great efforts directed towards enlarging the urban built-up area, development zones, new urban districts and multiple ring roads, without much efforts on tapping the full potential of existing urban land. Statistics from MLR indicate that the actually total supply of state-owned land for construction was 7,305 km^2 in 2013, up by 2.7% year on year, among which there were 2,100 km^2 used for industrial production, mining and warehousing, 651 km^2 used for commerce and services, 1381 km^2 for residential housing and 3,173 for other purposes, up by 1.4, 27.9, 20.5 and 6.3% respectively. From 2011 to 2013, there were evident increases of state-owned land supply for construction purposes, with the average annual land supply above 6,500 km^2 during this period.

China's total area of farmland reached a new historical low of 1.8254 billion *mu* (15 *mu*=1 ha) in end 2008. Afterwards, thanks to land consolidation, reclamation and adjustment of survey standards, the total area of farmland spiked up, reaching 2.031 billion *mu* by end of 2009, which then kept dropping slightly in the following few years. The downward trajectory is much steeper for the farmland per capita. China's farmland per capita is 1.59 *mu* in 1996, and fell to 1.52 *mu* in 2009, which is less than half of the world average (3.38 *mu*) (see Fig. 2).

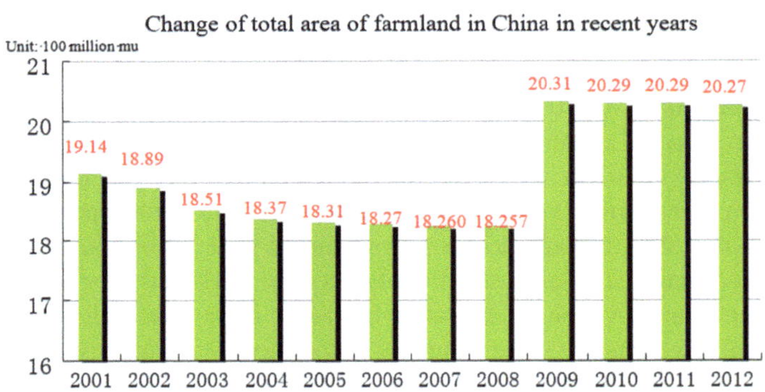

Fig. 2 Change of total area of farmland in China in recent years

In the long run, reckless expansion of land for construction will inevitably pose serious threat to the stability and sustainability of local agricultural production. In particular, as local governments become increasingly reliant on the revenue from sales of land, the scale of land supply will see solid increases, which will stimulate the expansion pace of urban land and thus exacerbate the tense relation between land for construction and protection of farmland.

(iii) **Low plot ratio in urban areas and low output ratio per unit area of land**

Compared with developed countries, the plot ratio is relatively low in China's urban areas, which means urban land is not fully utilized. Statistics show that the plot ratio of urban areas is 2 in Japan, 1.6 in Hong Kong, 1.2 in Taiwan and only 0.78 in China's mainland. Although China has several large cities like Beijing, Shanghai and Shenzhen, with rapid growth of urban population, it still lags behind those developed countries. China should further enhance economical and intensive use of urban land, tap the full potential of land resource and strive to catch up with developed countries.

During the period from 1980 to present, China has seen rapid economic growth and radical progression of urbanization. Some study and analysis indicate that every 1% of economic growth will cost a country around 300,000 *mu* of farmland. Compared with Japan in its rapid growth period, the land demand arising from every 1% of GDP growth in China is almost 8 times the figure in Japan. Currently, the comprehensive land use per capita in China's mainland large and medium-sized cities has already surpassed 120 m^2, which, in comparison with international metropolitans, is much higher—only 78 m^2 in Tokyo and only 37 m^2 in Hong Kong. It can be obviously seen from the above-mentioned data that extensive land use and low intensity are very common in China's urban areas, which results in low output ratio per unit area of land.

(iv) **Severe pollution of land environment potentially threatens land utilization**

High speed urbanization in recent years has brought severe land pollutions. Some companies operate with rusty facilities and obsolete technologies, without systematic environmental planning, which has caused irreversible damages to the urban ecological environment and a series of environmental issues such as soil erosion, air pollution and deteriorated water and environment quality. When promoting urbanization, some cities focused on economic benefits and GDP growth without paying much attention to environmental protection. Land pollutions pose potential threat to further development and utilization of land resource.

Additionally, with the advancement of urbanization, urban population has been steadily growing, generating a large amount of household garbage, which not only takes up plenty of land but also pollutes the ground water and surrounding environment, and thus severely undermines daily production and everyday life. In a considerable number of cities and town, excessive utilization of ground water has led to subsidence of land, piling up garbage is very commonly seen, and due to financial constraints, local governments cannot guarantee timely and effective measures against environmental pollution and leave the ecological environment to continuous deterioration.

(v) **An inadequate land use supervising and restraining system results in frequent occurrences violations in land use**

Under China's current economic system, government has complete monopoly over the primary market of land. Only for the sake of their own interests, some regional governments can be bold enough to violate laws and regulations, e.g. use agricultural land for non-agricultural construction projects, expanding the development zones without proper approval, recklessly building various types of new development zones, land acquisition, land supply and project execution without going through the necessary review and approval procedures as required by law. In some towns or townships, government not only owns land, but also assumes the administrative role and operative role for land. A full set of administrative authorities is not properly set up, and scope of duty is not clearly defined. In some areas, there is not even a specific land administration organ but only one or two land administrators. Under these circumstances, loose supervision and constraint over land seems inevitable.

MLR statistics show that there were 83,000 violations against land use laws and regulations across the nation in 2013, with 41,000 ha of land involved, among which there were 12,000 ha of farmland—up by 35, 28.2 and 14.4% respectively. There were 58,000 official cases reported and set up for further investigation, reaching a historical new high, with 36,000 ha of land involved—also relatively high from a historical perspective, among which there were 11,000 ha of farmland—up by 57.7, 29.8 and 17.3% respectively.

6 Thoughts on Improving Urban Land Utilization Intensity

Land, the origin of people's livelihood and the base of development, is a non-renewable, valuable resource. Economical and intensive land use is a long-term, dynamic process as well as a complicated and systematic project. How can we utilize land resource in an economical and intensive style, make use of land in a scientific and rational way, optimize the benefits of land use and satisfy the needs of land from different income groups or various purposes? The key to this question is system and institution innovations.

6.1 To Formulate a Rational Overall Land Utilization Plan and Urban Development Plan

Overall land utilization plan is the "steering wheel" and general guideline in land administration, which serves as the statutory basis for administrative review and approval for land use, scale control and land use purposes. We must give full play to its guiding role and make overall arrangement of various land usages. Efforts must be directed towards making a rational macroscopic plan of urbanization based on the capabilities of resources and environment to sustain development, developing city agglomerations with a scientific plan based on the comprehensive transportation network and information network, strictly controlling the scale of land used for urban construction, making meticulous demarcation of permanent basic farmland, setting reasonable boundaries for confining urban development, optimizing internal spatial structure of cities, promoting compact and intensive urban development, and improving the utilization efficiency of land and space. The overall land utilization plan should start with the three objectives in sustainable land use—ecological rationality, economical feasibility and social acceptance, aimed to coordinate the relation between land for construction and farmland as well as the relation between land for industrial development and land for other construction purposes. In addition, land use planning should not only focus on the spatial arrangement of land resource, but also the reasonable temporal allocation.

Urban planning means to rationally organize and coordinate various land usages and construction projects in urban areas in order to promote both cultural and ethical progress and material progress and to make cities and towns the perfect habitats with rational layout, necessary supporting infrastructure, neat, picturesque environment and flourishing culture. It can regulate the relations between buildings as well as the relation between buildings and environment through control of how land is used and to what extent it is used, and thus ensure the speed of urban development keep in line with regional conditions. Rational urban planning should be practical construction plans under the guidance of regional planning and planning of urban systems, with specific details about functional positioning. It should be in line with current market demand but also be proactive, focus on its economic benefits and feasibility, and play a leading role in guiding the allocation of urban land resource.

6.2 To Set Up a Standard System and an Evaluation System, and Enhance Standardized Control

Efforts must be directed to setting up a control system of indicators for economical land use planning, an evaluation system for economical land use planning and a system of land use standards, that is, (1) to improve the territory and space planning system so that rational and feasible economical land use indicators and standards become the key content in planning, (2) to establish an evaluation system for economical land use planning with evaluation, monitoring and alerting sub-systems for different planning standards, planning hierarchies and planning types, and (3) to expand the research and application scopes of land use standards to cover various sectors of the national economy such as major infrastructure, new industries and sectors aimed to improve the people's livelihood.

6.3 To Mobilize Existing Land Resource and Improve Land Utilization Efficiency

As urbanization progresses, the total area of land for urban construction projects will reach its "ceiling". Given the strict control over this total, efforts for higher land use intensity must be focused on the current inventory of land available for urban development. A mechanism of incentives and constraints must be established to encourage and regulate redevelopment of low-efficiency urban land use, which features overall planning, government guidance, market-oriented operation, public participation, and shared benefits. Efforts should also be directed towards reinvigorating and utilizing existing urban land for construction projects, setting up a mechanism of incentives for reclaiming existing construction land for other purposes, pushing ahead the transformation and protective development of old urban districts, decrepit facilities and villages inside cities, and giving full play to the roles of government land reserve in reinvigorating low-efficiency urban land use.

Some developed cities like Guangzhou and Shenzhen have made sound explorations in redevelopment of the current inventory of land. Policy-wise, Guangzhou rolled out the *Opinions on Accelerating the Transformation Work of "Old Urban Districts, Old Villages and Obsolete Facilities*", which provides regulative norms and policy guidance for renovating work on these existing used land. Shenzhen city released the *Overall Plan of Reforming the Land Administration System in Shenzhen* and the *Methods for Refreshing the City of Shenzhen*, with overall arrangements for issues like balance between industrial development and land administration, between market orientation and government regulation, etc. Practices of existing used land redevelopment in Guangzhou and Shenzhen has proven that a quadrupled mechanism with "government policy, participation of enterprises, market-oriented operation and profit allocation" is the key to successful redevelopment work.

Another key aspect in mobilizing the inventory of land is to strengthen the supervision and management of idled land. Related government authorities should carry out all-round surveys, have a clear picture of relevant statistics, manage idled and desolated land according to national regulations, and mitigate the constraints of land element. For newly approved projects, procedures should be in place to ensure prompt start of construction, with key focuses on rate of disbursement, and no deferment is allowed unless under special circumstances. For projects that have acquired land use certificate but is yet to start construction, a deadline should be set, otherwise the granted land should be withdrawn. For land acquired but idled or not fully utilized for longer than a specific period, an idling fee should be imposed or the land use right be withdrawn. For land idled but not long enough to be taken back, efforts should be directed towards mobilizing such land resources by various means such as consolidation, swap and replacement, tapping the full potential of existing land resource, and making sure "every inch of land is fully utilized for the optimized effect". In the meantime, guidance and incentives should be provided to enterprises for improving land use intensity per unit area of land and increasing plot ratio.

6.4 *To Push Forward Land Market-Oriented Reform and Give Full Play to the Role of Market Principles in Resource Allocation*

Efforts should be directed towards market-oriented reforms of land markets and building an integrated urban-rural construction land market. Since its reform and opening up to the world, China has set up a characteristic, relatively mature market of state-owned land for construction. However, by far, there are still many weak links across the market, mainly including: (1) relative high proportion of administrative allocation, which accounts for 36% of total land supply, (2) prevalent administration malpractices, and (3) improper pricing mechanism for industrial land, sometimes the land is sold at a price lower than the purchasing price.

It is necessary to further reform the system of compensable use of state-owned construction land, including: to expand the scope of compensable use of state-owned land, to gradually implement the compensable use policy for infrastructure and social undertakings that are of a business operation nature; to reduce allocation of land not used for public welfare; to apply the compensable use policy (e.g. requiring annual rent of land) for land gained through administrative allocation but used in for-profit projects; to fully implement the market-oriented allocation principles in the supply of various compensable usages of land; employ land rent and price leverages and promote economical and intensive use of land. It is proven in history that land resource allocation giving full play to the market's role is the best way to stimulate economical and intensive land use.

6.5 *To Enhance Environmental Improvement and Step Up Effort Toward Ecological Progress*

In order to ensure economical and intensive use of land resource during the urbanization process, it is necessary to enhance control, improvement and management of pollution sources, to meet the prescribed standards of pollutant emissions, to strictly control the development scale of completed projects that cause pollutions, and to make sure that the disposal of pollutants meet relevant requirements. Then it is also important to undertake preventative work against land pollution, take precautionary measures, strengthen the rule of law, guarantee a virtuous cycle of urban land use from an ecological and environmental friendly perspective, and achieve sustainable development of land resource. Urban areas with the right conditions should fully draw on the underground space. Making use of urban underground space is the most effective way to achieve higher land use efficiency, save land resource, increase urban green belts, maintain historical and cultural landscapes, realize vertical traffic separation of pedestrians and vehicles, expand the capacity of infrastructure and improve urban ecological environment.

6.6 To Build a Supervising and Controlling System Over the Full Process of Urban Land Use and Strengthen Publicity Effort in Promoting Advanced Models and Exemplary Initiatives

To establish and optimize the land use supervising and management system with close links between "ex ante", "in action" and "ex post", covering the whole process of examination, approval, supply, use and development, and coordinated by relevant authorities. The focus of land management should shift from solely on administrative examination and approval toward on both examination & approval and supervision, from ex post penalty to ex ante precautions as well as ex post penalty. Efforts should also be direct towards improving the dynamic monitoring and measuring system of land use, enhancing timely monitoring and tracking management over land development and utilization, building an investigation and penalty coordination mechanism for land use violations, establishing and improving various systems such as case information sharing, case transfer and joint efforts on major cases, etc., and giving full play to all involving parties as a whole. It is also important to step up the efforts in ascertaining responsibilities, investigate every major violation cases that come to light, impose proper punishment and expose the cases to the public.

To step up efforts in promoting and advertising exemplary models of economical and intensive land utilization. It is necessary to summarize the successful lessons learnt from the regions with outstanding achievements in economical and intensive land utilization, and to strengthen the promoting and advertising effort. Proper technologies and models should be developed for economical land use in different industries and sectors. By summarizing, advertising and promoting exemplary practices, we can gradually achieve the goal of improving the land utilization intensity across the whole society.

Land use is a matter that has a long term influence on future generations. Economical and intensive land use and solid measures to protect farmland are not only the requirement of sustainable development but also the indispensable condition in achieving a new type of urbanization and building a harmonious society. We must have a fresh mind with enhanced awareness, take actions to increase the intensity of construction land utilization, and create a harmonious, beautiful and sustainable living environment for future generations.

Chapter 7
Study of Low-Carbon Development Path for Small and Medium-sized Cities

Global climate change has become a topic that draws close attention in the international community, and adopting the path of low-carbon economic development by seeking a balance point between development and emission reduction is the inevitable choice. In essence, low-carbon development requires human activities to feature low input, low pollution, low emission and high output, so as to integrate economic, environmental and social benefits and the system of human society, system of science and technology, and system of natural ecology.

Low-carbon city refers to "cities where the economy is dominated by low-carbon industries and production, residents adopt and promote low-carbon life, and government takes low-carbon society as the construction blueprint. The purpose of low-carbon city development is, on the premise of continuously improving the quality of life, to achieve a model of urban construction and social development that is beneficial to reducing carbon emission by changing the economic development model, consumption concept and lifestyle."[1] Low-carbon city stresses the promotion of low-carbon concept pushed by certain plans, policies and systems. With low-carbon technologies and products as the basis and the production and application of low-carbon energies as the main means, it promotes extensive public participation in city development activities that boost local economy and improve people's quality of life, thus contributing to global carbon emission reduction.[2]

There are a lot of small and medium-sized cities in China, which, as an important secondary engine for economic growth, are critical for China's overall economic development. Compared with large cities, small and medium-sized ones are better at driving local economic growth that is centered on county economy, effectively increasing farmers' income and promoting land transfer, and boosting the integrated development of first, secondary and tertiary industries in local areas. As the

[1] Dai Yixin, "Evolution and Primary Analysis of the Concept of Low-carbon Urban Development," *Modern Urban Research 11* (2009): 7–12.

[2] Liu Zhilin, Dai Yixin, Dong Changgui and Qi Ye, "Concept and International Experiences of Low-carbon City," *Urban Development Studies 16*: 1–7.

© Social Sciences Academic Press and Springer Nature Singapore Pte Ltd. 2018

X. Li and X. Liu, *Green Development Model of China's Small and Medium-sized Cities*, Research Series on the Chinese Dream and China's Development Path,
https://doi.org/10.1007/978-981-13-0779-9_7

conjunction point between urban and rural economic areas, small and medium-sized cities are relatively independent and their comprehensive functions decide that they play several irreplaceable special roles in urban-rural economy and social development. Such a characteristic is good for facilitating exchanges between urban and rural areas, gradually breaking the duel economic structure in China, addressing the conflicts between dual economies, and eventually promoting integrated urban-rural development.

In light of the general background of low-carbon economy and the important role of small and medium-sized cities, promoting low-carbon construction of those cities can push low-carbon economic development across the board and ensure economic sustainability in China. Nowadays big cities all attach great importance to low-carbon development and have made great efforts to adjust industrial structure and eliminate outdated production capacity. Those efforts have proven fruitful and also squeezed the room for further emission reduction. On the other hand, low-carbon development of small and medium-sized cities has often been neglected while they, because of their large number, actually play a decisive role for the nation's overall low-carbon development. Therefore, small and medium-sized cities cannot take the old development path of high pollution, high energy consumption, and treatment after pollution. Meanwhile, as many of them are in the growing stage, they can take low-carbon approach into account as an important factor in their industrial layout and urban design, so as to fundamentally ensure sustainable development.

1 Main Problems for Low-Carbon Development of Small and Medium-sized Cities

Environmental problems are prominent. Since the subsidy for environmental pollution control is limited, effective recovery mechanisms of "waste water, waste gas and solid waste" haven't been established, a prevention and treatment system of them is lacking, pollutant recovery and utilization ratio is low and pollution prevention and control is weak. Pollution takes place faster than prevention and control. The awareness of eco-environmental protection is weak, green spaces are lacking, and environmental pollution remains a prominent problem.

Weak economic foundation and government financial strain result in limited capital support for low-carbon city development. Economic development in small and medium-sized cities is limited, where construction capital mainly comes from government investment thus investment and financing channels are limited, so it's hard to accumulate capital to complete low-carbon industrial layout and industrial cluster upgrade, which impedes the speed and potential of developing low-carbon small and medium-sized cities.

Enterprises are under heavy pressure of low-carbon development as they stand at the low end of the industrial chain. As high housing price, traffic congestion and air pollution become increasingly serious in big cities, the quickly rising cost has forced enterprises to move to small and medium-sized cities, which, however, can hardly attract high-tech non-pollution industries due to backward infrastructure and other conditions. In particular, many small and medium-sized cities in western China, with their cheap production factors and favorable resources, have taken over a lot of industries transferred from the eastern coast. Most of those industries are primary processing of energy and raw materials, including many high-energy-consuming and high-pollution ones, which bring challenges to local low-carbon development.

The promotion of low-carbon technologies is slow, only a small proportion of enterprises apply those technologies, and specific fund is lacking in that area. While there are not many high-tech enterprises or specific research institutes that specialize in low-carbon economy, most enterprises have a weak awareness of research innovation, haven't realized the development potential and values of low-carbon economy, and are unwilling to proactively upgrade technologies due to the absence of incentives and government supervision. Correspondingly, environmental products are of low added values and there is no valid support for environmental talents and technologies.

Notwithstanding, small and medium-sized cities have obvious comparative advantages in developing low-carbon economy.

First, they feature a large agricultural ratio and sound ecological conditions. Second, they are in the middle stage of industrialization, so the industrial adjustment and transformation toward low-carbon economy features little historical burden, low cost, small resistance and high speed, and it's relatively easy for them to form special development models and differentiated competitiveness. Third, they have rich clean resources such as natural gas, geothermal, wind energy, hydropower and rural biogas and therefore great potential in developing and utilizing clean energies. Fourth, whether it's big cities in developed regions or small and medium-sized cities in less developed regions, low-carbon economy is in the starting stage. As they are standing on the same starting line, developed cities don't always have advantages and the key lies in who holds the "key" to success first. In fact, big cities are in a "weight-carrying race" because they have to pay a high cost for energy conservation, emission reduction and environmental governance.[3]

2 Paths of Low-Carbon Development for Small and Medium-sized Cities

Since low-carbon economy is an economic model, it has to bring benefits. More than that, as the upgraded version of traditional economy, it should guarantee economic benefits from a more systematic and long-term perspective. Most small and

[3]Liu Yang, Tang Renwu and Li Chuan, "Low-carbon Path for Small and Medium-sized Cities in Western China with Luzhou as Example," collection of papers for 2010 Annual Meeting of Chinese Public Administration Society and "Innovation in Government Administration" Seminar, December 2010.

medium-sized cities face arduous tasks of eliminating poverty, achieving prosperity and developing economy. If they cannot find a low-carbon economic development model that suits the local area and only spend money on pollution control and popularizing environmental concept, low-carbon economic development will be nothing more than empty talk.

2.1 Reforming Traditional Industries to Reduce Carbon Emission Intensity

2.1.1 Developing Low-Carbon Agriculture

Agriculture holds vast room for low-carbon economic development, including water conservation and reducing non-point source pollution.

The agricultural development model should be transformed. With comprehensive and circular resource utilization and agricultural eco-environmental protection as the focuses, we should conserve land, energy, water, fertilizer, seed, pesticide and manpower when planting corn, rice, wheat and cash crops, and reduce agricultural non-point source pollution and the generation of agricultural wastes. We should also pay attention to environmental technologies of water and soil conservation and environmental protection, foster the idea of resource conservation and environmental protection among farmers and agricultural enterprises, and strongly promote circular, eco-friendly and intensive agriculture and other agricultural forms that are conducive to resource conservation and environmental protection, so as to achieve agricultural sustainability.

A green, low-carbon and smart agricultural network should be established. We should continuously upgrade agricultural infrastructure, advance modern agricultural equipment and raise its use efficiency, optimize the planting structure, cultivate fine and high-yield crops, and promote advanced agricultural technology. With IT and Internet of Things (IoT) as the carrier, we should make full use of IT network, and leverage on smart and accurate low-carbon agricultural production to keep its quality traceable and monitored from beginning to end.

Bio-resource utilization and pollution-free treatment of livestock and poultry excrements should be carried out. Of all by-products of agricultural production, straw is the bio-resource of the widest distribution and largest output. It can be reused directly in the farmland or recovered and recycled, but the former approach is too time- and labor-consuming and the latter involves a high transportation cost. Therefore the comprehensive utilization of agricultural straw should be promoted by means of policy guidance, technical support and incentive mechanisms. For instance, straw's plant fiber can become agricultural resources through gasification or other technical means, be processed into feedstock and fertilizer with biochemical technology, or serve as a good alternative for packaging material, disposable tableware, building material and other products. At present, ever more livestock and poultry excrements are produced as large-scale breeding develops rapidly in the countryside, causing ever more serious pollution. Pollution-free treatment and recycling of those excrements is an important way of achieving low-carbon agricultural development. Biogas digester can be built, where the excrements go through anaerobic fermentation and pathogenic bacteria is killed, so that the excrement is less polluting to air and water resources and regional environment is purified. Biogas can also provide the energy for cooking, lighting and other everyday needs, thus reducing the use of fossil energy, saving resources and protecting the environment.[4]

2.1.2 Developing Low-Carbon Industry

According to statistics of total energy consumption by industry in 2010, in the category of energy consumption for production, primary industry consumed the least energy that accounted for only 2% of the total, followed by tertiary industry whose energy consumption accounted for 15% of the total. More than 70% of energy consumption took place in the secondary industry, in which manufacture was the most influential factor in carbon emission.[5] Industrial production consumed a lot of resources and energies, so developing low-carbon industry was key to low-carbon city development. For small and medium-sized cities where industrialization started quite late, they should give full play to their advantages, start at a high point, stress low-carbon economy, and develop industries featuring low energy consumption, low emission and low pollution, with a view to sustainable development.

Efforts should be made to adjust industrial structure, upgrade traditional industries and foster emerging ones. Different industries use different kinds of resources, adopt different processes and feature different resource intensity, so their influence on carbon emission also varies greatly. Generally speaking, capital-intensive industries have a larger intensity of energy consumption and carbon emission than labor-intensive and technology-intensive ones. For instance, industries like petrochemical, metallurgy, non-ferrous metals and paper making feature "high energy consumption and high emission", those like foodstuff, agricultural and by-product processing and textile are of medium energy consumption and carbon emission intensity, while high-tech industries like electronic and communication equipment manufacturing, apparatus and instrument, and pharmaceutical manufacturing have a low reliance on energy and small carbon emission intensity. Small and medium-sized cities should make choices carefully, actively engage in links with high added values in the processing and manufacturing chain, combine the optimization of new industries with the reform of existing ones, and work hard to introduce and build high-quality new industries. They should focus on strategic industries that fit the functional position-

[4]Zhang Wenxu, "The Study of Evaluation and Countermeasure of Low-carbon Town-community of State Farms in Heilongjiang Province," thesis paper for master's degree at Northeast Agricultural University, 2011, p. 43.

[5]Zheng Changde and Liu Shuai, "Analysis of Carbon Emission and Economic Growth Based on Spatial Econometrics," *China Population, Resources and Environment* 5 (2011): 80–86.

ing of local areas, eliminate highly polluting industries by force, push for continuous industrial restructuring, and strive to create a new industrial landscape characterized by more sophisticated high-tech industries, stronger advanced manufacture, and improved traditional industries. They should adhere to innovation-driven development, hold fast to the core driving force of innovation, strengthen enterprises' capability of independent innovation, create a pro-innovation eco-system, gather innovative resources and foster innovative players, combine science, technology and economy more closely together, and shift the economic growth model from production-factor-based to technological-innovation-driven.

With the optimization of resource utilization method and improvement of resource utilization efficiency in the center, we should make great efforts to develop an industrial chain of circular economy, gather industries in industrial parks, and reinforce the recycling of green packing materials, packing waste and plastic waste. Water conservation projects should be accelerated such as reuse of reclaimed water and rainwater collection, industrial energy and water consumption standards should be developed, and the threshold of corporate energy consumption indicators should be determined to regulate and screen enterprises, so that every enterprise will work toward the goal of low-carbon development. The energy and water consumption performance of key corporate users should be analyzed and evaluated regularly to help them work out plans for improving energy efficiency, and save energy and water. Those of backward production process, serious pollution and are hard to reform will be phased out.

2.2 Guiding Low-Carbon Development with Plans

The general development plan for small and medium-sized cities is usually delayed, and some towns still suffer from irrational layout, insufficient infrastructure, chaotic development and construction, low-level redundant construction, serious resource damage, backward town management, and the phenomenon of "dirtiness, disorder and poor governance". A scientific and rational plan is critical for the low-carbon development of small and medium-sized cities in that it can effectively raise the utilization ratio of relevant infrastructure, avoid redundant and excessive construction, and reduce the waste of capital, resources and energy.

2.2.1 Overall Urban Layout Plan

Traditional urban spatial layout always went for large scale, which was not only a waste of land, but also put a big strain on resources, environment and traffic in the downtown area, made production, life and recreation inconvenient, and led to a high-carbon economy featuring high energy consumption, high pollution and high emission. Clustered layout, which is another layout approach, features clear division and balanced distribution, rational use of inter-cluster space, connection between peripheral areas and central greenbelt, and proper relation between different clusters and between clusters and the downtown. This approach gives full play to cluster advantages, makes reasonable and efficient use of energies and reduces carbon emission.[6]

In many small and medium-sized cities, the layout of industrial land is too scattered due to lack of proper planning and restriction, which not only wastes land, but also expands pollution. They should build industrial parks and development zones in a concentrated area and arrange related industries close to each other, so as to make more intensive use of land, facilitate lateral cooperation between enterprises engaged in related industries, form industrial chain, make efficient use of water resources and energy, and largely reduce carbon emission.

Some small and medium-sized cities have natural elements like original river, lake, mountain and forest, which are important ecological resources. They should incorporate those resources in the general framework of urban spatial layout, keep the ecological landscape of the local area, and make natural view part of the cityscape. Upholding the philosophy of eco-security-based construction, they should choose the construction area carefully, make reasonable residential and commercial development in light of land functions, and strictly control construction capacity in order to achieve multi-win results in ecological, landscape, social and economic benefits.[7]

2.2.2 Plan for Public Service Facilities and Service System

In the plan for small and medium-sized cities, especially for communities, public service facilities and auxiliary facilities are quite weak, or they are only planned but never built, and land for public facilities like business and finance, culture and entertainment and market is scarce, causing great inconveniences to people's life and commute and aggravating carbon emission and pollution. So public facilities such as road, plaza, park and market should be rationally planned and built to serve enterprises and residential communities.

Low-carbon service system should be established in towns. First, the capability of small and medium-sized cities of garbage treatment should be bettered. The cleaning and transportation of garbage should be mechanized and classified and garbage itself should be recycled or treated in pollution-free ways. Second, gas supply system in small and medium-sized cities should be improved. They should start with gas development and utilization, expand the scope of gas utilization, introduce low-carbon equipment to gas producers and reduce carbon emission. Third, heating network structure in small and medium-sized cities should be optimized and energy-saving projects should be promoted. Fourth, water-saving projects should be carried out for water supply and drainage in towns. Drainage facilities should be better built and managed, and drainage system should be improved to separate rainwater

---

[6]Zhu Guangyin, Zhu Qimei and Wang Luyu, "Study of Relation between Urban Plan and Low-carbon Development of Small Cities," *Ecological Economy1* (2013): 45–48.

[7]Yang Hui, "Exploration of Low-carbon City Concept in Control and Planning of Small Cities," *Architecture & Culture 2* (2014): 52–55.

from sewage. Drinking water and production and domestic water will be supplied separately by making rational overall water supply arrangements. Water quota management will be applied and existing water-saving equipment will be managed for circular use.[8]

2.2.3 Traffic Plan

Road network should be rationally planned and constructed. Road network plan in small and medium-sized cities has the following prominent problems: the ratio between main road and secondary main road is too high, branches are far from enough, and roads for resident use are lacking and cannot meet the demand for walking and cycling. A rational traffic network layout requires the proper match of road levels. In road network of big cities, the length ratio of expressway, main road, secondary main road and branch is 1:2:3:6, the latter two accounting for more than 70% of total road length in city plans, while for road network in small and medium-sized cities, the length ratio of main road, secondary main road and branch is 1:2:6, and the last one should account for at least 60% of total road length. Meanwhile, through traffic and urban traffic should be separated to improve efficiency.[9]

Public transit should be prioritized because it can reduce energy consumption and carbon emission, mitigate pollution and congestion. A public transit system should be built that suits the scale and spatial layout of small and medium-sized cities, and public transit networks should be connected, interacted, extended and supplemented to widen public transit coverage in towns, raise its operating efficiency and create an integrated public transit network system. According to relevant laws and rules, great efforts should be made to promote franchised operation system of public transit, lower its operation cost, improve service, and preserve order in that market to guarantee the lawful rights and interests of both operators and passengers. Measures such as the adoption of both bus rapid transit (BRT) and regular public transit, increase of bus frequency and extension of night operation can be taken. City roads should be designed according to local conditions to provide continuous areas for residents to commute, relax, rest and exercise.

Walking and cycling should be encouraged. For a small and medium-sized city, planning and designing atraffic system that's friendly for pedestrians and cyclers is an important aspect of building a low-carbon city. They should establish the green public bike service system, fully consider residents' needs, efficiently distribute road resources, follow the principle of intensive use, pay attention to greening of road

[8]Lang Di, "Study of Low-carbon Development of Small Towns in Qitaihe," thesis paper for master's degree at Jilin University, 2013, p. 39.

[9]Zhu Guangyin, Zhu Qimei and Wang Luyu, "Study of Relation between Urban Plan and Low-carbon Development of Small Cities," *Ecological Economy1* (2013): 45–48.

construction and ecological function, and make rational layout for small plazas and public service facilities in areas suitable for walking and cycling.[10]

2.2.4 Plan for Greenbelt System

Forest land, bushes, woods, grassland and wetland are all good carbon sinks. Regarding ecological type, forests have a strong carbon sink capability that makes up for 2/3 of the entire land ecological system.[11] City greenbelt is able to sequester carbon, release oxygen, reduce the carbon emission of landscape itself, mitigate the city's heat island effect, cut construction energy consumption and guide green traffic. Therefore, a good plan for urban greenbelt system is very important for lowering carbon emission, improving ecological environment, purifying cityscape and raising people's living standard.

On one hand, small and medium-sized cities need to actively promote regional ecological protection, control and governance, build forest parks that involve returning farmland to forest, grassland and wetland, and start with preventing ecological aggravation and degeneration to improve and recover natural ecological environment. On the other hand, garden construction should be stepped up in towns, city development should be harmonized with surrounding natural environment, and a looped network of urban green corridors should be built wherein multiple layers of green blocks are evenly distributed. The "greenway" planning model can be adopted. Greenway is a planned, designed and managed lined network of land use system that carries ecological, entertaining, cultural and aesthetic functions, and is a sustainable land use approach. The greenbelt width on both sides of main roads should be controlled, so that the greening in newly built areas and old city areas are closely connected to provide residents with continuous space for recreation and rest, and greenways can realize smooth connection between greening environment inside the city and the natural environment outside it. Besides, to enrich the functions of greenway, make its construction operable, and give full play to small cities' advantage in small size and close functional connection, greenways should be organized in close proximity to public centers at all levels, thus preventing them from becoming an empty shell because of limited functions. As a result, spatial unification between greening, recreation, public service and life can be achieved, and the use efficiency of greenbelt and public service facilities can be largely enhanced.[12]

---

[10] He Xindong and Zhuang Guiyang, "Practices of and Thoughts about Low-carbon Plans of Small and Medium-sized Cities in West China," *China Population, Resources and Environment S1* (2011): 482–485.

[11] Dong Zuoji, "Low-carbon Plan for Land Resources," *Urban Development Studies 7* (2010): 1–5.

[12] Yang Hui, "Exploration of Low-carbon City Concept in Control and Planning of Small Cities," *Architecture & Culture 2* (2014): 52–55.

2.3 *Promoting Use of Renewable Energy and Supply of Low-Carbon Energy*

The energy goal of low-carbon cities is reducing energy demand and using low-carbon energies. The energy supply structure in small and medium-sized cities in China that is focused on coal-fired electricity won't change fundamentally in the short term. To make sure that energy supply can meet the demand for economic and social development, the near-term task is to speed up the use of natural gas in cities, retrofit power plants for heat-electricity co-generation, and raise the overall energy utilization ratio. We should also actively promote the exploitation and utilization of renewable and new energies such as solar power, biomass energy, wind power and hydropower, optimize the general structure of urban energy supply, and boost low-carbon energy supply. The aim is to replace, to the largest extent, coal and oil resources, the consumption of which makes up a large proportion in towns, and implement and promote low-carbon strategy in small and medium-sized cities.

The vast rural areas hold large room for low-carbon energies.[13] Low-carbon strategy for small and medium-sized cities has to address the potential energy demand that is about to emerge in the vast rural areas, remote areas and small and mediums-sized towns. For instance, household appliances of all kinds are popularized in the countryside, and modern "air conditioning" technology has been promoted to the countryside too in the hot south, imposing great energy pressure on small and medium-sized cities. The best way to meet that demand is to energetically develop distributed energy supply systems, including power and heating supply, so as to largely raise energy utilization ratio. But if the energy comes from coal, oil or natural gas, that will go counter to low-carbon development and energy cost will increase considerably. Distributed energy supply should be developed according to local conditions and fully leveraged on local resources. In other words, it means building "a strategic emerging industry that should be explored urgently in the vast rural areas and small towns, namely a new energy system in which the 'small smart grid' comprised of 'solar power + wind power + small hydropower + biomass energy + small pumped storage power station + small and medium-sized energy storage + battery for small and medium-sized electric vehicles' is the 'center' of power and heating supply." While electricity is easy to transmit, thermal energy usually involves massive transmission losses. To supply electricity to the countryside and small towns, it's best to establish "smart" grids of different scale and level, ranging from micro grid, small grid to medium grid, large and super-large smart grid. As to heating supply, heating pipes should be shortened as much as possible, and the best way to supply domestic heat to the countryside is solar cooker and low- and medium-temperature solar boiler, which features low energy consumption, low cost, low price, and the ease of extensive application and promotion in the vast rural areas, remote areas and small and medium-sized cities. To meet the large demand for production heating in the

---

[13]He Zuoxiu, "Sure Route to Low-carbon Economic Development in Beijing-Tianjin-Hebei Region," collection of papers of 2010 Forum on Coordinated Development of Beijing-Tianjin-Hebei Region, p. 71–78.

countryside, the best way is building small and medium-sized heating/power plant, namely distributed co-generation power plant of "solar power generation + straw or biogas power generation" that can raise the utilization ratio of primary energy by a large margin.

2.4 Intensifying Publicity for Building Low-Carbon Society

Publicity should be intensified. Promote low-carbon economy and consumption in families, schools and communities through TV, radio, newspaper and other media to popularize and enhance ecological awareness in the public. Relevant departments should also broaden the channels for public participation in low-carbon ecological city construction, listen to public opinions and respect their wishes, so as to keep them fully motivated for building a low-carbon ecological city.

The government's exemplary and guiding role should be brought into play, use of official car should be regulated, energy-saving renovation should be implemented on government buildings, high-efficiency equipment should be prioritized in government purchase, and more recycled paper and similar resources should be used. During city construction, relevant departments should employ multiple approaches to step up publicity and make the public more aware of the importance of developing green economy.

Relevant parties should work together to intensify the publicity of low-carbon concept. Low-carbon construction of small and medium-sized cities isn't a simple and abstract government behavior, but is the common obligation and responsibility of the whole society. It cannot rely on solely the government, but should be carried out through the collaboration of government, NGOs, enterprises and residents of small and medium-sized cities under government guidance and pursuant to low-carbon principles.

Low-carbon life should be upheld among residents. Residents' low-carbon lifestyle and actions constitute an important part of low-carbon city construction. We should inherit and carry forward traditional low-carbon living habits, avoid energy waste, emission increase and pollution aggravation, reduce energy consumption and carbon emission in everyday life, enhance the education of low-carbon concept in institutions, schools and public service bodies, and popularize this concept in the whole society to expand its influence.

3 Realistic Problems that Should Be Considered in Low-Carbon Development of Small and Medium-sized Cities

3.1 Center of Low-Carbon City Construction Is Raising Carbon Productivity

Low-carbon urban industrial system doesn't reject all high-energy-consuming and high-carbon-emitting industries. It is an opportunity to carry out technical upgrade and renovation of those industries and create the market foundation for low-carbon technological innovation. Even new energies have to be measured by whether they can improve carbon productivity, an indicator that helps evaluate the energy conservation and emission reduction performance of small and medium-sized cities where high-energy-consuming enterprises and industries take a large proportion.

3.2 Planning for and Construction of Low-Carbon City Cannot Be Superficial

Before low-carbon city, other concepts such as "forest city", "garden city", "green city" and "eco-city" were put forward and many cities jumped on the bandwagon, but all those concepts stayed on paper only and city construction wasn't fundamentally changed. At present, some cities want to hype up the concept of low-carbon economy as a strategy to improve government image, enhance city brand, secure support from superior authorities and attract business and investment, but concrete low-carbon practices are mostly sporadic and tentative, and a systematic framework for low-carbon economic development hasn't been established. We should avoid such a situation.

3.3 Interests Should Be Balanced in Low-Carbon City Construction

Just as we can take low-carbon city as a new development of city planning in the low-carbon age, it, like city planning, is also a mechanism of interest balancing. First, central and local interests have to be balanced when implementing national policies on energy conservation and emission reduction. The central government initiated the goal of cutting CO_2 emission per unit GDP by 40–45% in 2020 from the 2005 level. This goal has to be broken down to local governments on all levels, and small and medium-sized cities won't be exempted just because they are less developed. Moreover, as small and medium-sized cities develop, especially those in backward areas in central and western China, their carbon emission will increase at a high pace for a certain period, so local and central governments need to communicate about that to balance the interests. Second, the interests of a city's long-term and short-term development should be balanced. In the long term, low-carbon development is the inevitable trend for cities and its pros outweigh the cons, but in the short term, it requires massive input from local governments in many aspects, while the effect may not be visible until a long time later. How to balance the conflict here tests the local government's resolve to build a low-carbon city. At last, the interests of government, enterprises and the public should be balanced. In current China, government pursues good performance, enterprises pursue profits and the public has higher demands on the environment they live in, but government efforts to improve performance may sometimes turn into simple and crude administrative orders, such as limiting power supply by force in order to meet the target of energy conservation and emission reduction, which seriously affects production and life. These conflicts have to be prevented and balanced.[14]

In sum, in the current age when low-carbon development has become a mainstream consensus in the world, low-carbon development of small cities faces both great opportunities and severe challenges and restraints. Low-carbon economic development relies on the adjustment of industrial structure, energy structure and consumption structure, has to be supported by policies and regulations and bolstered by technological innovation. Despite their late-mover advantage for building low-carbon cities and developing low-carbon economy, small and medium-sized cities face bigger difficulties because they lag behind in urban infrastructure and social and economic support, so enterprises, government and the society have to make joint efforts. Enterprises should continuously make innovations and apply low-carbon technology and build low-carbon industrial structure, the society has to create a consumption model consistent with low-carbon development, and the government should develop policies, laws and market mechanisms that encourage low-carbon development. Studies on low-carbon city development are in a starting stage in the world, and existing research results are concentrated on big cities, so studies on the low-carbon development path for small and medium-sized cities are to be deepened in the future.

[14] He Xindong and Zhuang Guiyang, "Practices of and Thoughts about Low-carbon Plans of Small and Medium-sized Cities in West China," *China Population, Resources and Environment S1* (2011): 482–485.

Chapter 8
Green Education Boosts Green Development

Cities are in ever fiercer competition for development today. The sustainability of a city's economic development decides its developing potential, and such sustainability is affected and restrained by resources and ecology. As resource environment becomes ever harsher, only cities that develop in the low-carbon and green direction are sure to become green with lasting developing potential and competitiveness. They should stick to green development by making green strategic plans, building green infrastructure, and through other measures, but the premise is that all social members in the city have a certain level of green awareness, green knowledge, green skills and green quality, which mainly depend on education. Agenda 21 expressly stated that "education is critical for promoting sustainable development and improving the capacity of the people to address environment and development issues", which indicates that green education on sustainable development can give a strong impetus to green city development, and this has received growing attention from more countries and cities. When the 12th International Congress of Educating Cities was held in the theme of "Green Environment, Creative Education" in Changwon, Republic of Korea in April 2012, city government employees and education scholars from 33 countries and regions discussed how to develop and improve the green environment in cities through creative education. At the international conference on environmental education held in Australia in 1999, some participants proposed to create a community of urban environmental education because environmental education could promote sustainable city development. The call for promoting green city development with green and sustainable education is getting louder.

© Social Sciences Academic Press and Springer Nature Singapore Pte Ltd. 2018

X. Li and X. Liu, *Green Development Model of China's Small and Medium-sized Cities*, Research Series on the Chinese Dream and China's Development Path,
https://doi.org/10.1007/978-981-13-0779-9_8

1 Theories and Practices of Green Education in the World

1.1 Formation and Contents of Green Education

Before the 21st century, education was always regarded as the way for students to obtain knowledge and become more competitive, especially for the country to become more competitive, but it turned out quickening the human step of trying to conquer nature, so much so that natural environment was drastically damaged during excessive conquest and exploitation. The Man and the Biosphere Programme (MAB) conference held in Paris in 1968 raised the awareness of environmental education for the first time in the world and creatively initiated a pro-environment education program, and the idea of education began to change. In 1975, the UN held an international working symposium on environmental education in Belgrade, at which a global framework document on environmental education—Belgrade Charter—was announced. In 1977, Tbilisi Declaration, which was called a milestone in environmental education development, was created at the Intergovernmental Conference on Environmental Education. It further specified the nature and characteristics of environmental education and put forth specific purposes, goals, and implementation principles. In 1992, the United Nations Conference on Environment and Development held in Rio De Janeiro suggested that education should turn to focus on sustainable development, enhance public awareness of it, and provide related training. In 1994, UNESCO proposed to integrate environmental education, development education and population education. In 2002, the UN General Assembly decided to designate the period from 2005 to 2014 as the Decade of Education for Sustainable Development (DESD). From the Biosphere Conference in Paris to the present day, the international community has deepened reflections on human development model, review of modern industrial civilization, and contemplation on the future form of existence. It is generally agreed that the focus of education should shift from conquering, exploiting and utilizing nature to viewing it as a partner that needs protection and interaction and pursuing common prosperity between man and nature, so that it can be combined with the idea of sustainable development on a larger scale. In this process, green education came into being, which is based on and preceded by environmental education and has extended to the sustainability of eco logical environment, human life and economy and society along with the development of modern human civilization. Some scholar said that green education refers to educational practices that include education on ecology, environmental protection and sustainable development as well as their penetration and radiation to other disciplines and subjects.

1.2 Empirical Explorations for Green Education by International Cities

In the mid-20th century, some countries and cities began to explore the development of green education and have achieved remarkable results. This fully demonstrates education's irreplaceable importance in the sustainable development of nations and cities, and the importance is mainly reflected in the following aspects.

1.2.1 Advocating and Stressing Green Education with Laws and Policies

The governments of many countries and local areas have specified the necessity of green education on the level of laws and policies, providing strong guarantee for attaching importance to and implementing green education during city development. The US was the first country that guaranteed the implementation of green education with legislation. Its institutionalization of green education started with the *National Environmental Education Act* formulated in 1970, and the legal system for it was basically established in 1990 when the new *National Environmental Education Act* was passed. The system provided for many aspects including the development, implementation, evaluation and popularization of environmental education courses, setup of field environmental education centers, and in-service training in that area. It effectively regulated the construction and management of green education organizations in the US and pushed for the creation and improvement of relevant mechanisms in that area, such as investment, incentive and public participation.

According to a report submitted to the Congress in 2005, the implementation of *National Environmental Education Act* notably promoted the progress on environmental education in the country. Japan's legislation on green education started with the *Basic Environment Plan* of 1994, based on which the *Law for Promoting of Environmental Education* was passed in 2003. The *Law* elaborated on the three aspects of conducting environmental activities, motivating passion for environmental protection and implementing environmental education, specified and coordinated the duties and obligations of national government, local governments and civil societies, ascertained the scope of public green education, and stressed the idea of green education and sustainable economic and social development.

Australia laid down detailed provisions on green education by releasing national action plans that had a similar effect to legislation, but some local governments there guaranteed the implementation of green education with laws even earlier. For instance, New South Wales issued green education laws in the 1990s, including *Education Trust Act 1990*, *Environmental Trust Act 1998*, and *Protection of the Environment Administration Amendment (Environmental Education) Bill 1998*.

1.2.2 Implementing Green Education in Multiple Ways Suitable for Different Age Groups

First of all, most countries and cities that set store by green education believe in "education starts with children" and have developed colorful basic green education for middle schools, primary schools and kindergartens by combining various educational forms. ① Contents of green education are incorporated in the syllabus and textbooks for middle schools. Sweden, for instance, included the idea of environmental protection in Biology Syllabus for Middle Schools in 1962, and in the current national syllabus, over half of the courses during compulsory education specifically require environmental education. ② Non-fixed courses and outdoor natural education are combined and local resources are used to let students perceive, observe and experience nature. Lyon in France carried out a green education program that built pre-schools on the river and taught the students to respect nature and be responsible for it through riverside education. ③ Urban environmental education plans targeting teenagers and children are carried out. To popularize knowledge about reducing greenhouse gas (GHG), Strasbourg of France designed a local climate plan targeting pupils and kindergarteners to foster their awareness of environmental protection. Mexico's Zapopan carried out an early childhood education program about urban garbage that taught children about waste discharge and recycling. Children learnt to recycle things and discard plastic and glass bottles separately through simple games.

Second, since institutions of higher education are cradles that cultivate high-caliber talents for the society, many European and American countries attach great importance to developing flexible and diverse higher-level green education. ① Efforts are made to enrich and diversify the teaching of green courses, continuously update, add and delete major courses, coordinate and integrate the green concepts of multiple disciplines, popularize green education among non-majors, and set up a lot of compulsory and optional courses. For instance, 41% of universities in Canada have opened green courses in science and engineering departments, and most universities have established departments of environment, biology and geography. ② Green education practices are implemented in large quantities. For example, Germany's Hamburg once carried out the famous fifty-fifty project that requested education authorities to return half of the money saved by school faculties and students through waste reduction to the school for its free use. This project significantly enhanced the effects of green education and was widely supported across the nation. ③ Measures like green university management and green campus plan are adopted to build green universities. For example, Britain's University of Strathclyde is developing a campus environment management system that complies with Britain's BS7750 environmental management system. Many American colleges worked out independent eco-protection plans, and presidents of about 400 colleges signed an agreement on CO_2 emission reduction and carbon equilibrium on campus.

At last, since every resident more or less participates in green city development and is affected by it, it is necessary to conduct green education among all social members regardless of age, gender and occupation in order to achieve the goal. An effective approach adopted by most countries is enhancing the publicity of green knowledge by building social environmental schools, urban study centers, green communities and other green public facilities and venues. For instance, many communities in Japan built environmental education centers that had multiple green and environment-friendly facilities to directly deliver the concept of environmental protection to the public and urge them to live and act green. ROK's Changwon created the "Earth Protector" climate change education center that provided environmental education programs for different age groups. Spain's Barcelona built an environmental education school named "solar plant" that provided residents with rich knowledge and information about renewable energies, urban environment, sustainable environmental protection, etc., and provided resources to help other organizations with the same purpose.

1.2.3 Raising Green Educators' Competence and Skills with Diversified Training

Some countries realized at an early date that a strong faculty is a forceful guarantee to promote green education, so they have relied on teachers' associations and trainings by colleges and professional institutions to provide green education training for teachers with different backgrounds, and organized pre-service, in-service and further trainings for green education faculty.

Environmental faculty training is one of the key contents of teacher training in Holland, which is carried out through cooperation among teacher training organizations, schools and teachers. The training strategy and courses are planned in light of the school's independent capability and teachers' occupational inclination, and training contents include teaching methods, knowledge acquisition, and helping teachers to expand their teaching philosophy. Portugal founded the Environmental Promotion Society in 1993 to carry out on-campus training programs and organize environmental education faculty training, and created training centers for primary school and kindergarten teachers to provide them with pre-service training on environmental education, covering protection of cultural heritage, climate change, solid and liquid garbage treatment, water pollution, among others. Every teacher had compulsory courses. The University of Wisconsin and University of Michigan in the US made environmental education one direction of pedagogical education, opened four-year specialized courses to train teachers in that field, and conferred them certificates for environmental education. Australia implemented green education training in three forms—pre-service training, postgraduate education and in-service training, and asked green educators to not only understand green education, but also grasp certain green knowledge. It also incorporated sustainable life education in faculty training, and the Environmental Education Association formulated the *Plan for Environmental and Development Education in Faculty Training* to guide the trainings.

1.2.4 Guiding Government and Public with Multiple Green Projects and Plans

Implementation of city plans and projects largely affects and guides the residents' behaviors and activities. Some foreign cities have carried out city plans and projects beneficial for ecological environment, energy conservation and emission reduction to guide and teach residents to adopt a green lifestyle.

Based on a bike leasing program, France's Paris launched Autolib, an electric vehicle sharing program, in 2011 to reduce air and noise pollution in the city. The program provided four seaters powered by LMP (Lithium Metal Polymer) battery, and participants only needed to show their ID card, driver's license and credit card to sign an online contract with customer service representatives. The fee was charged by day, month or year, or by hour according to different leasing plan. The program was so good for cutting traffic cost and convenient that more people paid attention to and participated in it, and it has attracted more than 6,000 users so far, which is expected to rise to 80,000 users in the future. In 2011, London held an exhibition of environment-friendly and energy-saving cars, at which new energy vehicles (NEVs) of 17 brands were exhibited, and the city planned to build 25,000 NEV charging stations to promote the vehicle. This measure increased people's interests in NEV and more than 2,000 NEVs have been registered so far. In 2008, ROK's Changwon launched the famous public bike program that realized self-service leasing of public bikes. To make the program more popular among residents, it also adopted auxiliary measures such as "resident bike insurance", "employee commute allowance" and designating the "bike day". At the moment, this program has nearly 120,000 members and the bikes have been used 4.63 million person-times accumulatively, not only cutting residents' traffic cost and the use of motor vehicles considerably, but also making great contributions to reducing air pollution and GHG emission and preserving a green urban environment. Urban public transit program also drew the attention of Sao Paulo of Brazil, which replaced the diesel system of its buses with renewable energy and drive system, and committed to reducing the use of fossil fuel step by step at the annual reduction rate of 10%. The initiative was launched in 2009, and by 2018 when decrement reaches the peak, all buses in the city will use fossil fuel alternative systems.

2 Green Education in Chinese Cities

2.1 Status Quo of Green Education in Chinese Cities

National government is the main driving force of green education in China. It adopted the top-down approach centered on environmental education and the nation realized the importance of green education quite late. After the work meeting on environmental education was held in 1992, a national framework of it was gradually established.

In 1996, the Publicity Department of the CPC Central Committee, Ministry of Education and Ministry of Environmental Protection jointly printed and distributed the *National Action Outlines for Environmental Publicity and Education* and launched a green school campaign nationwide. As of the end of 2008, 42,000 middle schools, primary schools and kindergartens across the country became green schools, 705 of which received national commendation. In 2003, Ministry of Education officially promulgated the *Syllabus of Environmental Education in Middle and Primary Schools* and *Guide on Implementing Environmental Education in Middle and Primary Schools*, and officially incorporated environmental education in the new courses of national basic education in 2004. To promote green education, Chinese government actively worked with enterprises and international organizations. For instance, it participated in the UNESCO Project on Education for Environment, Population and Sustainable Development (EPD). In 1997, Ministry of Education, World Wildlife Fund (WWF) and BP jointly conducted a 10-year "green education program for middle and primary schools", which benefited more than 5 million person-time students and helped 21 schools build environmental education centers, covering 23 provinces, autonomous regions and municipalities across the country. In 2007, China joined the Foundation for Environmental Education (FEE), regularly held training classes for eco-school projects, and launched the international eco-school project. About 1,000 teachers have participated in the training so far, qualified member schools are granted an eco-school green flag, and 81 schools received the flag in the first batch.

Under the leadership of national government, provinces and cities in China also conducted green education activities. In response to the national call for building green schools, almost all provinces and cities organized and urged local middle and primary schools and kindergartens to participate in green school construction, application and evaluation. In addition to national evaluation, provincial, municipal and county-level evaluation of green schools was also added, and some cities even held regular environmental education trainings to improve teachers' competence in that area. Cities like Beijing and Wuhan worked to build and select "green communities" since 2006. Beijing took the initiative to launch the *Green Community Manual*, Shanghai built "green accounts" in communities, and Ningxia Hui Autonomous Region held training classes for building "green community". Cities like Shanghai and Guiyang took an active part in the international eco-school project and made explorations in certain schools on a trial basis. Many large and medium-sized cities were voluntarily promoting and expanding green publicity and education across the city by holding all kinds of green activities and exploring relevant policies. In 2009, Chongqing Environmental Culture Promotion Association successfully held an environmental photography contest in the theme of "Livable Chongqing, Green Home" to urge all walks of life to participate in green city development. Wuhan held a lot of environmental performance contests for youths every year to enhance their green awareness, and Guangzhou organized "environmental technology summer camp" and "environmental technology practice youth camp" several times for middle and primary school students to improve their green awareness and practical skills. In

2005, Shanghai issued the *Guiding Outline of Life Education in Middle and Primary Schools of Shanghai*, which incorporated life education in green education, and explorations started for green education centered on life education.

2.2 Existing Problems

Having realized the importance of green education, countries and cities in the world have carried out multi-dimension explorations and practices and achieved great results, largely promoting their sustainable development. This further proves that while advocating the green and sustainable development of cities in China, all-round popularization of green education cannot be ignored and must be implemented urgently. Analysis of the current status of green education in China showed that it is quite backward at the moment, progresses slowly and has many problems.

First of all, both central and local governments have a vague and perceptual understanding of the nature and role of green education, and they haven't truly realized what green transformation of education essentially means and how important it is for sustainable development. As a result, they paid little attention to the formulation of regulations and policies on green education. Only Ningxia issued *Regulations on Environmental Education* in 2011, and no national law has been issued on that topic. This resulted in a wide disparity between cities and urban and rural areas in the implementation of green publicity and education, and the publicity and education approach wasn't regulated. Considering the fact that policies are usually made and implemented in a top-down way in China, green education started late in the country, and local governments and the public have a low green awareness in general, it is especially important for the nation to support green education with laws and policies.

Second, in most Chinese provinces and cities, basic education is focused on teaching subjects for examination, and green education features a small proportion and poor effect. Although the Ministry of Education printed and distributed the *Syllabus of Environmental Education in Middle and Primary Schools*, and more than 20 provinces and cities published reference books in that area, good teaching materials on green education are still lacking and existing ones contain outdated knowledge, lagging far behind the current development of green education. Most schools still adopt the traditional teaching method of knowledge cramming without much practical experience, and teaching materials only cover ecological environment but barely cultivate the concept and commitment to green environment. This is not good for students to form green awareness and flexibly grasp and use green knowledge.

Third, China has been in the stage of fast economic growth and accelerated urbanization for a long time, so the public is accustomed to thinking with economic factor in the center and their participation in green education activities is quite passive. This shows how urgent it is to conduct green education for all in China, and government needs to adopt proactive guiding mechanisms and measures. However, the nation, especially local governments, hasn't really put nationwide green education in an important position. They just organized media publicity and held simple activities, which was too superficial and not very effective when the public green awareness relies heavily on government motivation and guidance.

At last, green education teachers are of a low competence level in general and teachers in different areas vary greatly in competence. Organizations and courses are lacking in China that provide green education training for teachers of different types, so is a standard teacher training system. According to a survey, only 5,000 or so Chinese are qualified to teach courses of higher-level environmental education, which is not enough to meet the demand for specialized education, not to mention green education for all students. Meanwhile, about 88% of the teachers in China haven't received systematic pre-service green education training, and only 9% of them have received in-service training.

3 Suggestions on Promoting Green Education in China

3.1 *Directing More Attention and Capital, Formulating Laws, Policies and Systems of Green Publicity and Education*

Chinese government should draw on foreign experience from countries like the US and Japan in legislating for green publicity and education. It can first explore to establish laws and rules about environmental education that suit China's national conditions, specify the concept, contents and role of environmental publicity and education, and stipulate and restrict the leading organizations, promotion scope, behavioral norms, publicity and education, approval and evaluation mechanisms in that respect. While legislation is in process, it can select pilot cities and encourage and support the formulation and implementation of local regulations, which is a creative and helpful attempt and preparation for national legislation and will eventually lead to that.

Another major obstacle that impedes the implementation and development of green education in China is lack of funding. Central and local governments should prioritize green education in government budget and fund grant and intensify planning for it. Meanwhile, duties and rights in green publicity and education should be clarified for environmental protection departments, education and publicity departments and other administrative departments at all levels. They should strengthen cooperation and coordination, work out and carry out forceful guiding policies, effective working mechanisms and reward and punishment systems, and improve green publicity and education.

3.2 Establishing Green Education Teacher Training System, Improving Teachers' Green Competence and Teaching Skills

China can also draw on the experience of European countries in founding relevant organizations such as green education association and special teaching and research institute, formulating corresponding management measures and coordination mechanisms, and working with colleges, NGOs and international organizations to provide systematic training for teachers in provinces, cities, counties and villages nationwide. We can establish diverse teacher training, examination and evaluation systems, provide trainings, by way of pre-service, in-service and further training, with different focuses to teachers on different levels considering their different demand, and provide for compulsory and optional courses as well as credit and assessment arrangements.

Besides, the urban government's role in education and guidance should be intensified and trainings for government employees should be stepped up to raise the green education level. A green education training system should be explored that targets government employees on various levels, whereby the approach varies according to region, time, type and level of the trainees, and trainings contents should focus on teaching and discussion about green culture, system, policy, and international experience.

3.3 Raising Green Education Level in Schools at All Levels, Encouraging Education Innovation

For basic education, education authorities and schools should adopt new ideas and views about sustainability, organize the development of scientific and advanced green teaching materials, and update them in a timely manner. Based on the characteristics and advantages of the city where schools are located, we, by referring to experience from European and American countries, should utilize local museums, parks and forests and organize field activities such as countryside experience, so that students can embrace nature, feel green environment, understand it and discover problems, thus fostering their green awareness and commitment.

For green education in colleges, the idea of green college should penetrate all aspects of the school, including construction facilities, management and operation. Basic courses such as eco-environmental protection and life education should be listed as compulsory or designated optional courses, and green practices should be carried out among all students and faculty to foster their green awareness and help them build green ethics and values. In addition, practices and researches should be intensified in natural disciplines like ecological environment to raise students' specialized skills and foster their capability of evaluating and addressing environmental issues and sustainable development.

3.4 Expanding Scope of Green Education, Taking Effective Steps to Enhance Green Awareness and Actions of All

All city governments should draw on international experience, foster a green culture through multiple channels and ways, including developing lifelong environmental education, opening green knowledge websites, building green social universities, designating green anniversaries and printing and distributing brochures. They should continue to step up green publicity and education to all social members, and use green city plans, policies and projects to guide the public to choose a greener way of life.

To promote green education in cities, we shouldn't just rely on the government, but should mobilize all social forces. Municipal governments should actively introduce international green organizations, encourage and support local green NGOs and green enterprises, strengthen the construction of green communities, enhance public participation mechanisms, and reinforce the cooperation and interaction of all social organizations and members, including government, enterprises, communities, families and individuals, in various green activities and projects.

Chapter 9
Experience and Lesson of Green City Development at Home and Abroad

In face of realistic problems such as climate change, environmental pollution and energy crisis, the whole world is reflecting on the traditional development model, lifestyle and consumption pattern and exploring new development model and lifestyle, so as to mitigate damage to nature, enhance nature's bearing capacity, slow down exploitation of natural resources, and search for paths for man-nature harmony and economic and social sustainability. Many regions have gathered successful experience in their exploration for green development.

1 Typical Cases of Green Development Explorations at Home and Abroad

Application of green energies: Sun City in Heerhugowaard, Holland. With 3000 small houses, covering an area of 120 ha, and surrounded by a 177-ha green park for residents' recreation and entertainment, this is the first region in the world that meets the standards of Kyoto Protocol and the largest residential area of zero CO_2 emission. The Sun City is designed on the core principle of "holistic landscape" to reflect ecological friendliness, leisure and beauty. It builds a lot of energy-saving houses with energy-saving materials and its electricity comes from green power. One is solar power, which means solar panels and related facilities are installed on rooftops and outer walls. Apart from self-supply, 44% of the solar power produced by this community is fed into the grid. The other one is wind power, which provides 6.9 MW of power for the community. Local residents are very supportive of Sun City even though the construction and facilities are expensive, and the massive application of PV products is encouraged by the government. Property owners in Sun City only have to pay 10% of the housing price, while 90% of the construction capital comes from European and provincial energy companies and municipal government, which is expected to be recovered in 7 years.

© Social Sciences Academic Press and Springer Nature Singapore Pte Ltd. 2018

X. Li and X. Liu, *Green Development Model of China's Small and Medium-sized Cities*, Research Series on the Chinese Dream and China's Development Path,
https://doi.org/10.1007/978-981-13-0779-9_9

Development of green industries: Baoding, Power Valley in China. In 2006, Hebei's Baoding set the strategic goal of building itself into the "Power Valley in China". To achieve that goal, it strongly developed industrial parks of energy conservation, PV and wind power by way of technology introduction and R&D, education and training, and commercial services, and worked hard to foster the six industrial systems of wind power, PV, biomass, power conservation, transmission and storage leveraged on the new energy and energy equipment industrial zone. It introduced a large number of high-tech enterprises that fitted the city's industrial development strategy, supported the development of enterprises in those industrial parks, and actively sought external resources. By becoming a pilot city of WWF, Baoding strived to build its industrial parks into state-level high-tech new energy zones. Baoding actively applied enterprises' products and achievements when making construction plans, such as using solar power to control traffic lights in the city proper, installing solar devices in residential communities, and building the world's first PV-powered five-star-rated hotel. Today Chinese cities like Wuxi and Dezhou are all developing solar power industry and implementing green development plans.

Strategy-driven: Sino-Singapore Tianjin Eco-city. Co-built by Chinese and Singapore governments, this is the first intergovernmental eco-city cooperation project in the world. It aims to become a sustainable eco-city featuring "economic prosperity, social harmony, environmental friendliness and resource conservation", and an administrative committee has been built based on the ideas of "three harmonies" (harmony between people, between humans and environment, and between humans and economic activities) and "three cans" (can be implemented, promoted and duplicated). Planned and designed by China Academy of Urban Planning and Design, the eco-city is operated following the principle of separating government administration from enterprise management, and the Sino-Singapore Tianjin Eco-city Investment & Development Co., Ltd (SSTEC) was established, a 50:50 JV by Teda Group and Keppel Corporation. To better guide its development and construction, Singapore Ministry of National Development set up an office in Tianjin Eco-city, and the two countries set up the vice-premier-level "Joint Steering Council Meeting" and ministerial-level "Joint Council". Being built in complete accordance with construction indicators developed by experts, the construction of Sino-Singapore Tianjin Eco-city was broken into 26 key indicators, based on which 51 core factors, 100 statistical indicators, 129 key links, 275 control targets and 723 specific control measures were developed to make its construction more quantified and scientific. The eco-city also made great efforts to bring in enterprises engaged in cultural creativity, science and technology R&D, finance and investment, and energy conservation and environmental protection, and has primarily established an industrial cluster dominated by green, low-carbon and circular industries.

Ecological restoration: Vastra Hamnen in Malmo. Vastra Hamnen used to be an industrial city created through refuse landfill whose ecological environment was seriously damaged, but now it is the first eco-friendly (low-carbon) demonstration zone in Sweden. At the end of the 20th century, environmental pollution was severe and regional industry declined. Taking the opportunity of hosting the first "European Housing Exposition" in 1995, Malmo turned the discarded industrial port into a new eco-zone. On one hand, it strongly enhanced the residents' awareness and competence of eco-environmental protection and fostered a "green culture". Children were taught to live in harmony with nature from kindergarten, people were encouraged to choose green traffic, and driving was considered shameful if it was less than 5 km. On the other hand, it stepped up infrastructure construction. Resources were utilized circularly and wastes were treated for recycling. Malmo sought to cooperate with colleges, science and technology parks and companies extensively, energetically introduced knowledge-intensive enterprises, and replaced abandoned manufactories with IT and clean-energy technology enterprises.

The Malmo government hired more than 20 construction companies and 30 design companies to participate in designing the city. They applied advanced technologies to create green buildings and traffic, limited the growth rate of cars in the city, strongly developed public transit and rail traffic, and energetically promoted green industries.

Community-driven: Halifax EcoCity. The Halifax EcoCity that won the International Eco-city Award in 1994 challenged the traditional business development model. Built according to the wish of community residents, the project was a "community-driven" eco-city and the first of its kind in Australia. Urban Ecology Australia (an NGO) and Eco-city Co., Ltd. jointly developed the project with strong support from the Education Association, Leasers' Association, industrial, environmental and community organizations, and other groups and participants. During the construction of Halifax EcoCity, its economic structure and lifestyle had to be eco-friendly. It was considered an example of best practice at the "city forum" of United Nations Conference on Human Settlements held in Istanbul in 1996.

Based on the "community-driven" independent eco-development model, Halifax EcoCity put forth 12 planning principles and 21 operating strategies. According to the design, great efforts were made to tap the potential of existing land, fully use existing technologies, strongly promote green architectures, make circular use of materials, extensively use new and renewable energies, and develop public and static traffic. The eco-city organized residents to make investment, renovation and construction by themselves, developed industries whose production purpose, process and products fitted the goal of ecological development, and conducted education and skill training on that topic for residents. It also built the "city eco-center" as the library, exhibition hall and consulting center for people to understand the plan, design and construction progress of the eco-city, and created the educative "eco-tourism".

2 Lessons from Green Development at Home and Abroad

First, capital was raised in multiple ways and green developed was promoted through projects. One of the important elements to promote green development is capital. When countries and cities around the world made explorations in that direction, they used project as the carrier and took various measures to encourage diverse capital to participate in green development. (1) Government investment, which means government investment plays a leading and guiding role and drives other investments.

Baoding government invested profusely to drive the development of related industries, and Vastra Hamnen used loan and grant from the EU to build demonstrate projects highlighting low carbon, energy conservation and ecological friendliness. (2) Corporate investment. In market economy, enterprises are main market players and important participants in green development. While exploring for green development, local governments, on one hand, actively sought to cooperate with enterprises and give play to their market role; on the other hand, they laid down rigorous requirements on the enterprises to force them to transform their production model. (3) NGO's support. Many NGOs used their own resources in specific fields to bolster local green development. Halifax EcoCity was initiated by NGOs and jointly developed by it with other organizations and civil groups. Beddington Zero Energy Development (BedZED) in London, the largest zero-carbon eco-community of Britain, was jointly created by Peabody, the largest non-profit charity housing federation in London, and professional environmental assessment company BioRegional. (4) Self-organized private construction, which is also an important force for green development as reflected in green consumption, green lifestyle, community construction and industrial development.

Second, policy support and encouragement, planning and design were stressed. Governments all strongly supported and encouraged local regions to implement green development plans, ranging from green industries to green community construction. A series of "green new deals" largely boosted local regions' confidence in green development and played a leading role. In the process of green development and construction, local regions stressed planning and positioning, comprehensively used various forces to scientifically work out the strategic goals, steps, and division of functional zones, and formulated a raft of rules and construction and evaluation standards.

Third, pilot explorations were conducted continuously to gather experience through practice. As different regions all actively explored the new concept of green development, there was no unified standard or model, so they had to apply advanced ideas into practice according to specific local conditions and development goals, in search for a suitable way through practice. There were pilot projects aiming for overall social development, in specific industries or focused on the handling of prominent problems.

Fourth, science and technology was given full play. While mature and practical technologies were applied in every aspect of people's lives, great efforts were also made to develop advanced technologies.

Fifth, exchange and cooperation was intensified and external support was sought. Countries and regions mostly depended on themselves and focused on local conditions, but they also paid attention to communication and exchange with the outside world, during which they could discover their deficiencies, draw on advanced experience and technologies, and actively seek external support to boost local green development.

Sixth, system and education were combined and social participation was stressed. Green development is a revolution of traditional production model and lifestyle, which requires not only the change of technology, but also the change of ideas and customs. While countries and regions adopted systems and compulsory measures to push the change, what was more important was intensifying education and utilizing public opinions, so that the public could fully realize the importance of local green development and an energy-saving and environmentally friendly production, living and consumption model could be created.

Chapter 10
Establishing the Compensation Systems for Use of Resources and for Damage to the Ecological Environment

With the rapid increase of urban population and fast progress of urbanization, the ecological environment is under rising pressure. The question of eco-environmental protection during urbanization has received ever more attention as it is of great importance for China's sustainable socioeconomic development. To implement the strategic deployments about comprehensively deepening the reform made by the 18th CPC National Congress, the Third Plenary Session of the 18th CPC Central Committee made the *Decision of the Central Committee of the Communist Party of China on Some Major Issues Concerning Comprehensively Continuing the Reform*. The *Decision* expressly stated that "in order to promote ecological progress, we must establish complete and integrated institutions and systems, use set rules to protect the ecological environment, improve the system of natural resource property rights and the system of natural resource utilization control, delimit the red line for ecological protection, implement sound compensation systems for use of resources and for damage to the ecological environment, and reform the ecological protection and management system." Compensation systems for use of resources and for damage to the ecological environment is a key component of green development and the system of ecological progress, a basic institutional guarantee for advancing ecological progress, a requirement made by comprehensively deepening the reform, and a symbol that China will adopt more market-based means to enhance eco-environmental protection. There will be strict economic restrictions on waste discharge and use of resources, which will be very meaningful for making sure that the exploitation and utilization of resources is within the self-recovering capacity of ecological system, thus ensuring sustainable development.

© Social Sciences Academic Press and Springer Nature Singapore Pte Ltd. 2018

X. Li and X. Liu, *Green Development Model of China's Small and Medium-sized Cities*, Research Series on the Chinese Dream and China's Development Path,
https://doi.org/10.1007/978-981-13-0779-9_10

1 Contents and Definition of the Systems

According to views of sustainable economics, natural resources and ecological environment, like goods that contain human labor, also have values. With socioeconomic development, the exploitation and utilization of natural resources such as land, mineral reserves, water, forest, sea, grassland, intertidal land and wasteland have become a major part of human life, and the property right deriving therefrom is a key aspect of social wealth and has drawn attention from all parties. On the one hand, natural resources belong to the whole society and constitute the shared material foundation for the continuation of human society, and right holders other than the property owner should be entitled to use those resources and share the profits. On the other hand, for natural resources to realize their values through use, the right of use must be determined due to its exclusivity. Paying for resource consumption requires that human life and production activities should be beneficial for the sustained utilization of natural resources. Instead of willfully damaging and demanding from the ecological environment, humans should use resources in an eco-friendly way, treat the environment nicely, and pay a due price or fees for the resource they enjoy based on their value and level of scarcity.

The compensation system for use of resources refers to the whole set of management measures that the state takes through compulsory means to regulate the actions of units and individuals that exploit and utilize natural resources and demand them to pay corresponding fees. This system is established according to the theory of public goods and of internalizing external diseconomy, based on the limitation, usefulness and value of environmental resources, and in light of the principle of sustainable development. This system correctly deals with the price difference between natural resources and their products, renewable and non-renewable resources, and of various resources such as land, water, forest and mineral resources. It puts in place a price mechanism that truthfully reflects the extent of scarcity and market supply and demand of resources, as well as the cost for environmental damage, and forms a reasonable price difference for natural resources.

Compensating for ecological damage, a concept that was created as a policy tool kit for environmental problems, is an important economic means that can realize compensated use of resources and effectively address environmental externalities. Pursuant to the theory of environmental resource values, ecological compensation charges actions or products that damage the ecological environment, compensates for or rewards those that protect it, compensates for people that suffer losses because of eco-environmental damage and protection, stimulates market players to voluntarily protect the environment, and coordinates environmental and economic development.

The system for damage to the ecological environment means that to preserve the stability of ecological system and prevent the destruction of ecological environment, the government adopts relevant policies and measures with the focus on economic adjustment and makes overall use of government, legal and market means to regulate production, operation and development activities that affect or may affect the ecological environment. It internalizes the externality of eco-protection, makes those who benefit from the results of eco-protection pay corresponding fees, provides reasonable return to investors in eco-environmental protection, improves the capability of producing and supplying eco-friendly products, incentivizes people to invest in eco-protection and increases the values of eco-environmental capital. As a result, eco-protection gradually becomes a voluntary action and its interests and benefits are realized.

Ecological progress concerns people's wellbeing and the future of the nation. The 18th CPC National Congress incorporated ecological progress in the five-pronged overall plan (covering economic, political, cultural, social, and ecological progress) for socialist cause with Chinese characteristics, and explicitly called for great efforts to promote ecological progress, build a beautiful country, and achieve lasting and sustainable development of the Chinese nation. Chinese president Xi Jinping emphasized that only the most rigorous system and rule of law can provide reliable guarantee for ecological progress. Institutional construction for ecological progress is not only a symbol of ecological soft power, but also a standard that measures the level of ecological development, in which the core content is establishing and improving the compensation systems for use of resources and for damage to the ecological environment. Establishing those two systems is good for innovating the resource and environment management model, reflecting the values of natural and eco-environmental resources, urging every social member and group to pay more attention to the natural environment we live in, and motivating eco-protecting actions. Against the background of resource shortage and serious eco-environmental pollution, the two systems make sure that the exploitation and utilization of resources is within the self-recovering capacity of ecological system, integrate economic and ecological development, address the conflict between economic and social development and eco-protection, and promote sound and fast economic and social development. They also match the ecological responsibilities borne by local areas with the rights they enjoy, alleviate and eliminate uneven regional development, and achieve coordinated regional development and social harmony. The two systems provide steady capital for eco-environmental protection, restoration and reconstruction, urge people to save resources, protect environment, and willingly invest in eco-protection, and enhance the capability of producing and supplying eco-products, so that the value of eco-environmental capital increases and humans and nature exist in harmony. They are of great importance for building a beautiful China and realizing the lasting and sustainable development of the Chinese nation.

2 System Establishment and Practices in Different Areas

The per capita resource possession by Chinese people is much lower than world average. Per capita possession of mineral resources is less than half of the world average, that of freshwater, farmland and grassland is 28.1, 32.3 and 32.3% of world average respectively, and that of forest is only 14.3% of world average. The traditional extensive economic development model resulted in serious resource waste, not only aggravating resource shortage, but also leading to prominent environmental pollution and other problems. It is estimated that in the eight high-energy-consuming industries in China, including iron and steel, non-ferrous metals, electricity and chemical industry, energy consumption per unit product is over 40% higher than world advanced level; energy consumption for heating per unit construction area is 2–3 times as much as that in developed countries with similar climate; industrial water recycle rate and mineral resource recovery rate is 15–25 and 20 percentage points lower than world advanced level respectively; and intensity of raw material consumption is 5–10 times as high as in developed countries. This is mainly caused by the old system of free or cheap use of resources. To fundamentally reverse the trend of ecological deterioration and achieve sustainable development, we have to straighten out the interest relationship between ecological protectors and destroyers, beneficiaries and victims. Upholding market mechanism, we should firmly promote the compensation system for use of resources and environment, and put in place a long-term mechanism for resource conservation and environmental protection, so that those who save resources and protect environment can benefit and those who waste resources and pollute environment will pay the price, and resources and environment can be used more efficiently.

2.1 Establishment Compensation System for Use of Resources

Socialist public ownership plays a dominant role in China, so the compensation system for use of resources means that under the premise that natural resources belong to the state, usufruct related with them including the right of use and benefit can be transferred at a price, namely interest exchange, compensation and distribution should be reflected by the payment of royalties, while the government, as the administrator, charges relevant taxes and fees on natural resource exploitations. The goal of building the compensation system for use of resources in China is to create a fair, open and just resource market, and a unified, open and orderly mechanism of initial resource distribution and tier-2 market transaction system. It is also to establish a resource circulation mechanism that facilitates government regulation and orderly market distribution, raises the efficiency of resource utilization, and guarantees economic and social sustainability.

On December 1, 1987, Shenzhen transferred a plot of land by auction, marking the first case of compensated use of resource after the People's Republic of China was founded. The First Session of the 7th National People's Congress (NPC) held in April 1988 passed the *Amendments to the Constitution*, whereby Item 4 of Article 14 of the *Constitution* was revised into "no organization or individual should occupy or trade land or otherwise engage in the transfer of land by unlawful means. The right of land use can be transferred according to law". This denoted the establishment of the compensation system for use of land, and land revenue became a major source of increasing government revenues and urban construction fund since then.

In 1996, the State Council issued the *Decision of the State Council on Several Issues Concerning Environmental Protection*, which put forth to establish and improve the compensation system for use of natural resources and an economic compensation system for restoring the ecological environment. The report made to the 15th CPC National Congress proposed to implement the compensation system for use of resources.

Article 9 of the *Constitution of the People's Republic of China* (amended in 2004) provided that mineral resources, waters, forests, mountains, grassland, unreclaimed land, intertidal land and other natural resources are owned by the state, that is, by the whole people, with the exception of forests, mountains, grassland, unreclaimed land and intertidal land that are owned by collectives in accordance with the law. The state ensures the rational use of natural resources and protects rare animals and plants. The occupation or damage of natural resources by any organization or individual by any means is prohibited. Article 10 provided that urban land is owned by the state; rural land and land in urban suburbs are owned by collectives unless they are owned by the state according to law; homestead, private plot and private hilly land are also owned by collectives. The state can expropriate land and provide compensation in accordance with the law for the sake of public interests. No organization or individual should occupy or trade land or otherwise engage in the transfer of land by unlawful means. The right of land use can be transferred according to law. Organizations and individuals should use land rationally.

In September 2006, the State Council approved Ministry of Finance, Ministry of Land Resources and National Development and Reform Commission (NDRC) to carry out pilot reform on the compensation system for use of coal resources in eight main coal-producing provinces including Shanxi and Inner Mongolia, marking a substantial step forward in China's reform for compensated use of resources.

On March 16, 2007, the Fifth Session of the 10th NPC passed the *Property Law of the People's Republic of China* (*Property Law*), which came into effect on October 1, 2007. Article 119 of the *Property Law* provided that the state shall apply a system of compensated use of natural resources, unless otherwise stipulated by law. Relevant laws such as *Law of Land Management*, *Law of Mineral Resources* and *Water Law*, as well as administrative rules of the State Council all laid down clear provisions about this. For example, Article 2 of the *Law of Land Management* provided that the use of state-owned land follows the principle of compensated use, except transfer of the right of use of state-owned land within the scope of law. Article 5 of the *Law of Mineral Resources* provided that prospecting and mining right follows the principle of paid acquisition, except the payment is exempted according to rules of the State Council. Article 7 of the *Water Law* provided that the use of water resource follows the principle of compensated use, except for water of the ponds and reservoirs belonging to rural economic collectives that is used by such collectives and their members.

The report to the 17th CPC National Congress reaffirmed the need to "establish and improve the compensation systems for use of resources and for damage to the ecological environment". The government work report in 2008 stated "reform the system of resource tax and fee, and improve the compensation systems for use of resources and for damage to the ecological environment". According to NDRC's *Opinions on Deepening Economic System Reform in 2008*, one of the key reform tasks that year was to establish and improve the mechanism of resource conservation and environmental protection. Efforts would be made to establish and improve the compensation systems for use of resources and for damage to the ecological environment, and study the levy of environmental protection tax.

On November 23, 2010, Ministry of Finance, NDRC and National Energy Administration (NEA) jointly issued the *Notice on Issues Concerning the Standard Management of Compensated Development and Use of Water Energy (Hydropower) Resources* (CZ [2010] No. 105), which demanded to strengthen the management of the collection and use of water resource fees, and standardize the compensation system for use of water resources. Several other rules and notices were also issued, such as the *Regulations on Water Permit and Collection of Water Resource Fee* (State Council Issue No. 460), *Notice of Ministry of Finance, National Development and Reform Commission and Ministry of Water Resources on Printing and Distributing the "Regulations on Collection and Use of Water Resource Fees"* (CZ [2008] No. 79), and *Notice of National Development and Reform Commission, Ministry of Finance and Ministry of Water Resources on the Charging Standard for Water Resource Fee for Central-level and Cross-province Water Conservancy Projects and on Other Relevant Issues* (FGJG [2009] No. 1779). According to them, local governments should strengthen the management of water resource fee collection, and make sure it is collected in time and in full and earmarked for water conservation, protection and management as required and for rational water resource development. Transfer, retention or embezzlement of the fee by any organization or individual is prohibited. Local governments were required to stop implementing their own policies on compensated development and use of water energy (hydropower) resources, strengthen the management of fee collection and use, and standardize the compensation system for use of water resources. The *Notice* specified that local governments should not make paid transfer of the right of water energy (hydropower) resource development of completed, ongoing and new hydropower projects, or charge transfer fee for the right of water resource development and use or charge hydropower development compensation from hydropower enterprises or project developers in the name of compensated development and use.

In 2012, the report to the 18th CPC National Congress proposed to enhance system building to promote ecological progress, and establish the compensation systems for use of resources and for damage to the ecological environment that reflect market supply and demand and resource scarcity, recognize ecological values and require compensation in the interests of later generations. In 2013, the Third Plenary Session of the 18th CPC Central Committee also stated that we should implement the compensation systems for use of resources and for damage to the ecological environment and reform the institution of eco-environmental protection and management.

2.2 Establishment of Ecological Compensation System

Chinese government started building the ecological compensation system by founding the afforestation fund in 1953. In 1993, the then State Environmental Protection Administration issued the *Noticed on Determining Pilot Projects of Eco-environmental Compensation* (abolished in 2002), which kick-started studies of and practical explorations for ecological compensation mechanism. Ecological compensation was levied on a trial basis successively in 685 counties (units) and 24 national natural reserves of 11 provinces and autonomous regions including Hebei and Liaoning.

In 2003, the CPC Central Committee and State Council issued *Several Opinions on Implementing the Strategy for Reinvigorating Northeast China and Other Old Industrial Bases*, which specified the need to "study and establish the mechanism of resource development compensation and assistance to declining industries." The communiqué of the Fifth Plenary Session of the 16th CPC Central Committee demanded the government, for the first time, to "establish the ecological compensation mechanism faster on the principle that whoever develops the environment should protect it and whoever benefits should provide compensation". This pushed the implementation of ecological compensation in China in full swing.

The *Decision of the State Council on Implementing Scientific Outlook on Development and Strengthening Environmental Protection* issued in 2005 and the *11th Five-Year Plan of the People's Republic of China on Economic and Social Development* promulgated in 2006 both urged to establish the ecological compensation mechanism at an early date. In 2007, the State Environmental Protection Administration issued *Guiding Opinions on Implementing Ecological Compensation on A Trial Basis*, which stated that pilot ecological compensation should be carried out in natural reserves, important eco-zones, areas of mineral resource exploitation and water environmental protection, and other key areas, and efforts should be made to set the standard for ecological compensation. It also put forward the principle for ecological compensation—whoever develops the environment should protect it, whoever damages the environment should restore it, and whoever pollutes the environment should pay the compensation.

The reports to the 17th and 18th CPC National Congresses and the *Decision of the Third Plenary Session of the 18th CPC Central Committee* all stressed the establishment and improvement of the mechanism of compensated use of resources and for damage to the ecological environment. At the moment, national, provincial and municipal governments have all worked out relevant systems and measures. On the central government, there is the system of forest ecological benefit compensation fund, grassland ecological compensation, ecological compensation for water resource and water and soil conservation, mine environment governance and ecological restoration responsibility, and transfer payment for key eco-zones.

The NPC standing committee passed a range of laws concerning ecological compensation, including *Law of Mineral Resources* (1996), *Forest Law* (1998), *Law on the Management of Sea Area Use* (2001), *Law of Sand Prevention and Control* (2001),

Water Law (2002), *Fishery Law* (2004), *Law of Land Management* (2004), *Law of Wildlife Protection* (2004), *Law of Animal Husbandry* (2005), *Law of Water Pollution Prevention and Control* (2008), *Law of Island Protection* (2009), *Law of Water and Soil Conservation* (2010), *Agriculture Law* (2012) and *Grassland Law* (2013). Among them, only *Forest Law* provided for the forest ecological benefit compensation fund system, while others only said that fees must be charged on environmental resource exploitation and utilization and eco-protection must be compensated. In 2010, the State Council listed the study and formulation of ecological compensation regulations in the legislation plan. 11 departments and units including National Development and Reform Commission, Ministry of Finance, Ministry of Land and Resources, Ministry of Water Resources, Ministry of Environmental Protection and State Forestry Administration formed a drafting team, and the draft regulations are now completed. The State Council has issued more than 80 ecological compensation regulations and policies covering natural reserve, returning farmland to forest, forest ecological benefit compensation fund, compensation for eco-environmental restoration in mining area, functional zoning across the country and regional eco-protection. They involved areas such as administration, macroeconomics, resource and energy, agriculture and animal husbandry, water conservancy and environment protection, and primarily set up the framework of ecological compensation system. The scope of ecological compensation expanded from development of wetland and mineral resources to river basin and water resource, protection of drinking water source, agriculture, grassland, forest, natural reserve, key eco-zone, region and the sea.

Establishment of ecological compensation system for forest and natural reserve started quite early. In addition to the aforementioned afforestation fund system founded in 1953, the State Council endorsed and forwarded the *Notice on Key Points of Economic System Reform in 1992* (GF [1992] No. 12) issued by the State Commission for Restructuring the Economic System in 1992, which specifically demanded to establish the forest pricing system and forest ecological benefit compensation system, and implement compensated use of forest resources. In 1993, the State Council issued the *Notice on Further Intensifying Afforestation and Greening* (GF [1993] No. 15), which pointed out the mechanism of afforestation and greening investment should be reformed and ecological benefit compensation should be collected. The new *Forest Law* implemented from July 1, 1998 explicitly stated that the system of ecological benefit compensation fund should be established in China. The *Implementing Rules of Forest Law* promulgated in 2000 provided that operators of shelter forest and special-purpose forest were entitled to compensation for forest ecological benefits, and the compensation fund should be founded with capital directly allocated from government budget. Since 2001, the state has spent RMB1 billion on pilot projects in 11 provinces, with another RMB30 billion on the compensation for returning farmland to forest and the planting of public welfare forest. 2001–2004 was the period when forest ecological benefit allowance was provided on a trial basis. In 2004, the central fund for forest ecological benefit compensation was officially founded, and Ministry of Finance and State Forestry Administration issued regulations for it, marking the official establishment of that system. According to articles of the *Forest Law*, Ministry of Finance and State Forestry Administration successively issued the delimitation methods for state-level public welfare forests and regulations on the central fund for forest ecological benefit compensation, providing compensation for 1.87 billion *mu* of land.

Regarding ecological compensation system for water resources and river basins, National Development and Reform Commission, Ministry of Finance and Ministry of Water Resources jointly issued documents to further raise the charging standard for water resource fee, and are studying to formulate regulations on the collection and use of compensation fee for water and soil conservation. In 2011, Ministry of Finance and Ministry of Environmental Protection issued the implementation scheme for pilot water environment compensation in Xin'an River basin concerning Zhejiang and Anhui provinces. The scheme specified the source of fund and standards and methods of compensation, and water environment ecological compensation across provincial administrative regions was conducted on a trial basis. In March 2013, the State Council approved the coordination scheme between the reservoir area and upper reaches of Danjiangkou to support coordination between Beijing, Tianjin and Hubei, Henan, Shaanxi, respectively water recipients and water sources on the middle route of the South-North Water Diversion Project.

Regarding ecological compensation system for mineral resource exploitation, the system of mine environment governance and ecological restoration responsibility was in place. The state allocated a special fund for the geological environment of mines to support local areas in governing the geological environment of mines that were left from history or whose mining right owner had passed away, and demanded that a certain proportion of the income from mineral product sales be allocated as cash deposit for mine environment governance and ecological restoration. After mineral resource tax was levied on the exploitation of mineral resources in the mid-1980s, mineral resource compensation fee was also levied in 1994. The *Implementing Rules on Law of Mineral Resources* implemented from 1997 made detailed provisions for water and soil conservation, reclamation and environmental protection during mine exploitation, and demanded miners that couldn't fulfill those responsibilities to submit to competent department the expenses needed to fulfill those responsibilities, hence the mine exploitation deposit system.

Regarding regional ecological compensation system, the system of transfer payment for key eco-zones was established, and its implementation has expanded to 466 counties (cities, districts). The state also provides subsidies for exploitation-prohibited areas, including natural reserves, scenic areas, forest parks and geological parks at the national level. The grassland ecological compensation system was established. As of the end of 2012, 1.23 billion *mu* of grassland was subsidized for grazing prohibition, and 2.6 billion *mu* of grassland enjoyed the grass-grazing balance reward.

2.3 Practices and Explorations by Local Governments

China's efforts to establish the compensation systems for use of resources and for damage to the ecological environment is mainly based on policy documents formulated by NPC and the central government and regulations issued by State Council departments. Provincial People's Congresses, governments and functional departments also formulated many local rules and policies in that aspect in light of local conditions, focused on the implementation of ecological compensation in areas such as forest, river basin, natural reserve, ocean and mineral resource development and also involving ecological compensation for wetland, agriculture, soil, prevention and control of desertification, water resource protection and grassland. For example, Shanxi, Shaanxi, Inner Mongolia, Yunnan and Hebei started related work before State Environmental Protection Administration began to levy eco-environmental compensation fee in certain provinces on a trial basis. To assist in the implementation of central forest ecological benefit compensation fund, provinces set up their own compensation funds successively and worked out the implementing methods and schemes. Zhejiang carried out pilot ecological compensation across the eight major water systems in the province. In February 2008, Liaoning Provincial Finance Department issued the *Implementing Methods for Ecological Compensation Policies in Key Areas of East Liaoning*, which designated the scope of regional ecological compensation, indicators and formula of compensation calculation, grant and management of the compensation fund, and duties of relevant departments. Provinces and autonomous regions including Heilongjiang, Liaoning, Jiangsu, Inner Mongolia, Anhui, Fujian and Jiangxi made progress on establishing the wetland ecological compensation system. Shandong's *Provisional Methods for Management of Compensation for Ecological Damages and Losses to the Sea* clarified for the first time the definition of compensation for ecological damages and losses to the sea, main subjects and scope of application, the levy, use, management and purpose of the compensation, and supervision and inspection of its levy and use.

Zhejiang took the initiative to improve the ecological compensation mechanism across the province and created the "Zhejiang mode". It issued regulations on special environmental protection fund for water sources, actively tried multiple forms of ecological compensation, and its lateral compensation took effects. In August 2005, Zhejiang issued *Several Opinions on Further Improving the Ecological Compensation Mechanism*, which made detailed provisions regarding the target, standard and form of compensation, source of fund, and main ways and measures of establishing and improving the mechanism. With Qiantang River basin as a pilot site, the province provided ecological protection subsidy for water sources and formulated supportive policies including local regulations on ecological compensation, administrative incentives and policies that supported relevant industries.

Qinghai did fruitful work on establishing and improving the compensation system for use of resources, which has already taken shape in certain key fields of resource development. Resource authorities preliminarily established the system of paid acquisition of mining right and paid exploitation of mineral resources. Whether it's the newly established mining right of coal or mining right that was obtained for free in the past, they should be paid now. Effective reform and explorations were also conducted in compensated use of water resources and other areas.

Gansu Provincial Environmental Sanitation Department suggested in 2010 forming a provincial coordinating organization of ecological compensation mechanism under the lead of the provincial government and comprising a number of resource authorities including development and reform commission, departments of finance, land resources, construction, agriculture and animal husbandry. The organization should study and formulate the ecological compensation framework in a centralized way, integrate various resource charges, found an ecological compensation fund, and implement compensated use of resources and ecological compensation.

In 2014, Hainan will push the reform of the compensation system for use of natural resources, conduct early research on the system of eco-environmental damages and accountability, and explore to carry out the damages system on a trial basis. It will also reform the ecological compensation system, organize to formulate regulations on the use of ecological transfer payment for key national eco-zones and assessing methods of eco-environmental quality in key national eco-zones in the central mountainous area, and apply the reward and penalty system whereby ecological transfer payment is linked with the assessment result.

Shandong made active efforts to establish the system of compensated resource use and ecological compensation. According to *Methods of Shandong Province of Air Quality Ecological Compensation*, if ambient air quality in cities improves and contributes positively to air quality improvement of the whole province, provincial government should compensate the municipal government; if ambient air quality in cities worsens and contributes negatively to air quality improvement of the whole province, municipal government should compensate the provincial government. According to the *Summary Sheet of Ecological Compensation for Ambient Air Quality in Shandong Province—2014Q1*, RMB70.29 million of compensation was provided to various cities, of which Yantai received the least of RMB320,000 and Liaocheng received the most of RMB9.5 million.

3 Problems and Challenges

3.1 Regulations and Regulatory Policy Documents Are Lacking or Contradictory

The *Constitution* is the fundamental law in China and the basis for making all other laws. It makes general provisions on the ownership and use of natural resources, but except for land, articles are absent regarding compensated resource use and ecological compensation. Since contents about those two issues are scattered in various laws and regulations formulated by both the central and local governments and even different functional departments on various levels, there aren't unified rules or institutional requirements in China. Existing laws and rules on compensated resource use and ecological compensation have different priorities and usually focus on a specific field, so different administrative regions and river basins have diverse concepts, execution norms and specific operation approaches. However, the holistic nature of the ecosystem decides that there is overlapping among different fields, such as the overlapping of water and river basin with forest, grassland, land and wetland. To address this problem, the state needs to intensify top-level design, issue unified and specialized laws and regulations, and effectively smoothen the interest conflicts among regions and fields, so that the compensation systems for use of resources and for damage to the ecological environment in China can be implemented according to laws and rules.

3.2 Fiscal and Tax System Needs Urgent Reform

In the current tax and fee system in China, what really reflects the principle of ecological compensation is waste discharge fee, eco-environmental compensation and deposit for mine environment restoration and governance. Other than that, there are local ecological charges on mineral resource exploitation, such as land reclamation fee, fee for the prevention, control and compensation of water and soil loss, forest vegetation restoration fee, afforestation fund, and forestry fund. As compensated use of resources is implemented in a larger scope, the determination of the ownership of natural and eco-environmental resources lags behind socioeconomic development. In the fiscal and tax system, that means the lack of definite design for the compensation systems for use of resources and for damage to the ecological environment, which leads to a number of problems, such as policy blanks in certain areas, the absence of standards and methods for assessing the value of eco-environmental resources that are generally accepted by stakeholders, low compensation standard and huge capital shortfall.

The current standard for resource tax and compensation fee doesn't reflect the supply, demand and scarcity of resources or take into account the social and environmental cost that resource developers should bear, so the standard is far lower than international common practice. Take mineral resource compensation fee for example. The average rate for it in China is 1.18% as opposed to the general rate of 4–8% in other countries.

Transfer payment from the central government is the main source of capital for ecological compensation, but it is insufficient because eco-environmental matters are not fully taken into account. The ratio of tax distribution between national and local governments isn't rational enough. As the system of compensated resource use is to be improved, economic benefits arising from resource exploitation cannot be given back to the area of exploitation through institutional arrangement. Therefore, while local government and the public don't benefit much from resource exploitation, they have to bear all responsibilities and outcomes, which leads to uneven development from region to region and a series of social problems. For instance, provinces like Guizhou and Heilongjiang, which abound in ecological and mineral resources, haven't received enough fiscal revenues, and such demonstrative effect has dampened local governments' enthusiasm to some extent.

The current economic accounting system in China makes physical quantity statistics of natural resources but doesn't quantify their value. Even if physical quantity and value are both incorporated to calculate natural resource assets, there is the problem of how to combine and balance the two measurements. In addition to listing proven reserves and the majority of natural resources currently possessed by the government under the category of ecological resource, we should also design accounting items for waste discharge right, atmosphere, water, land, mineral resource, forest, greenbelt and grassland.

3.3 Government's Management Functions Have to Be Adjusted

In the current system, protecting ecological environment is under the administration of several departments, including forestry, agriculture, water conservancy, land resource and environmental protection, which results in department-based interests and unclear division of responsibility. Since property right isn't clearly defined, the interests for contributors to and beneficiaries of natural and eco-environmental resources are unbalanced. The ecological compensation principle of "whoever benefits should compensate, whoever damages the environment should restore it, and whoever pollutes it should tackle it" isn't operable enough for clarifying the subject and target of responsibility and right.

Supervision of fund use isn't sound. Some local governments embezzled ecological compensation fund against rules, so the fund didn't play its due role or take the expected effect. Especially at the town and township level, compensation standard isn't unified due to multiple reasons, so its release cannot be open and transparent, leaving loopholes to lawbreakers. At present, the evaluation of ecological compensation effect takes place between the superior and the subordinate without an independent third-party evaluation organization, so the objectives and standards of the evaluation may be irrational.

While the compensation systems for use of resources and for damage to the ecological environment are being established, a public participation system hasn't taken form yet, nor is there an effective opinion feedback mechanism. As a result, supervision by public opinions isn't in place, and private right cannot impose reasonable check upon public right.

3.4 *Market Mechanism Is Weak*

China has preliminarily set up the framework of ecological compensation mechanism for forest, grassland, mine, and water and soil conservancy. However, the market transaction mechanism for compensated use of natural resources isn't well developed, and ecological compensation faces a series of problems including unreasonable, non-transparent and excessively low standards and indiscriminate approach. As a result, "excessive compensation" and "insufficient compensation" co-exist, and compensation measures become a mere formality during implementation.

The total sum of ecological compensation fund allocated by the central government has increased rapidly in recent years from RMB2.3 billion in 2001 to about RMB78 billion in 2012, and RMB150 billion had been spent accumulatively by 2012, more than half of the total quota. While fiscal expenditure cannot increase by a large margin, sustainable ecological compensation can only be guaranteed with market mechanism.

Confirmation of property right is the foundation for compensated resource use and ecological compensation, so it's urgent to change the reversed property right in natural and ecological resource management, and clarify the eco-protection responsibility due on property right owners. In a well-developed market economic system, the price of most natural resources can be adjusted through market transaction. Under uncertain conditions, eco-environmental resources are irreversible, usually generate sunk cost and comprehensive consideration of them is difficult. The resource price spontaneously formed in the market can only reflect the production cost of resource, but not its compensation cost and external cost, and cannot fully reflect the pricing principle of "fairness for later generations and reasonable compensation". Therefore, resource regulators must intervene in or adjust the market-based price of natural resources.

4 Policy Suggestions

4.1 *Establishing and Improving Relevant Laws and Regulations*

We should establish and improve relevant laws and regulations and include clauses about compensated resource use and ecological compensation in the *Constitution*. We should issue the *Ecological Compensation Regulations* and implementing rules at an early date to specify the responsibilities, obligations, rights and interests of the subject and recipient of ecological compensation, and use that as the legal basis for standardized operation. We should move faster to set up the ecological compensation standards, specify control variables and prevent randomness, so as to make sure ecological compensation is truly used for ecological restoration and protection.

4.2 *Improving Current Policies on Environment Protection Tax*

We should levy ecological compensation tax and a new environmental tax, adjust and improve the methods for the collection, use and management of taxes and fees for resources such as water and soil, mineral resources, forest and environment, and allocate a larger proportion of resource taxes to ecological compensation with a special emphasis on underdeveloped areas, important eco-zones, areas of water sources and natural reserves. In this way, we can use tax as a leverage to combine resource exploitation and use with eco-environmental protection, and implement ecological compensation in specific economic activities. By adjusting the price system, tax system and waste discharge charging system, we can put in place quantified standards, make requirements and impose restrictions on ecological compensation, and further clarify responsibilities and obligations following the principle of whoever develops the environment should protect it, and whoever benefits should pay the compensation. We should establish a multi-layered, multi-channel all-society common compensation mechanism under the overall leadership of the central government, and work out the lateral ecological compensation mechanism between regions. Priority should be given to underdeveloped areas, important eco-zones, areas of water sources and natural reserves in fund allocation, and special support should be given to regional, river-basin-based and key environmental projects and state-level forests where eco-environmental protection is particularly effective. In this way, we can put compensation to good use, motivate initiative, and advance the sustainable development of ecological compensation.

4.3 *Streamlining Administration, Delegating Power and Innovating Public Services*

Following the State Council's call for streamlining administration and delegating power to lower-level governments, we should innovate in public services, scale up government purchase of public services, strengthen supervision and management, and improve government work. In recent years, China has carried out Energy Performance Contracting (EPC) and trade of water right, waste discharge right and carbon emission right on a trial basis, formulated and improved auxiliary policies and systems, and made favorable progress. In particular, the carbon market has great potential and more efforts should be made in that area. China has issued the *Provisional Methods for Management of Voluntary Greenhouse Gas Emission Reduction and Trade* to guide enterprises to actively carry out voluntary emission reduction and trade in a standard way. We should adopt effective measures to encourage more enterprises to participate in that and create more market demand.

4.4 Establishing and Improving Market-Oriented Mechanism

We should establish and improve the market-oriented mechanism and give full play to the basic role of the market in allocating resources. First, we should innovate in the price formation mechanism for resource-intensive products and improve the pricing mechanism whereby the price is decided through consultation among government, enterprises and consumers. Second, in light of the interactive mechanism of price, tax, fee and rent, we should appropriately increase resource tax, facilitate the collection of environmental tax, improve the levy model, and explore to raise the cost of environmental pollution and reduce pollutant discharge by means of taxes and fees. Third, we should improve the system of ecological resource compensation and trade, develop environmental protection market, promote trade system for conserved energy, carbon emission right, waste discharge right and water right, and create a market mechanism that can attract private capital to eco-environmental protection.

Part III
Typical Cases

Chapter 11
Holding the Ecological Red Line, Writing a New Chapter of Development—Kunshan

In 2013, Kunshan's economic and social development displayed a sound status of progress and better quality amid stability. Income of urban and rural residents maintained a two-digit growth for ten consecutive years, local GDP reached RMB292.01 billion, a 9.7% growth from the previous year, and per capita GDP was USD28,700 and energy consumption per RMB10,000 GDP was 0.4 metric ton of standard coal, reaching the level of moderately developed countries and regions. Kunshan ranked 8th of all cities in the country regarding total import/export volume, and it was the only county-level city nationwide with public fiscal revenues exceeding RMB20 billion. Under the leadership of the CPC Committee and government of Jiangsu Province and Suzhou City, Kunshan thoroughly implement the guidelines of the 18th National Party Congress and the Second and Third Plenary Sessions of the 18th CPC Central Committee. Focused on the general goal of taking the lead in achieving modernization and the overall positioning of creating "a modern industrial city in the world, a harmonious and happy city in China, and a cultural and livable city in Jiangnan (south of the Yangtze River)", Kunshan is committed to "reform, opening up, innovation, responsibility and courage", strongly promoting the new Kunshan spirit of "dare to be No. 1 and the only one". It maintained steady and fast economic and social development, and obtained periodic results in and laid the primary foundation for basically achieving modernization ahead of others.

Strengthening ecological progress and environmental protection and exploring a green development path suitable for itself—those are the prerequisites for leading the way to basically achieving modernization in a sustainable way. Kunshan earnestly implemented the guideline of prioritizing environmental and ecological protection, worked hard to foster ecological advantages, and won a raft of awards in that area, including National City for Sanitation, National Garden City, National Pilot City for Ecological Development, Exemplary City for Environmental Protection, Exemplary City for Greening, National Ecological City, National City for Water Conservation and UN-Habitat Scroll of Honour award. Especially after the 18th CPC National Congress, Kunshan put ecological progress and green development in a more prominent position, implemented the five-pronged overall plan across the

© Social Sciences Academic Press and Springer Nature Singapore Pte Ltd. 2018

X. Li and X. Liu, *Green Development Model of China's Small and Medium-sized Cities*, Research Series on the Chinese Dream and China's Development Path,
https://doi.org/10.1007/978-981-13-0779-9_11

board, and explored a new green path of development-protection integration, with the focus on green, circular and low-carbon development. Kunshan strives to achieve all the 26 indicators of ecological development under five categories by 2015 and basically create the spatial layout, industrial structure, production model and lifestyle characterized by resource conservation and environmental protection. To that end, it has focused on the following aspects.

1 Reinforcing Green Awareness, Forging United Efforts for Green Development

First, fostering the awareness of green environment and putting ecological protection in a leading position. Of the 34 indicators under 28 subjects of 5 categories on basically achieving modernization ahead of others, eight indicators of four subjects were put under the category of "ecological environment", which accounted for 15% of the total points, in order to apply eco-environmental standards to all areas and the whole process of modernization drive. The city issued the opinions on accelerating ecological development and worked out annual action plan, made annual project plans for ecological and green development, environmental improvement and ecological progress, and prioritized those projects in the allocation of fund, materials and talents to guarantee their smooth progress. In 2013, the municipal People's Congress made ecological development the No. 1 motion, often debriefed progress on it and organized people's deputies to inspect relevant work, supporting the implementation of the motion with forceful supervision. Second, creating the atmosphere for green development and motivating public participation. The city carried out a series of green activities, such as exemplary public behavior day, green cycling and mass walking, held lectures and step up knowledge dissemination and publicity for green and ecological development, broadened channels for e-government and public supervision in that area, and gave play to all kinds of news media and interactive platforms including government microblog, online forum and People's Voice 110. The city strongly fostered and guided environmental NGOs and volunteer teams and advocated a lifestyle and consuming habits featuring civilization, frugality and environmental friendliness, so as to enhance "green and ecological consciousness" in the whole society. We organized meetings of netizens and residents in the theme of environmental protection, released microfilms in that theme, and invited residents to participate in environmental law enforcement, in an attempt to mobilize all Kunshan people to become the referee, supervisor and participant in ecological development. Third, consolidating ecological efforts for results of green development. The city advocated green and low-carbon travel, built bus-first traffic lanes, and provided 17,000 new public bikes across the city, which were borrowed and returned for more than 72,000 person times a day on average, and public transit undertook 24.2% of the city traffic. Kunshan has put 670 new-energy and clean-energy buses into use accumulatively, accounting for 46.9% of all buses, and built high-level energy-saving and green architectures on a trial basis. The central area of Huaqiao International Service Business Park was listed by Ministry of Housing and Urban-rural Development as a demonstration zone for green and low-energy-consuming architectures.

2 Attaching Importance to Planning and Guidance, Optimizing Spatial Layout for Green Development

First, improving the planning system for green development. The city government insisted that plans for water system, green land, resources and environment should be combined, systematically developed overall plans for the southern water town and ecological plans for open green space, tourist resorts and circular economic development, and urged for the integration of ecological plans with district plan, industrial plan and land plan. The city upheld the principle of priority to ecology, all-city planning and holistic district development, completed the new round of revision of overall city plan and the plan for green and ecological development, and created a clear and rational functional division and spatial layout covering several layers—central urban area, urban sub-centers, small cities and characteristic town, new-type communities, and natural villages. Second, controlling land development intensity. The city held fast to the red line of protecting natural and ecological resources such as important waters sources, wetland, water bodies and woods. Kunshan was among the first in the province to adjust and optimize key eco-zones. The city government decided the purpose and intensity of land development according to environmental capacity, scientifically allocated construction land, ecological land and reserve land for future development, and developed existing blocks in the four types of "prioritized, key, restricted and prohibited", so as to leave sufficient room for future development by leaving undeveloped land. Third, the city optimized the spatial layout of urban and rural areas. The government insisted on overall planning and construction of urban, rural and ecological areas, and comprehensively implemented the urban upgrade program with the focus on renovating old city areas, old towns, old industrial zones and old residential communities, in the endeavor to build a famous cultural and livable city in the south of Yangtze River. While making adjustments for "district-town interaction and cluster development", the city upheld the philosophy of "industries are concentrated in industrial parks, agricultural development goes for large scale, and residents are concentrated in communities". Kunshan also developed urban/rural public transit, environmental protection, municipal pipe network and other civil facilities in a holistic way, so as to seamlessly connect and integrate urban/rural infrastructure networks and optimize the spatial layout in both urban and rural areas.

3 Accelerating Transformation and Upgrade, Creating Green and Ecological Industrial System

First, continuously pushing green industrial development. The city insisted on innovation-driven and talent-led development, provided stronger support and policy guidance, carried out special land use programs, and promoted large-scale development of dominant and emerging industries, brand-name service industries and high-end industries. The output value from high-tech industries and emerging ones accounted for 47 and 39% of the total output value of all industries above designated scale, and added values from service industry accounted for 41.2% of local GDP. The city made planting and fertilization more scientific and targeted, and strongly promoted soil testing and formula fertilization. Thanks to those efforts, they have reduced the use of phosphate fertilizer and nitrogenous fertilizer by about 4 and 5% per *mu* every year, achieved win-win results in ecological agriculture with lower cost and higher efficiency, and effectively controlled non-point source pollution. Second, promoting intensive resource utilization. Following the requirement for "strictly controlling increment, controlling total amount and activating existing resources", Kunshan managed to make economic development less resource-and-energy intensive, intensified all-process frugality management, and promoted resource recycling and consumption reduction in production, circulation and consumption. They applied rigorous management and control system for intensive land use, promoted new energy conservation mechanisms more quickly such as Energy Performance Contracting (EPC) and carbon footprint, and placed special stress on energy conservation in key areas including construction, industry, public institutions and transportation. The city actively promoted district-town interactive development for industrial clustering, resource integration, advantage complementarity, functional sharing and win-win cooperation. The local GDP per square kilometer rose from RMB124 million in 2007 to RMB313 million in 2013, and foreign and domestic investment per average *mu* climbed up from USD502,000 and USD3.274 million in 2007 to USD680,000 and USD4.7 million in 2013. Third, continuously enhancing the eco-function of industrial parks. Upholding the guideline of "differentiated guidance, fitting local conditions and highlighting characteristics", the city energetically promoted clean production and green manufacture, implemented clean production licensing, and has cultivated 583 high-tech enterprises, 127 pilot enterprises of circular economy, 663 licensed clean production enterprises, and 620 ISO14000-certified enterprises accumulatively. They supported industrial parks in developing "big platform economy" and green and ecological renovation, and encouraged intensive land utilization, clustered industrial development and concentrated environmental governance. They have completed a national demonstration eco-industrial park, a provincial modern ecological park and a provincial modern ecological park of service industry, thus improving their general profitability, overall quality and ecological competitiveness.

4 Carrying Out Comprehensive Governance, Improving Quality of Green, Ecological Environment

First, energetically implementing energy conservation and consumption reduction. The city actively conducted energy-saving campaigns, made special effort to regulate industries such as electroplating, chemical industry, printing and dyeing and spraying, shut down and relocated 148 enterprises of serious pollution and excessive emission, and stopped 89 polluting projects. They sped up the elimination of backward production capacity, implemented rigorous environmental standard, conducted coal-to-gas renovation at coal-fired power plants, and conducted tail water treatment at all sewage treatment plants. We dismantled purse nets in lakes and rivers, strictly controlled non-point source pollution in agriculture, and applied pond culture with circulated water. In 2013, Kunshan's GDP made up 22.4% of Suzhou's GDP, energy consumption per RMB10,000 local GDP was reduced to less than 0.4 metric ton standard coal, while its discharge of four main types of pollutants was less than Suzhou's 1/10, and gross industrial output value per kwh electricity was RMB58.9, 1.7 times as high as the average level in Suzhou. Meanwhile, its industrial water recycle rate was 82.7%, and fresh water consumption per unit industrial added value was 7.43 m^3/RMB10,000. Kunshan was titled National Advanced City for Emission Reduction. Second, energetically implementing specific regulatory campaigns. The city paid special attention to industrial waste gas, dust prevention and control of buildings and exhaust gas, and carried out coordinated prevention and control of atmospheric pollution. All petrol-fueled taxis were retrofitted to be gas-fueled, and the city was the first in the province to prohibit high-pollution and high-emission motor vehicles from certain areas. By 2015, more than 90% Yellow Label Cars (high-emission cars) are eliminated, and the city has good air quality 75% of the year (calculated by AQI). Kunshan focused on the protection of key water sources, lakes and rivers, developed long-term working mechanism both along and across the river, and promoted comprehensive water environment governance. Sewage treatment facilities were built in all rural areas, and sewage treatment ratio in cities, countryside, districts and towns was 97.5, 98.39 and 92% respectively. Their farmland water conservation and pollution control technology was leading in the country, and they innovatively built ecological retaining walls on riverways. The city created the "dual water sources of rivers and lakes" and took the initiative to carry out in-depth treatment of drinking water in China. They also emphasized the construction of ecological green corridor along rivers, lakes, roads and areas of concentrated industries, added more than 10 million square meters of greening every year, and stepped up greening efforts in urban and rural areas, with urban green coverage ratio reaching 45%. Third, energetically building beautiful towns and villages. The city comprehensively implemented the garbage treatment system featuring "sorting in household, collection in village, transport through town and treatment in city" since 2007, and have built one domestic waste incineration power plant, two domestic sludge incineration plants, 22 urban sewage treatment plants, and 23 industrial solid waste treatment plants. They have achieved "one faucet for drinking water, one furnace for garbage incineration, and one grid for clean energy supply". Focused on environmental renovation and ecological restoration, they integrated ecological landscape in scenic attractions, historical sites and littoral areas and maintained the original outlook of the "land of fish and rice", Jiangnan water town and idyllic scenery. They carried out overall governance of rural environment and the "six-faceted" environmental campaign, promoted protection of ancient villages and village planning and construction in an orderly way, and completed environmental improvement of 905 natural villages, driving the construction of beautiful towns and villages to new levels.

5 Making Institutional Breakthroughs and Innovations, Improving System for Green, Ecological Development

First, improving the law enforcement and supervision mechanism. Focused on administrative enforcement, emergency response, mediation and handling of visits and petitions about environmental problems, and the levy of waste discharge fee, the city set up eight environmental teams respectively engaged in environmental monitoring, supervision, environmental impact assessment, emergency response, publicity and education, solid waste disposal, scientific research and nuclear radiation. They developed the environmental quality joint early warning mechanism that realized resource sharing and joint prevention and control. They led the way in incorporating "smart environmental protection" in environmental management and carried out dynamic enforcement and supervision with the help of modern electronic information technology. They connected the administrative service center with environmental business platform, so that all cases could be inquired, processed, submitted and supervised online completely. The city has built 12 automatic atmospheric monitoring stations, 17 automatic water quality monitoring stations and 1050 sets of online pollution source monitoring systems, thus weaving a "smart network" of environmental protection covering the whole city. They innovatively opened environmental police office and environmental court, created an interactive mechanism of environmental law enforcement, and sternly cracked down upon environmental violations. The city also strictly investigated and punished enterprises that discharged waste against the law with a view to eradicating anything that would impair the eco-environment. Second, improving the green examination and assessment mechanism. The city incorporated green and ecological development in the target-oriented responsibility system of economic and social development and leading cadres' performance assessment system, raised the weighting of ecological progress in district/town-level performance assessment from 11 to 15%, and set up the "Green Development Award" for districts and towns in particular. They designed the letter of responsibility for ecological development that had to be signed by corresponding leaders, set annual environmental goal for the mayor, and reinforced accountability mechanism to make sure all green development tasks and targets were accomplished. They brought public supervision into play, urged enterprises to disclose information about their environmental actions, and explored to establish the environmental credibility system and green credit for enterprises. The city improved the administrative supervision system for green and ecological development, strictly implemented environmental impact assessment of major projects and regional plans, and gave environmental department the veto power. They also selected 10 Best Enterprises for Green Development every year, and set examples for energy conservation, emission reduction and clean production. Third, improving the investment and reward mechanism. Following the principle of "government guidance, diverse investment, public participation and reward and punishment", they established and improved the diverse investment mechanism with corporate and government investment playing a leading and guiding role and participation from private capital and financial institutions, while 10% of financial increment was used for ecological development. In the past three years, ecological and environmental investment of the whole society increased by more than 10% on annual average and exceeded RMB23 billion. In 2013, RMB141 million was spent on ecological compensation, and the philosophy of "whoever benefits should protect the environment and whoever pollutes it should pay the compensation" was applied. According to the principle of "two-way compensation", the city issued schemes to provide for and explain environmental and resource compensation, and created and improved the payment system for fiscal transfer of ecological compensation. They explored to establish the trading system of pollutant discharge permit and its compensated use, pushed pilot trade of waste discharge right and its compensated use, and improved the sewage treatment mechanism of "quality-based pricing", so as to make sure water from sewage treatment plants is up to quality standard.

A sound ecological environment is the fairest and universally beneficial public product. Going forward, Kunshan will keep up the sense of responsibility for stimulating development and the mission of improving ecology for the people, enhance its sense of duty, and diligently implement all measures to promote smooth "green" work. They will hold up high the brand of "ecological Kunshan", act faster in building an environmentally friendly and resource-saving society, and create an upgraded version of Kunshan. It is their aspiration to make Kunshan a beautiful and livable home where ecological and economic development is coordinated, rural landscape and urban cityscape improve in parallel, and humans and nature exist in harmony.

Chapter 12
Building an Ecological Garden City—Suining

June 19, 2012 is a memorable day in the history of Suining. On that day, the name Suining was mentioned at the Global Forum on Human Settlements (GFHS) of Rio+20 held in Brazil's Rio De Janeiro for winning the honor of "Global Green City". This international honor reflected international organizations' recognition of Suining's persistence in green development concept and building a green and ecological city, and was the outcome of the leadership and decision of Suining CPC Committee and municipal government and the joint efforts of all residents of the city.

Today's Suining is a modern and ecological garden city. In recent years, it firmly upheld green development concept, focused on urbanization for the people, and implemented "town optimization" and "environmental improvement" of the "six city rejuvenation programs". It built a modern garden city in downtown area and an ecological idyllic city across the board, and made unremitting efforts to improve environmental quality and promote sustainable development. In face of resource restriction and the dilemma of environmental bearing capacity, Suining has never stopped thinking about how to explore a new model of green city development from the planning perspective, how to push the construction of a resource-saving society, how to ensure the city's sustainability, and how to apply green thinking and ideal to city planning, design and construction and to every part of the city.

Suining has won a range of honors such as National City for Sanitation, National Garden City, Excellent Tourism City of China, National Demonstration City for Livability, National Ecological Demonstration Zone, National Exemplary City for Greening, and National Exemplary City for Environmental Protection. By turning advantages in ecological resources into advantages in ecological capital, Suining has blazed out a new path of green development, and building a modern ecological garden city complies with its positioning to become a global green city.

© Social Sciences Academic Press and Springer Nature Singapore Pte Ltd. 2018

X. Li and X. Liu, *Green Development Model of China's Small and Medium-sized Cities*, Research Series on the Chinese Dream and China's Development Path,
https://doi.org/10.1007/978-981-13-0779-9_12

1 Governing Environment, Improving Quality

The ever more disorderly human activities have brought certain impacts to urban and rural environment. To curb this trend, Suining adopted the path of combining government guidance with social investment, and launched comprehensive urban/rural environmental governance to ensure a happy life for residents, with the focus on demolishing skirt buildings, demolishing and renovating physical enclosure walls, and regulating architectures.

Urban/rural environmental governance is a complicated work of wide involvement and countless difficulties. Suining focused on six aspects in urban environmental governance. (1) On the principle of government leadership and market operation, it renovated and demolished the skirt buildings of about 1200 households in 24 locations of the city. (2) It adopted a series of measures to increase green coverage in the city and achieved "there is greening wherever it's possible" in the city proper. It built more than 20 parks including Binjiang Park, Quhe Park, Hedong Wetland Park and Suining Union River Guanyin Cultural Park, and launched ecological greenbelt construction including China Health Valley, Rose Valley and Shengping Island, increasing the city's green coverage ratio to more than 40%. (3) Following the principle of "bagging at home, classification in community, government support and market operation", Suining built garbage sorting stations in units, communities and neighborhoods through enterprises to classify, collect and treat domestic waste, and pilot demonstration projects made primary progress. (4) Suining conducted overall cityscape governance according to the general requirement of "improving urban functions, enhancing urban quality", and launched four specific campaigns targeting visual pollution, store signs, rolling door and physical enclosure wall. It carried out the "face washing project" for the city to varnish outer walls of buildings and beautify architectural facades in an attempt to coordinate the colors of architectural facades on main streets. It also worked hard to control dust in the city, encouraged model and standardized construction sites, renovated city roads, promoted solar energy-saving road lamps, and eliminated blind angles and dead zones of city hardening. (5) Suining made great efforts on environmental protection. It invested nearly RMB500 million in building and increasing environmental sanitation facilities, built sewage and garbage treatment plants, separated rainwater and sewage pipes in new city area, and intercepted all sewage discharged from the old city area to Guanyin Lake. As a result, domestic sewage treatment ratio reached 84%, and water quality in all water functional zones met the standard. (6) Suining provided public bikes in the city. It completed the 30 km-long urban public bike network around Guanyin Lake and Union River in 2011, which had 38 service outlets and 790 bikes, and more than 12,000 bike cards had been issued to residents. Public bike has become a beautiful view in the city. Phase 2 of this project is already under way, which, when completed, will extend the service range to about 100 km with 109 service outlets and 2290 bikes, better facilitating resident's green travel and making their life greener and happier.

2 Building Sound Ecological Planning System, Stressing "Green Planning"

Suining hired first-grade planning institutes from China and abroad to comprehensively revise the general city plan, formulated and implemented plans for traffic, land utilization, ecological construction and industrial development in a holistic way, and made systematic plans for ecological infrastructure. It created an ecological planning system with *Conceptual Plan for Modern Ecological Garden City* as the basis, *General City Plan* as the overall outline, *Green Land System Plan* and *Water System Plan* as the main body, and plans for various wetland parks, scenic spots and district regulatory plans as branches, providing scientific references for ecological protection and construction. Spatial layout of townships and direction of industrial development are critical for building low-carbon and ecological cities. In the process of city construction and development, Suining tried hard to avoid "blind pursuit for large scale" and replace "reinforced concrete forest" with mountains, waters and natural forest. On one hand, Suining insisted on clustered city development and actively created green and ecological new areas. According to the spatial development strategy of "extension in south and north, development around lakes, expansion in east and west, and construction along mountains", Suining created the urban layout of "one city, two districts and five clusters", and the clusters were separated by natural mountains and rivers but connected through express passages. Each cluster tried to build an "industry-city complex" integrating urban communities, industrial parks and ecological protection zones in view of the philosophy of "three in one and industry-city integration". On the other hand, Suining launched the "green town campaign" to build "green towns" and "happy and beautiful new villages". Since 2014, it has launched 20 key green towns and 100 happy and beautiful new villages every year under the idea of "town-park integration, industry-village integration and coordinated development". It wanted to build green towns and beautiful new villages with all-round functions, appealing environment and suitability for both business and living, and actively explored a new urbanization model whereby ecological agricultural parks, green towns and new village settlements could develop in parallel and unison.

3 Giving Up Projects for Environment

While speeding up development, Suining paid close attention to changing the development concept. It didn't just focus on the speed of growth, but more on the quality of growth; not just on the quantitative increase of materials, but more on cultural enjoyment of the people; not just on what is achieved now, but more on leaving a favorable development environment for later generations.

To protect wetland and water systems in the city, Suining resolutely gave up many economically profitable projects. It lost some economic benefits in the short term, but protected the environment that we lived in the long term. Suining planned and developed ecologically sensitive zones and particularly important blocks in strict accordance with the standards for modern ecological garden city. It originally planned to build the Tangjiadu power station, but since it would cause major impacts on the city's wetland and water systems, the municipal CPC Committee and government abandoned the plan for increasing several square kilometers of construction land and cancelled the project without hesitation. The planning for Shenglian Island of Guanyin Lake in the city proper went through 11 rounds over 10 years, and eventually the scheme from a British company was selected that positioned the island as a primitive ecological museum. Shengping Island was positioned as an ecological garden city complex in the theme of training and education for ecological protection and ecological business, and Xijiazhou and Wujiazhou refused a lot of real estate projects to develop ecological wetlands.

Suining is clean not only because the city is tidy and orderly, but also because of its creation and preservation of greening. It is the continuous greenbelts and wetland parks in the city proper that make the city charming, lively and vigorous, make people enjoy its cleanness and freshness, and make them want to stay. Suining's fascination is just right.

Chapter 13
Watertown on the Plain, Ancient Cultural City—Green Yangzhou

At the end of 2013, Jiangsu provincial government conferred Yangzhou the "Ecological Achievement Award for Green Jiangsu 2003–2012". As a typical water city on the eastern plain of China, Yangzhou created a green city of forests and waters in itself by following natural laws, and benefited its people with ecological development. At the moment, Yangzhou has 1.53 million *mu* of forests across the city, forest and wetland coverage ratio reaches 51.5%, green coverage ratio in completed areas of city proper is 43.34%, and per capita park greening is 19 m^2.

1 "Green Living Room" for Every Resident

Green at the gate—this is the biggest ecological benefit created by Yangzhou government for the residents; 19 m^2 per capita park greening—this means every resident has a "green living room". Yangzhou CPC Committee and government have always attached great importance to forestry. Especially in the 21st century, as the rapid economic and social development and people's rising living standard posed higher demand on ecological environment, they took forestry development as an important part of ecological improvement, put it in a more prominent position, and explored a path of sound and fast green development for urban and rural areas on the water plain based on local conditions, by making scientific plans and highlighting key points, and through step-by-step implementation. Since 2003, Yangzhou has developed *Forestry Development Plan of Yangzhou*, *Urban Green Land System Plan*, *General Urban Afforestation Plan*, among others. In light of its characteristics as a "plain water town and ancient cultural city", it set the goal of "creating a green city, building a land of forest and water", and explored the path of "water, road and forest networks", of "picturesque countryside, forest-rich city and urban-rural integration", and of "vernacular trees, natural arrangement and maximal utilization".

To guide residents to "plant, protect, love and support greening" voluntarily, Yangzhou took afforestation as the fairest and universally beneficial livelihood

© Social Sciences Academic Press and Springer Nature Singapore Pte Ltd. 2018

X. Li and X. Liu, *Green Development Model of China's Small and Medium-sized Cities*, Research Series on the Chinese Dream and China's Development Path,
https://doi.org/10.1007/978-981-13-0779-9_13

project to increase income for urban/rural residents and enhance ecological benefits, and energetically promoted it with innovative mechanisms and under the idea of "greening of the people, by the people and for the people". When this idea was truly driven home, it would become a habit for people. Statistics from forestry department showed that about 11 million trees were planted in urban/rural areas during the planting festival every year, 80% of which by residents themselves. According to the *Three-year Action Plan for Green New Yangzhou*, the city planted 50,000 *mu* of trees in 2013, including 35,000 *mu* of continuous forests, tended 100,000 *mu* of forests, built 15,000 *mu* of high-efficiency forests (of flowers, tea leaves, fruits, etc.), as well as 100 provincial demonstration villages for greening, one provincial wetland park or forest park, and one provincial education base for ecological civilization. Making afforestation and ecological center the focus and highlight of ecological development, Yangzhou brought into full play afforestation's two roles of "boosting economy, improving environment", and made strong efforts to achieve the goal of "ecology for the country, good image for the city, wealth for property owners and health for residents".

2 Promoting the Application of Green Buildings

Implementing the concept of green, circular and low-carbon development and launching green building campaign is of great significance for transforming the urban/rural construction model, transforming and upgrading construction industry, addressing energy and resource restriction, making urban and rural areas more ecological and livable, and fostering strategic emerging industries such as energy conservation, environmental protection and new energy. The city government sped upefforts to build an "innovative, refined and happy Yangzhou". To do that, they applied ecological ideas to the whole process of urban/rural construction, and firmly seized the important period of strategic opportunities presented by urbanization and the new countryside construction. They upheld the guideline of "comprehensive efforts with priorities, specific guidance in view of local conditions, targeted guidance, market operation under government guidance, and combination of short-term and long-term interests". They formed the idea of life-cycle development, took concrete steps to change urban/rural construction model, and raised the efficiency of resource utilization, making positive contributions to building a resource-saving and environmentally friendly society.

During the 12th Five-Year Plan period, Yangzhou planned that projects that meet green building standards will have the total area of more than 4 million square meters, including an increase of 850,000 m^2 in 2014, an increase of 100,000 m^2 in Hanjiang District, Jiangdu District and Yizheng each, an increase of 80,000 m^2 from Gaoyou and Baoying County each, an increase of 350,000 m^2 in Guangling District, and an increase of 40,000 m^2 in Yangzhou economic and technological development zone. By 2015, all new buildings in towns of the city will be designed and built according to one-star-rated and higher-level green building standards; by

2020, 50% of new buildings in towns of the city will be designed and built according to two-star-rated and higher-level green building standards. At the end of the 12th Five-Year Plan period, the city will have established a sound administrative regulation system, technical support system and market service system for green buildings, and created technical routes and work mechanisms for green building with Yangzhou characteristics.

Promoting large-scale construction of green buildings with a strategy that combined overall guidance with priority efforts. Since 2014, green building standards will be implemented across the board for four types of new projects—low-income housing, government-invested projects, projects in provincial demonstration zones, and large public buildings, while other new projects will be encouraged to follow those standards too.

Actively building demonstration county (city, district) for green building. All areas were planned and developed following the concept of resource-saving urban/rural construction that's green, low-carbon, ecological, smart and livable. Gaoyou and Jiangdu Districts will strive to become "demonstration county (city, district) for architectural energy conservation and green building" of Jiangsu Province in 2015.

Pushing for local demonstration of green building. The city supported the upgrade of Guangling New City to be a "provincial demonstration area for architectural energy conservation and green building", which should build 430,000 m^2 of green buildings in 2014. It also accelerated the construction of Linggang New City, the municipal economic and technological development zone, to be a "provincial demonstration area for architectural energy conservation and green building". Its implementation scheme will be reviewed in 2014, and 500,000 m^2 of green buildings will then start construction.

Promoting green buildings in small towns and the countryside. While building a new countryside, the city strongly promoted solar energy, envelope-enclosure thermal insulation and other practical energy-saving technologies for rural housing, and developed centralized heat supply through biogas and straw gasification in livestock farms, main grain producing areas and concentrated settlements of more than 300 households. In 2014, they will build a group of provincial demonstration villages for green rural housing, and in 2015, every agricultural county (county-level city and district) across the city will have such a village. They also encouraged eligible townships and towns to apply for "national small town of green and low-carbon development" and "demonstration town for comprehensive planning in Jiangsu Province".

Expanding the application of renewable-energy buildings. The city further pushed the architectural application of renewable energies including solar energy, superficial geothermal energy and biomass energy. During the 12th Five-Year Plan period, 7 million square meters of new renewable-energy buildings will be built. Yangzhou aimed to build energy stations in Guangling New City and the economic and technological development zone, so that renewable energies can be used in concentrated and continuous areas.

Reinforcing energy conservation management in public buildings. They laid a solid foundation for regulating architectural energy conservation, improved the system of energy consumption statistics and public notice and energy auditing for public buildings, and improved the municipal monitoring platform of architectural energy consumption. They also improved the energy conservation management of public buildings, promoted architectural energy management system in demonstration zones and projects, and strictly implemented relevant rules regarding air conditioning temperature control in public buildings.

Accelerating energy-saving renovation of existing buildings. They renovated existing public buildings for energy conservation. When office buildings of government bodies and large public buildings were decorated, expanded, added with more floors or fortified for seismic purpose, energy- and water-saving measures should be adopted. Eligible buildings should meet one-star-rated green building standards as a whole, and for those that were only partially renovated, the renovated part should meet certain green building requirements. For office buildings of government bodies that were approved to carry out energy-saving renovation, the expenses were included in the fiscal budget of the same-level government. Yangzhou's aim was to renovate 1.5 million square meters of public buildings for energy conservation in the 12th Five-Year Plan period. Meanwhile, the city also renovated existing residential buildings for energy conservation on a trial basis. Governments at all levels should incorporate energy-saving renovation of existing residential buildings in the annual plan for old neighborhood renovation and effectively implement the plan. The work was focused on the renovation of flat roofs into slope roofs, of outer envelope enclosures and of old doors and windows, with considerations for solar-power water heating, energy-saving passageway lighting and other renovation projects. Eligible buildings could have overall energy-saving renovation. The aim was to renovate 450,000 m^2 of existing residential buildings in the 12th Five-Year Plan period.

Developing green building materials. They encouraged the development and use of high-performance concrete and high-strength rebar, promoted high-strength rebar of 400 MPa grade and above, strongly developed premixed concrete and mortar, and strictly prohibited concrete and mortar mixing at construction sites in the city proper. By 2015, some townships will prohibit on-site mortar mixing and 30% townships will reach the standard for demonstration township of bulk cement; production and use of clay solid brick will be prohibited across the city, production and use of wall materials with over 20% clay will be limited, and bricks made of river sludge will be promoted. In 2014, all towns of the city will prohibit the use of clay products.

Yangzhou implemented the most rigorous eco-environmental protection system, motivated the transformation of development model with ecological development, and made clear that every county (county-level city, district) should build at least one ecological center of more than 10 square kilometers. As projects such as "green city" and "clear water, blue sky" were carried out one after another, an ecological and livable environment is becoming Yangzhou's most precious resource and No. 1 brand.

Chapter 14
Integration of Culture and Nature—Ningguo

Located in the southeast of Anhui, Ningguo is one of the key mountainous counties and cities in the province. Covering 2,487 km^2 with a total population of 380,000 people, Ningguo is known for being a land of "80% mountain, 10% water, 5% farmland and 5% road and park". Since its location doesn't give it any advantage, the city has accurately positioned itself in recent years and explored a path of innovative, comprehensive and green development suiting its actual conditions. It was titled "top 100 small and medium-sized cities in China" for five years in a row and "top 10 resource-saving and environmentally friendly small and medium-sized cities in China" for three years in a row, and it is a category-one city of scientific development in Anhui in terms of overall economic strength. As a forerunner of county-level economic development in Anhui, Ningguo adhered to the centerline of changing development model, always followed the concept of ecological development, and made strenuous efforts to build an ecological city. Focused on economical and intensive land use, green and low-carbon development, and building an ecological and livable city, Ningguo has made great achievements in its new-type modernization drive.

1 Developing Circular Economy, Promoting Green Development

1.1 Optimizing Spatial Layout for Industries

In view of the defects of county industries that they are spontaneous and concentrated, Ningguo worked faster to shift from homogeneous and disorderly industrial layout in the county to function-based orderly layout, and made strategic adjustments and improvements of the city's general industrial layout. It tried to create a new big development landscape whereby industrial development and resource and environment are coordinated, industries are highly concentrated, industrial advantages are

© Social Sciences Academic Press and Springer Nature Singapore Pte Ltd. 2018

X. Li and X. Liu, *Green Development Model of China's Small and Medium-sized Cities*, Research Series on the Chinese Dream and China's Development Path,
https://doi.org/10.1007/978-981-13-0779-9_14

prominent, enterprises are distributed rationally, and regional features are distinct. First, Ningguo was the first in Anhui to delimit ecological functional zones. It divided the whole city into four main functional zones—agricultural and tourism zone, natural reserve, business and cultural zone, and high-tech industrial zone, and specified their positioning and main direction. It also established the ecological compensation mechanism that took into consideration a range of factors such as each zone's ecological value, ecological protection cost and opportunistic cost of development, and made comprehensive use of administrative and market means to adjust the interests of stakeholders in each zone. Second, according to the requirement for "economic base, base industrialization and industrial cluster", Ningguo, based on the existing industrial foundation, created a general layout to take over industrial transfer centered on the city proper and supported by Ningguo economic and technological development zone, port ecological industrial park, and Qinglongwan ecological tourism resort, known as "one center, three clusters". Third, on the principle of efficient industrial concentration, Ningguo scientifically guided similar industries to be located nearby and pushed the construction of "park in park". Aimed to become a demonstration zone for low-carbon and circular economy, the port ecological industrial park, on the principle of efficient industrial concentration, planned to build a group of specialized industrials parks engaged in energy-saving building materials, new energy application and electronic information. In this way, the port ecological industrial park will truly become a place where materials are used efficiently and circularly, enterprises complement each other, wastes are more fully recycled, and it exists in harmony with the surrounding natural and residential environment.

1.2 Building Modern Industrial System

Ningguo shifted industrial development from the model of high investment, high pollution, high energy consumption and low output to that of low investment, low energy consumption, low pollution and high output, and transformed economic growth from extensive to quality-oriented model. First, it fostered high-tech industries focused on advanced manufacture, reformed and upgraded traditional industries, and optimized and upgraded resource allocation worldwide through technological innovation, restructuring and capital operation. It moved faster to develop mainstream industries such as application of new materials and new energies and advanced manufacture, actively developed leading industries like medical equipment, created emerging industrial clusters, and cultivated new growth poles. Second, it prioritized green industries focused on health and recreation. Ningguo launched the agricultural industrialization program, sped up the construction of agricultural ecological technology demonstration park and food industry park, fostered and supported leading agricultural enterprises, and strived to develop a national demonstration base for agricultural industrialization. It energetically developed modern forestry and organic green agriculture, scaled up green and organic food production bases, stepped up efforts on agricultural quality and safety and product brand, achieved holistic development of agriculture, forestry, animal husbandry and fishery, and created the most famous production and supply base of organic and green food in the country. Taking the construction of south Anhui international demonstration zone for tourism and culture as an opportunity, Ningguo accelerated scenic area development, tapped the connotations of farming culture in depth, integrated agricultural production factors with natural landscape resources, and advanced the interactive development of related products covering business and vacation, recreation and health maintenance, and sightseeing, in the effort to become a national demonstration zone for ecological tourism. Third, Ningguo strongly developed modern service industry focused on creativity economy. It prioritized production service industries such as finance, logistics, high-tech service and business service, and improved output rate by attracting and allocating quality resources. It energetically developed headquarters economy and pushed it forward more quickly on the premise of not occupying more resources or damaging the environment. Ningguo also explored new business forms in the service industry such as e-commerce, online CBD and carbon trade, and raised the development level of modern service industry.

1.3 Developing Circular Economy

Ningguo upheld the concept of circular economy, which was a form of scientific development, actively built an ecological industrial network, established a mechanism for enterprises to circularly use and share energy, materials, infrastructure and information, and minimized waste discharge and maximized economic, eco-environmental and social benefits. After years of efforts, Ningguo's circular economic development made notable progress, and an industrial system of circular economy was primarily established with 26 demonstration enterprises, 10 engaged in agriculture, 13 in industry and 3 in service.

2 Building Ecological and Livable City

On the principle of "culture-nature harmony", Ningguo, while developing the city, is committed to bringing healthy natural ecology and better urban services for its residents. It achieved green and coordinated city development by formulating urban plan on a high starting point, accelerating urban development on a high level, and implementing urban management with high efficiency.

2.1 Formulating Urban Plan on a High Starting Point

City planning should have some vision. According to the strategic positioning of "building a modern ecological small and medium-sized city", Ningguo invited world-renowned design institutes such as Research Center for Eco-Environmental Sciences of Chinese Academy of Sciencesand Shanghai Tongji Urban Planning and Design Institute to plan and design the city. The overall scheme reflected first-class concept of integrating ecological and industrial civilization, and applied modern ideas such as ecology, environmental protection and resource conservation.

City planning should be systematic. Various sub-plans should be unified and coordinated to form a comprehensive and scientific planning system that fits reality and reflects individuality.

2.2 Accelerating Urban Development on a High Level

Under the general guideline of "improving the main city area, expanding in the east and west, optimizing the south, moving towards the north and cluster development", Ningguo upgraded the old city area, accelerated developing the Chengbei new area, and planned the Hexi new area on a high starting point. It also stepped up construction of public facilities such as city roads, natural gas pipeline, city parks and water environment works, improved the city's auxiliary functions, and enhanced its strong catalytic role.

Ningguo established the traffic network rationally. Under the great traffic strategy stressing "road connectivity with other regions and auxiliary functions within the city", it made active efforts to establish a modern 3D traffic system featured by external connectivity, internal smoothness, convenience and high efficiency.

It improved public service facilities. Ningguo stepped up construction of public facilities such as natural gas pipeline, city parks and water environment works, and pushed the construction of water supply and drainage, power and communication facilities in a holistic way, thus raising the city's public service level.

It promoted landscaping. Ningguo always made ecological environment and landscaping an important part of city construction and earnestly implemented the strategy of "prospering the city through ecology". (1) It fully utilized natural mountains and waters to build public greenbelts according to local conditions, and built and improved many parks. (2) Ningguo's urban road greening ratio reached 100%. Roadside trees were of diverse types focused on vernacular ones, and landscaping complied with the road nature, so that people could enjoy nice views wherever they went. (3) To guarantee a favorable living environment, Ningguo set strict greening land indicator—greening ratio in newly developed communities should be above 35% and that in renovated old communities above 25%. The total greening area in all residential communities across the city is 44.7 hectares today. (4) Shelterbelts were built along both sides of the provincial highway in the city proper and both banks of Dongjin River and Xijin River, playing an important role in fending off wind and dust, improving air quality, and reducing the city's heat island effect.

Chapter 15
Building a Beautiful Pixian County with Improved Ecology, Higher Standard and Greater Affluence

Located in the center of Western Sichuan Plain and the northwestern suburb of Chengdu, Pixian County is one of the key gravity irrigation areas of Dujiangyan, an important passageway from Chengdu to famous scenic areas including Dujiangyan, Mount Qingcheng, Huanglong and Jiuzhaigou, and a crucial protected area of drinking water source for Chengdu. Covering 438 km^2, the county has 16 towns (subdistrict offices) and 218 villages (communities), and had 966,900 households of permanent population and 588,500 registered residents at the end of 2013. With its overall economic strength ranking among the top 10 counties in the province for 19 years in a row, Pixian County has won a series of honors, including China's top 100 counties for basic economic competitiveness, China's top 100 cities with greatest investment potential, national model county, China's top 100 counties for scientific development, national ecological county, and national demonstration county for recreational agriculture and countryside tourism.

To prosper the county through ecology and promote scientific development was to build "a beautiful Pixian County with improved ecology, higher standard and greater affluence" around the positioning of "water-rich city of Sichuan and ecological Pixian". "Improved ecology" refers to the appearance of beautiful Pixian, "better quality" is its "soul" and "greater affluence" is its "essence". Their specific connotations are as follows: (1) Conspicuous ecological advantages mean that based on the current sound ecological foundation, Pixian County will work harder to improve the ecological environment and exert its advantages, so that its 400+ km^2 become an open natural scenic area and ecological park, ecological advantages in pleasant environment are translated into the greatest competitiveness that drives economic development, and the county becomes the top destination for travel, consumption, living and business startup. (2) Prominent industrial characteristics mean that "ecological" and "high-end" are the distinct characteristics of local industries, which feature zero pollution, limited land occupation, large output value and high benefits and constitute an ecological industrial system underpinned by ecological agriculture, ecological industry and modern service industry. (3) Simultaneous urban/rural development means the mechanism that coordinates urban/rural development is improved, efforts to build

© Social Sciences Academic Press and Springer Nature Singapore Pte Ltd. 2018

X. Li and X. Liu, *Green Development Model of China's Small and Medium-sized Cities*, Research Series on the Chinese Dream and China's Development Path,
https://doi.org/10.1007/978-981-13-0779-9_15

modern city and modern countryside proceed in parallel, and equal access to basic public services is realized in a wider scope. Pixian therefore becomes a paragon for urban/rural coordination in the city and even the whole province. (4) Profound culture means that the profound and diverse culture of Pixian County is fully displayed and cultural undertakings and industries flourish, giving the county a distinct cultural spirit and individuality and obviously reinforcing its cultural soft power. (5) Affluent and healthy life means that urban and rural residents have more income, society is more harmonious and peaceful, and residents live a more comfortable and leisurely life, making the county one of the first to achieve a moderately prosperous society in all respects.

To achieve those goals and build a beautiful Pixian, the county has to persist in the developing philosophy of "ecology first, quality paramount, livelihood as the basis and simultaneous progress on industrialization, informatization, urbanization and agricultural modernization". "Ecology first" means that when decisions are made and projects are launched, the top consideration is protecting the environment and ecology. Efforts must be made to urge all towns and departments to pursue "green GDP", cadres on all levels to strive for "green performance", enterprises to adopt the "green production outlook", and the society to practice "green consumption". "Quality paramount" means higher standards should be set and adopted in industrial development, urban/rural construction and environmental improvement, placing stress on quality, special features and connotations to create exquisite and top-grade projects and products.

1 Improving Ecological Environment

To build a beautiful Pixian County, ecological environment is the foundation. According to the requirement for "building big parks, creating big scenic areas" and taking the construction of a national demonstration county for ecological development and a national garden county as an opportunity, the Pixian government, while protecting the beautiful view of the "garden in west Sichuan", stepped up efforts on ecological restoration and environmental improvement. They aimed to build a picturesque "Pixian County of abundant water, extensive greenbelt and fragrant flowers", where ecological system is improved and water and air quality in the county and main city proper is better guaranteed.

The first thing is cleaning the water. An old Chinese saying goes that the benevolent like mountains and the wise like rivers. Water is the symbol of a city's vitality, resilience and quality, and having clean water means to make water both clean and within reach. Focusing on the eight rivers in the county, the government launched a number of projects to dredge rivers, protect banks, cut off sewage and build forest belts around rivers, so as to re-establish the river's natural outlook with clear water and green banks, and make sure every river is a belt-like garden and flowing scenery. In particular, a batch of high-quality cultural water views and littoral spaces were planned and constructed along sections of Tuojiang River that passed the urban planned area, and they became new landmarks that enhanced the city quality. The county strongly implemented water source protection projects and relocated farmers living in drinking water source protection areas in a planned way, drew the ecological red line, built ecological wetlands and conservation areas, and turned water source protection areas into typical areas of ecological and organic agriculture and new destinations of ecological tourism. In 2013, Pixian County launched 13 water source protection projects including wetland expansion, relocation for ecological protection and preservation projects, built 350 *mu* of water conservation forests and wetlands, and adopted digital supervision and grid-based management of drinking water source protection areas across the board. Conformity rate of drinking water source reached 100%.

The second is increasing green area. The county strongly implemented greening projects in urban and rural areas, ecological vegetation restoration and landscaping, planted a lot of big trees on a large scale, and created a beautiful environment of extensive green trees, colorful flowers and perennial views, turning the place into a natural oxygen bar. Whether planting flowers or trees, they took into account quality, cost, innovative mechanism and public participation, and the flowers and trees must be easy to survive and nice to look at. While keeping the original vegetation, they built a number of greenbelt parks and street landscapes for sightseeing and recreation by "planting trees wherever possible, where old buildings are demolished, and in 3D approach", giving "every street a special view, every road its unique characteristics". In particular, the several important trunk roads were built into landscape and ecological demonstration belts with a high standard. Known as the "city of azalea", Pixian County should plant all kinds of azaleas to enhance its charm. Exerting its advantages as national "hometown of bonsai" and a planting base of flower and nursery stock, Pixian raised the quality of local greening, and carefully arranged and tended to flowers and nursery stocks planted along roads to make them well-spaced and proportioned, so that residents and tourists could fully enjoy the idyllic view of west Sichuan. It also pushed the demolition for and construction of round-county ecological zone, and made it a high-standard "ecological pearl" of Pixian and even Chengdu according to requirements by the municipal government.

The third is waste treatment. The key to this is controlling the source and addressing both the root cause and symptoms. Pixian County set rigorous ecological and environmental standards for new projects, resolutely rectified, even shut down, enterprises of excessive pollution and discharge, and made sure all ecological and environmental indicators were met. They strictly controlled the intensity of water pollutant discharge, improved environmental protection infrastructure, which significantly strengthened the capability of sewage collection and treatment, and severely punished direct and secret sewage discharge. Pixian comprehensively advocated green and low-carbon consumption, promoted the use of energy-saving technologies and products, called for a healthy and environmentally friendly lifestyle, and actively built low-carbon demonstration zone. In 2013, Pixian addressed pollution of the Tuojiang River Basin and stenchy rivers like Yangliu River, dredged 293 km of key waterways, conducted sewage cutoff at 46 outfalls to Qingshui River, and suspended about 400 enterprises (institutions) that discharged pollutants against rules to take corrective actions.

The fourth is restoring order. Pixian County carried out overall urban/rural environmental improvement to maintain an all-round and consistent clean and tidy outlook of urban and rural areas. Focusing on the peri-urban areas, small lanes, villages inside cities and community courtyards, they launched contiguous environmental improvement and non-point source pollution governance in the countryside in an in-depth and consistent way in order to eradicate "dirtiness, chaos and poor governance". They placed equal emphasis on material progress and cultural and ethical progress, and especially improved the restricting and supervisory mechanism involving public participation, thus creating a sound atmosphere of "development of the people, by the people and for the people" and raising the city's cultural quality and management level. In 2013, Pixian County successfully created five provincial demonstration villages for good environment and four for sanitation.

2 Upgrading Industrial Development

To prosper the county with ecology, the core is ecological economy. Following the guiding thought of building an "ecological economic zone", Pixian strongly pushed tertiary industry in the ecological and high-end direction and tried hard to make industrial structure "light", development model "green" and economic quality "better". The aim is to blaze out a path of "industrial multiplication" with Pixian characteristics featuring maximized overall benefits and minimized resource consumption, and strengthen the industrial underpinning for a beautiful Pixian.

Upgrading ecological urban agriculture and focusing on high-quality agricultural products and deep processing. Following the guideline of "ecological, safe and high-end", they strongly developed organic, demonstrative and sightseeing agriculture, headquarters of agricultural technology companies, and deep processing of agricultural produce. The goal is to make green organic agriculture account for more than 60% in the county and deep processing rate of agricultural produce exceed 50% in three years, thus maximizing agricultural added values. The county specifically developed a number of pollution-free, green and organic agricultural bases, improved the tracing and inspection system for the quality and safety of agricultural produce, fostered the reputation for producing safe agricultural products, and built green food supply bases serving big cities. They also developed modern facilities and efficient demonstration agriculture including high-end seeds and biological, export-oriented and factory-style agriculture, and cultivated and bolstered a large number of agricultural technology demonstration farms. The county upgraded flower and nursery stock industry and developed a group of high-quality planting bases in that aspect, focused on creating boutique nursery stock demonstration zones integrating cultivation and R&D, sightseeing, exhibition, and trading. According to the guiding thought of "interaction between primary and tertiary industries and integration of culture and tourism", they supported and encouraged family farms, modern manors, countryside inns and recreation clubs in various forms, advanced the upgrade of countryside tourism, and created first-class demonstration resort for countryside recreation. In 2013, Pixian signed and introduced 13 agricultural industrialization projects, had four new leading enterprises above municipal level, and developed three new family farms. As of the end of 2013, it had completed 8,730 *mu* of organic agricultural bases and 6,225 *mu* of protected agriculture accumulatively, and deep processing rate of agricultural produce reached 44.5%. Pixian was listed as a national county for comprehensive agricultural development.

Strengthening ecological industry. The county facilitated concentrated, cluster and intensive development characterized by "environmental friendliness, low carbon, high technology and high end", strongly pushed the adjustment, transformation and upgrade of industrial structure, and promoted "three shifts"—industrial chain shifting from low end to medium and high end, horizontal industry shifting to building industry, and enterprises shifting from traditional processing and manufacturing to high-tech headquarters. The county optimized leading industries, vigorously developed industries featuring eco-environmental friendliness, sound growth and sustainability such as medical equipment manufacturing, bio-engineering and new pharmaceutical technology, electronic information and electric machinery, and introduced a number of famous Chinese and foreign enterprises to create the initiator effect of industrial cluster. They upgraded specialty industry of Sichuan cuisine, worked out the three-year action plan for that with the aim of "achieving RMB10 billion industrial value from Sichuan cuisine industry and RMB10 billion from broad bean industry", pushed group development of broad bean industry at a faster pace, and stepped up innovations in Sichuan cuisine industrial chain and products. They made special efforts to build a complete industrial chain covering "R&D, production, logistics, processing, delivery, sales, and sightseeing", and became the center of Sichuan cuisine industry in the whole province. In the meantime, government and enterprises both stepped up input to build a complete food inspection system and effective government supervision system, and strengthened publicity in an endeavor to build the Sichuan cuisine industrial park into one of safe food. They advocated innovation-driven development, took faster steps to improve the technological innovation service system and venture investment system, and urged enterprises to set up innovation platforms, concentrate innovative resources and translate technological findings in order to build high-tech parks and an innovative city. They accelerated IT reform and upgrade of traditional industries like machinery manufacturing, and adjusted and cleared out low-quality and low-efficiency enterprises that occupied a lot of land but with small output and contributions, thus raising the industrial park's management level and yield per unit area. According to the requirement for "industry-city integration", they worked hard to improve production and living service functions of the industrial park and transform it into a new industrial area. In 2013, Pixian introduced 10 new major projects including CEC and Huawei-iSoftStone, completed and put into production nine ones, had 20 new industrial enterprises above designated scale, 15 new high-tech enterprises, and six new engineering and technology research centers and corporate technology centers above municipal level, as well as six academician (expert) innovation workstations. It was titled a national demonstration county for IPR and 2013 national advanced county for scientific and technological progress.

Improving service industry. Observing the laws governing the development of service industry, they developed advantageous service industry with local characteristics and used it to gather both customers and stores, drive up the development level of service industry, and change its backward status. Leveraging on their resource advantages, they energetically develop specialty service industries targeting the Chengdu market, such as specialty catering, cultural creativity, education and training, tourism and recreation, and quality agricultural and sideline products, and plan, build and renovate a group of influential specialty blocks, scenic zones, markets and industrial parks, so as to establish the brand of Pixian service industry. They make special efforts to develop the city's only education and training industrial zone, introduce and gather a batch of high-end training organizations from home and abroad, and create a base of education and training headquarters and a training base of high-caliber and skillful talents in Chengdu. They focus on the "subway and express railway" corridor and city clusters and following the requirement for "rational layout, appropriate scale, optimized structure and perfect auxiliary functions", they made overall plans to build a series of urban complexes and community business complexes and created modern CBDs including key business areas and shopping malls, so as to foster a new business center in west Chengdu. Leveraging on key areas like Deyuan new area, they built auxiliary facilities serving the high-tech western area and strongly promoted production service industries related with advanced manufacture, including finance, insurance, R&D, design, service outsourcing, and business service, so as to achieve large-scale development. They also optimized the real estate structure and encouraged ecologically friendly high-quality apartment buildings, high-end communities and commercial properties, in order to attract high-caliber talents, improve local population structure and boost local buying power. In 2013, Pixian introduced 18 major service projects such as Wanda Shudu Plaza and Chongqing Department Store, sped up construction of 16 projects including the financial center, completed key service projects such as Longcheng International Phase 1 and Xipu Bailun Plaza on schedule, registered 13 new service outsourcing companies, and built two 3A-rated scenic areas—Sichuan cuisine experience park and Zhanqi Mother Farm Season 5. Pixian was among the "10 Best Recreational Counties in China 2013" and was titled "2013 Beautiful China Destination for Eco-tourism", and was listed as one of the "Most Beautiful Tourist Attractions in China 2013".

Chapter 16
Most Beautiful Bay on Yangtze River, Most Attractive City in Jiangnan—Zhenjiang

Zhenjiang is a famous historical and cultural city with more than 3,000 years of history. Thanks to its unique locational advantage at the confluence of rivers and favorable ecological environment with mountains and forests, Zhenjiang was an important commercial port and traffic hub in the lower reaches of Yangtze River in history, a city where southern and northern cultures met and merged and that led the development of prosperous Jiangnan (south of Yangtze River). After reform and opening up, it experienced rapid economic and social development and became much stronger economically, but rapid development came with unprecedented pressure on resource and environment and challenges to sustainable development. Zhenjiang is the smallest and least populous city in Jiangsu Province with relatively insufficient resources. To lead the way in modernization and overtake its early-starting peer cities, it had to achieve ecological and knowledge-based transformation of economic and social activities. The aim to build a national model city for environmental protection urges it to improve the environmental quality. For all these years Zhenjiang always put environment first, insisted on green growth, adopted the path of scientific development, and took building the model city for environmental protection as an important carrier for implementing the scientific outlook on development and building a harmonious society, as a major instrument for making ecological progress and transforming economic development model, and as a crucial platform for building a resource-saving and environmentally friendly society. By working hard on urban construction, environmental improvement and protection, Zhenjiang achieved environmental and economic progress simultaneously and provided new capability and space for its sustainable development.

© Social Sciences Academic Press and Springer Nature Singapore Pte Ltd. 2018

X. Li and X. Liu, *Green Development Model of China's Small and Medium-sized Cities*, Research Series on the Chinese Dream and China's Development Path,
https://doi.org/10.1007/978-981-13-0779-9_16

1 Improving Work Mechanism

The municipal CPC Committee and government established and improved the work mechanism for environmental protection that featured "leadership by government, responsibility of competent department, regulation of environmental authority, management of enterprises, participation of the public, and supervision by public opinion". Environmental protection was high on the government agenda, for which the system whereby "top Party and government leader is in overall charge, main leader is responsible, competent leader takes care of specific matters, and four departments make joint efforts" was adopted. Executive government meetings often discussed work in this area and solved many hotspot issues and difficulties. The municipal People's Congress and People's Political and Consultative Conference listened to environmental work report every year, inspected and supervised related work, exchanged opinions with the government and relevant departments, and provided suggestions and urged for their implementation, which promoted the in-depth and solid environmental protection work. Departments of municipal government and local governments performed their duties of environmental protection in the respective area or system, and guaranteed the balanced and coordinated development of environmental work across the city.

Reinforcing the government accountability system for environment and incorporating environmental performance in the work assessment of local Party and government leaders. By implementing mayor's (district director's) environmental target agreement, the municipal government reinforced target-oriented responsibility system, formulated *Duties and Work System of Municipal Environmental Protection Committee* and *Main Duties and Targets of Members of Environment Protection Committee*, adopted the "one post, dual responsibilities" system for main leaders of relevant departments, and signed environmental target agreements level by level. Functional departments passed on the pressure and broke down tasks level by level, and a thorough responsibility network was established, both laterally and vertically. The municipal government developed methods for assessment, reward and punishment, and responsible units and individuals were rewarded or punished according to assessment results. It also pushed for the accomplishment of mayor's environmental target agreement through such means as supervision, inspection, regular reporting and annual assessment.

Zhenjiang continuously optimized the structure of fiscal expenditure. Municipal finance includes an environmental protection fund that increased by more than 20% every year, and Danyang City, Jurong City and Dantu District that are located in the Taihu Lake basin have spent over 10% of incremental fiscal revenues on water pollution prevention and control in the region and basin for years. The leverage of fiscal fund was very effective and environmental protection investment was made featuring "government guidance, social participation, diversified investors and market operation". In 2010, municipal finance raised RMB125 million for environmental protection and attracted private investment through market operation and other measures. The city's total environmental investment that year reached RMB7.387 billion.

The municipal CPC Committee and government also invested heavily to tackle key and difficult problems in environmental work. In 2007, the city spent RMB70 million on Jinhe Paper's emission reduction, largely mitigating environmental pollution in the eastern region. In 2008, it spent nearly RMB230 million on resident relocation and resettlement as well as environmental governance in the Level-1 water source protection area in Runzhou, and RMB450 million on improving water supply to guarantee safe drinking water in the area. The government also invested more than RMB6 million in advanced membrane treatment process for in-depth treatment of leachate from refuse landfill.

The municipal CPC Committee and government attached great importance to the construction of environmental protection organizations and the building of regulatory capability. All seven cities and districts across Zhenjiang established independent environmental protection administration, and environmental branches in Jingkou, Runzhou and the new area were under vertical management. Environmental supervision branches were elevated to deputy division level; remote online monitoring network was established, whereby state-, province-, city- and county-controlled key pollution sources across Zhenjiang were basically under digital management; and professional regulators such as municipal petitioning and reporting center for environmental protection, environmental emergency investigation center and radiation and environmental supervision stations were set up. An environmental regulation system covering all villages and towns of Zhenjiang was established and improved. More than 60 new full-time or part-time township-level environmental specialists have been hired in the past five years, enlarging the team from 20-plus people in 2004 to the current 80-plus people, and the environmental regulation network is extending to townships and the countryside, consolidating groundwork at grassroots level.

2 Promoting Green Development

To promote studies and practices of green economy in the Yangtze River Delta, Zhenjiang municipal government and Jiangsu Department of Commerce co-hosted the Jinshan Summit on Green Economy in Yangtze River Delta in July 2010. Government officials from relevant departments and experts and scholars from United Nations Environment Programme (UNEP) attended the summit, at which a new strategy was put forward—the Yangtze River Delta should speed up transformation and upgrade and develop green economy with Zhenjiang as a pilot city. Green growth became the new direction of Zhenjiang's development.

Environmental control was moved forward. Intensifying environmental management of construction projects is an important way of controlling pollution at source with the focus on prevention. In the past few years, Zhenjiang CPC Committee and government strengthened the construction of various industrial parks, issued relevant policies, encouraged and guided enterprises to build plants in industrial parks, and took faster steps to make pollution treatment more intensive, professional and market-oriented. It applied strict environmental impact assessment in business attraction and investment invitation, implemented scientific environmental impact assessment and law-based approval, and tightened environmental standards in terms of industrial policy, overall planning and pollutant discharge, so as to prevent environmental pollution and ecological damage at source. All projects entering the industrial parks had to pass the environmental impact assessment.

Industrial structure was optimized. The city formulated and implemented the *Implementing Opinions on Accelerating Building a Green Business Invitation System*, and strongly carried out the "100 billion and 10 billion program" (industries worth 100 billion and enterprises worth 10 billion), "technological renovation of 1,000 enterprises" and "5 + x" multiplication program for emerging industries. They strived to develop five emerging industries including new energy, new materials, electronic information, aviation manufacturing and marine engineering, as well as modern service industry, the latter's added values doubling in three years.

Industrial layout was improved. To further improve environmental quality in the city, the municipal government, in light of urban construction and enterprises' technological renovation, issued specific favorable policies to relocate polluting enterprises from the city proper to industrial parks. While relocating them, it was made clear that what was relocated "were the enterprises, not their pollution", and "pollution in another place" was expressly prohibited. Instead, the enterprises were asked to improve production process, expand production scale and lower pollutant discharge according to the requirement that "facilities of pollution prevention and control must be designed, built and put into operation simultaneously with the main works of construction project". As a result, a number of polluting enterprises located in populous areas and scenic zones were relocated, including Zhenjiang Coking and Gas Group, Zhenjiang Shipyard, Titanium Dioxide Plant, and Shangtie Zhenjiang Cement Plant, and more than 20 of them were asked to stop or change the line of production.

Clean production was promoted. Zhenjiang incorporated clean production performance in the assessment of mayors and combined it with the "striving for excellence" program. It earnestly implemented the *Notice on Promoting Clean Production in Key Enterprises* ([2010] No. 54) issued by the Ministry of Environmental Protection, broke down and assigned clean production targets every year, worked out implementing schemes and conducted publicity and training, which achieved good results. To date, Zhenjiang has inspected and licensed 228 clean production enterprises and conducted clean production auditing of all those engaged in heavy metals, effectively urging them to improve efficiency and reduce pollution. On that basis, Zhenjiang also actively guided enterprises and development zones to participate in pilot circular economy projects and environmental management certification. Today it has 17 provincial-level pilot units of circular economy and six municipal-level ones, and a large number of enterprises have passed ISO14000 certification.

3 Creating Green Mountains and Clear Waters

In recent years, Zhenjiang has persistently guided the revision of various plans with the concept of eco-environmental protection, and developed its long-term development strategy by following natural and ecological laws to lead urban development. According to the bearing capacity of resources and environment, existing foundation for and future potential of development, the city was divided into priority development area, key development area, limited development area and area prohibited for further development. The advantages of each functional area were brought into the fullest play and protection, construction and management became more targeted.

Mountains and rivers are special features of Zhenjiang and the soul of this ancient city. To make its mountains greener, rivers clearer and turn the historical and cultural city into the most livable ecological garden city, Zhenjiang CPC Committee and government decided to invest RMB7 billion in a two-year "green mountain, clear water" campaign to improve the environment of 11 mountains and three riverways in the city proper. Houses on Mount Huashan, Mount Xiangshan and Mount Shizi were relocated, dilapidated buildings that were inconsistent with the plan were demolished, and efforts were made to address landslide, restore ecology and improve scenery. The mountains that used to be covered by garbage became open natural parks for residents to recreate and exercise.

The urban space featuring southern city and northern water was carefully designed. Aiming to create "the most beautiful bay on Yangtze River and most attractive city of Jiangnan" and based on Zhenjiang's unique geography that it's surrounded by mountains in the south and adjacent to a river in the north, an 8.8-km^2 central area was built in the Nanxu new city that served as the new administrative, business, cultural and sports center of Zhenjiang. The 16-km^2 Mount Nanshan became Zhenjiang's largest park and "lung of the city", and Jinshan Lake scenic area highlighted an 8-km^2 waterscape, which created the most beautiful bay on Yangtze River and set an example of ecological restoration for coastal cities at home and abroad. By bringing green mountain and clear water back into residents' life, Zhenjiang fully demonstrated its features as a "city of mountains, forests and rivers" and being "picturesque, ecological and livable".

In the past two years, Zhenjiang invested nearly RMB40 billion every year in urban construction. Xijin Gudu Street, a national cultural relic protection site, took on a new outlook after careful and meticulous restoration, making "a passage through time" a reality. The downtown Binjiang Avenue connected three mountains like three pearls and the old reed beach became a tranquil riverside wetland, and the elaborate west gate of Mount Nanshan made people more deeply feel the mountain's unique charm. Construction of city plaza made major headway, and Huashanwan Plaza and Shanxiang Plaza were fine venues for residents' recreation and relaxation, while road and community greening also made great progress.

After long years of unremitting efforts, the environmental quality in Zhenjiang has been obviously and continuously improved. Air quality is above national Level-2 standard, quality of drinking water source for the city proper is fairly good among cities on the Shanghai-Nanjing route, acoustic pollution is better controlled, green coverage ratio in established areas is raised, urban and rural environment is bettered, and the city's capability of sustainable development, overall strength and people's happiness index are elevated to a higher level.

Chapter 17
Building an Ecological and Happy Nan'an

Located on the southeast coast of Fujian, Nan'an abuts Quanzhou's downtown area in the east, adjoins Xiamen's special economic zone in the west and looks across to the island of Taiwan. It is an ancient prefecture with a history of more than 1,750 years, the starting point of "Maritime Silk Road" and an emerging modern city in the Economic Zone on the West Side of the Straits. Covering a land area of 2,036 km^2, the city has 23 townships and towns, three blocks and one development zone, and a registered population of 1.54 million people. There are also more than 3.5 million overseas Chinese and compatriots in Hong Kong, Macao and Taiwan with Nan'an origin, as well as more than 300,000 entrepreneurs and businessmen with Nan'an origin distributed all over the country, making Nan'an a famous hometown of overseas Chinese in China and one of the main ancestral origins for Taiwan compatriots of Han nationality. In recent years, the overall strength of Nan'an was continuously enhanced. In 2013, it ranked 34th among the top 100 small and medium-sized cities in China for overall strength, 23rd among the top 100 for investment potential, 31st among the top 100 for competitiveness, and 14th among the best county-level cities in Chinese mainland selected by Forbes. It is one of the fastest-growing and most vibrant areas in the Economic Zone on the West Side of the Straits. Upholding the scientific outlook on development, Nan'an strongly implemented the strategy of "prospering the city with ecology" and made great efforts a build a national ecological city while adjusting economic structure and developing green economy. By pushing urban infrastructure construction, they improved the functions of living communities, built beautiful villages, improved ecological environment, consolidated new drive for development, and blazed out a path of integrated urban/rural development with local characteristics as a hometown for overseas Chinese. Thanks to the united efforts of relevant departments on all levels and all residents, they comprehensively accomplished all tasks and passed the acceptance inspection of the Ministry of Environmental protection to become a national ecological city in January 2013, the first county-level city in Fujian Province to pass the inspection.

© Social Sciences Academic Press and Springer Nature Singapore Pte Ltd. 2018

X. Li and X. Liu, *Green Development Model of China's Small and Medium-sized Cities*, Research Series on the Chinese Dream and China's Development Path,
https://doi.org/10.1007/978-981-13-0779-9_17

1 Carrying Out Ecological Industrial Projects

Upholding the guideline of circular industrial development, Nan'an moved faster to upgrade traditional industries and foster high-tech ones, and actively established a modern industrial system. (1) It worked hard on energy conservation and consumption reduction and strongly developed circular economy, took a series of measures such as structural, engineering and management emission reduction, pushed water gas desulfurization and phenolic wastewater treatment in the ceramic industry, and uprated the working load of domestic sewage treatment plants. The city stressed the exemplary and demonstrative role of key enterprises in clean production, completed clean production review and approval for 15 enterprises, guided 115 ones to apply for ISO14000 certification, and promoted clean production to the whole society. Nan'an was titled "Demonstration City for Circular Economy in Fujian Province", 10 enterprises including Haolian Building Materials and Fujian Minfa Aluminum were designated as provincial pilots for circular economy demonstration in the 12th Five-Year Plan period, and Xiejin Building Materials was a demonstration enterprise for energy conservation in Quanzhou. (2) Nan'an strengthened pollution control, integration and upgrade of the stone industry. On one hand, the city stepped up pollution control of the stone industry and regulated pollutant discharge of enterprises in that industry. The 1,567 approved and licensed stone material producers in Nan'an all realized 100% production wastewater recycling and "zero emission". On the other hand, it planned 11 areas where architectural coating and stone material producers were concentrated and two transitional areas for them, totaling 83,800 *mu*, to provide a good platform for the development of stone industry. Nan'an introduced and supported projects that made overall use of rock flour and gravel and prioritized them in land supply. At the moment Nan'an has 135 enterprises that make overall use of rock flour and gravel, which use 2.1 million metric tons of them a year and generate RMB1.56 billion of annual output value, with the overall utilization ratio of rock flour being 65% and that of gravel exceeding 90%. (3) The city energetically carried out pollution control in electroplating, the auxiliary production link for plumbing industry. Nan'an invested RMB520 million in Huayuan Electroplating Zone in Shuitou town and introduced and used China's most advanced "membrane treatment" technology for electroplating wastewater. After technical treatment, more than 60% of electroplating wastewater in the zone can be recycled, its discharge can be reduced by 1.7 million metric tons a year, and recovered heavy metals such as nickel, copper, chromium and zinc that can be worth as much as over RMB20 million. (4) The city emphasized the construction of demonstration parks such as coastal stone industry park and PV and information industry park. Upholding the circular economic model, they demanded enterprises in industrial parks to use land intensively and control energy and resource consumption as well as pollutant discharge comprehensively. They were also asked to develop production technologies, processes and products featuring low energy and material consumption, low pollution, recyclability and capability of safe disposal, so as to achieve clean production, steady and standard pollutant discharge, and industrialized, green and ecological industrial parks.

2 Carrying Out Ecological Agricultural Projects

Making full use of the advantageous geography, unique climate conditions and rich ecological resources, Nan'an vigorously developed efficient and ecological agriculture, pushed agricultural transformation and upgrade, and adopted the path of ecological agriculture characterized by resource sharing, complementarity and circular utilization. Its modern agriculture has been notably improved in terms of scale and competitiveness. (1) Enlarging and strengthening specialty agriculture. Eight production bases of specialty agricultural produce were built across the city, covering food, vegetables, fruits, edible fungus, tea leaves, animal husbandry, aquaculture and flowers. Among them, there is the 18,000-*mu* ecological tea farm and 17 tea leaf producers with organic certification whose total certified tea farm area reaches 4,200 *mu*. The city has 22 leading agricultural enterprises above Quanzhou municipal level, five specialized agricultural trade markets, 149 farmers' cooperatives, 65 pollution-free, green and organic certificates for food, and 10,000-*mu* standardized production base. (2) Taking solid steps to control pollution arising from livestock and poultry breeding. It properly delimited development zone and prohibited zone for livestock and poultry breeding, and made sure all breeding farms in the prohibited zone were closed. It pushed for standardized and large-scale pollution prevention and control facilities on breeding farms. Medium and large-sized pig farms built comprehensive treatment facilities like biochemical and biogas ones, while other breeding farms all adopted ecological models such as "pig-biogas-orchard (farm, forestry)". Pollution in livestock and poultry breeding industry was effectively addressed. (3) Promoting biogas in rural households. Biogas has been installed in 6,410 new rural households, driving them to renovate their kitchen, toilet and pigsty. (4) Promoting "five news" (new variety, new technology, new fertilizer, new pesticide and new machine) in agriculture, focusing on the promotion of new technology, new pesticide and new fertilizer, which resulted in less intensity in the use of pesticide and fertilizer.

3 Carrying Out Ecological Tourism Projects

In the main theme of "successful hometown, new city on the west side of Taiwan Straits" and aiming to create a number of ecological tourism brands such as "celebrities of Nan'an", "religions of Nan'an", "ecological Nan'an" and "creative Nan'an", the city accelerated the integration of ecological tourism resources, strongly expanded the tourism market and achieved flourishing ecological and cultural tourism industry. It has spent RMB370 million successively on protective development and ecological restoration of natural landscape around multiple scenic areas to make sure the tourism resources were sustainable. Those scenic areas included Wurong Park, Lanxi Wetland Park, Liuhu Park, Nanshan Park, Shuitou Wuliqiao Wetland Park, Fengchao Ecological Resort, Lefeng Yinshan Ecological Tourism Zone, Luodong Valley Tourism Zone, Yefei's Hometown Red Ecological Tourism Zone, Mount Wutaile Tourism

Zone, Luoshan Provincial Forest Park, and Mount Tianzhu Tourism Zone. Quality tourist attractions such as Zheng Chenggong Historic Site, Mount Jiuri, Cai's Residence (demonstrating ancient architectural skills), pilgrimage to Lingying snow peak of Fengshan, and Mount Tianzhu Resort are very popular among domestic and foreign tourists. Mount Jiuri was listed as a national 5A-rated scenic area in 2012.

4 Carrying Out Ecological Forestry Projects

The city issued policies and measures to step up the planting and protection of ecological forests. To realize a forest coverage ratio of more than 46.92% and the forestry stock of 2,772,800 m^3, and make Nan'an an ecological city of beautiful environment, advanced forestry, prosperous forest culture and harmony between humans and nature, relevant departments on all levels innovated working mechanisms and forged a stronger sense of responsibility. (1) Nan'an government issued the *Implementing Opinions on Further Accelerating Forestry Development* in August 2013. In addition to provincial fiscal fund, extra fund will be provided for three years from 2013 to advance forestry development. (2) The city promoted non-burning afforestation and pushed the shift from clear cutting to selective cutting in order to prevent water and soil loss and protect biodiversity. Fiscal fund will be provided for three years from 2013 to replace clear cutting with selective cutting. Meanwhile, fast-growing species like huge end eucalyptus and other types of eucalyptus are not encouraged for afforestation to avoid the singleness of species.

Improving the ecological compensation mechanism and strengthening ecological protection in key areas. (1) On the principle of "whoever develops the environment should protect it; whoever benefits should pay the compensation", Nan'an chose ecological compensation models according to local conditions, kept improving government regulation of ecological compensation, gave full play to market forces, mobilized social participation and gradually increased ecological compensation, so as to institutionalize and regulate it. (2) The city actively explored ways of inter-regional ecological compensation, created favorable institutional and policy conditions for the development of less developed townships, and stepped up support for poverty alleviation through ecological development so that farmers could step from poverty to prosperity. (3) The city raised the cost of land use properly by charging forest resource compensation fee, limited irrational forest consumption and guided scientific, reasonable and economical use of forest land. According to regulations issued by the provincial financial and forestry departments, they started charging forest resource compensation fee from 2013 for the use of commercial forests in key ecological areas and provincial-level and state-level ecological non-commercial forests at the rate of RMB30, RMB60 and RMB90/m^2 respectively.

Making overall plans for the planting of ecological forests and promoting coordinated forestry development. (1) Upholding the philosophy that "enjoying both economic benefits and ecological development", the city accelerated the "four greens" campaign (green city, green township, green path, green barrier), and pushed the reform of forest right system solidly. In 2013, they completed 59,700 *mu* of afforestation and greening, more than the tasks assigned by the province and Quanzhou, including 6,900 *mu* of renewed artificial forests, 43,000 *mu* of restored and replanted forests, and 9,800 *mu* of "four greens" projects. (2) The city strengthened forestry law enforcement and supervision and improved the forest fire prevention and mitigation system. Afforestation should proceed in parallel with fire prevention. In 2013, it invested RMB4.059 million in fire prevention and planted 1,090 *mu* of fire-prevention forests. (3) The city strongly called for afforestation. In the past three years, townships and towns (neighborhoods) of Nan'an invested 2.49 million man-days in planting 8.07 million trees accumulatively.

Quickening steps of transformation and upgrade to develop modern ecological forestry economy. The government issued policies to upgrade traditional forestry processing, foster leading forestry enterprises and develop professional forestry cooperatives. Nan'an also strongly developed flower industry, understory economy, ecological forest tourism and forest cultural industry, explored new sectors of forestry and bolstered non-wood utilization industry. (1) Developing flower industry. For three years from 2013, it will support enterprises licensed to engage in seed production and operation to develop floriculture and apply the same water and power rate to them as that for general agriculture. (2) Developing understory economy. Nan'an accelerated the development of under-forest planting, breeding, product collection and processing, tourism, and warehousing and trade, including forest medicine, fungus, poultry, bird, vegetable and bee, aiming for "all-dimension forestry operation with understory supporting the forestry". For three years from 2013, they will support six municipal-level enterprises engaged in understory planting and breeding every year. (3) Developing ecological forest tourism and forest cultural industry. Leveraged on the advantages in forest landscape resources, the city encouraged private investment in ecological forest tourism, planned selected travel routes, created "Forest Home", and fostered ecological tourism brands for forest recreation, health care and experience. For three years from 2013, the city will support two demonstration Forest Home outlets every year.

5 Carrying Out Ecological Protection Projects

1. **Accelerating environmental infrastructure construction in urban/rural areas**

(1) Domestic sewage treatment system was continuously improved. The city built sewage treatment plants in the city proper and was the first in the province to build it in townships. Today a domestic sewage treatment system has been established covering all urban/rural areas across the city, in which the sewage treatment plants in the west and south are in operation and those in the north and east will be put into trial operation in September 2014. It also adopted multiple approaches to dispose of domestic sewage in townships according to local conditions. Altogether 1,113 inte-

grated PE domestic sewage treatment facilities have been installed across the city, and six artificial wetlands (e.g. Lantian village of Kangmei town), four biological oxidation ponds (e.g. Xinmin village of Jiudu town) and two oxidation ditches (e.g. Kengnei village of Matou town) were completed and put into use. (2) Garbage collection and disposal system covered all urban/rural areas of the city. The city built and put into use the garbage incineration power plant in the city proper with the daily incineration volume of 600 metric tons, and built 35 auxiliary garbage collection and transfer stations. "Collection in village, transfer through town and disposal in the city" was comprehensively achieved, and innocent treatment rate of urban domestic waste reached 99.56%.

2. **Strengthening protection of drinking water sources**

(1) Strictly restricting projects along river basins. The city urged for the shift from "business attraction and investment invitation" to "business attraction and investment selection", and prohibited projects that didn't comply with industrial and environmental policies. In particular, heavily polluting industries like chemical industry and papermaking was prohibited on the upper reaches of Jinjiang River. (2) Delimiting areas of concentrated drinking water sources. So far the city has delimited 11 protected areas of concentrated drinking water sources, three above county level and eight of administrative township level, and set up 59 signs in level-1 and level-2 protected areas. (3) Carrying out water supply projects to effectively solve the problem of production and domestic water in three economic heavyweights—Guanqiao, Shuitou and Shijing. The water supply pipes in those three towns totaled 47.329 km and cost RMB368 million, crossing 28 villages of four townships and towns. Phase 1 of the project was completed, accepted and put into use in 2013, with a total investment of RMB267 million and supplying 172,000 metric tons of water per day. (4) Carrying out drinking water projects step by step to effectively solve the safety problem of drinking water. As of June 2014, RMB119 million was invested in drinking water safety projects for 18 townships and towns, providing safe drinking water for about 226,000 people. (5) Intensifying comprehensive governance of basin-wide pollution. The city conducted overall environmental improvement around Shanmei reservoir, water environment improvement in Zhabeiqu protected area of drinking water source at Jinji Bridge, and Nangaoganqu sewage cutoff project. With these intensified efforts to address prominent water pollution problems, the city made considerable achievements in drinking water source protection.

3. **Intensifying prevention and control of industrial pollution**

The city tightened pollution control in industries such as papermaking and ceramics, reinforced environmental supervision and cracked down hard on environmental violations. Main industrial pollution sources reached 100% conformity rate. (1) Shutting down 17 paper mills of backward capacity and completing in-depth wastewater treatment in 18 ones whose production wastewater all met discharge standard. (2) Addressing pollution in ceramic enterprises. The city strongly promoted gas station desulfurization methods, and 48 ceramic enterprises built wastewater coagulation and sedimentation tanks, phenolic water treatment facilities and desulfurization and de-dusting facilities, or shifted to natural gas (clean energy). As of June 2014, the city went all out to promote the LNG substitution program in ceramic industry, and 58 ceramic enterprises completed LNG substitution, pipe laying and gas contract signing, eight shut down. (3) Building an automatic environmental monitoring center, which consisted of three modules - video monitoring, online monitoring of key pollution sources, and downtown air quality monitoring. Altogether 51 enterprises across the city have installed 160 “Mega Eyes” video monitoring devices, and 19 state-, provincial- and Quanzhou-level key enterprises as well as five Nan’an-level ones all realized online pollution source monitoring.

4. **Reinforcing conservation of water and soil resources**

On the principle of “respecting local conditions, taking targeted precaution, eradicating hazards and benefiting the people”, the city made overall plans for mountain, river, farmland, forest and road in light of city conditions with small river basins as the unit and areas of water and soil loss as the focus. It implemented water and soil resource protection solidly with biological measures as the main approach in conjunction with engineering and agricultural measures. (1) Reinforcing reservoirs. In the past three years, the city reinforced 95 dangerous reservoirs including a mid-sized Sunta reservoir, 13 small (I) type reservoirs and 81 small (II) type ones, costing RMB297 million in total. (2) Harnessing small and medium-sized rivers. The city invested RMB160 million in harnessing six small and medium-sized rivers, including Meishan section of Dongxi River, Shuitou section of Shouxi River, Luncang and Yingdu sections of Xixi River, Shishan section of Shixi River and Luodong section of Luoxi River. A total length of 27.7 km of waterway was addressed and 16.9 km embankment was built. (3) Conducting major flood control projects. The city conducted the Nan’an section of Jinjiang River flood control project, which involved eight embankments of Dongxi and Xixi rivers and totaled 34.28 km with a planned investment of RMB555 million. The testing section, namely the left bank of Phase 3 project in Nan’an city proper, is already under construction with a total investment of RMB94.55 million, and 4.24 km of newly built embankments and two new drainage sluices. (4) Conducting soil testing and formulating fertilization. Based on soil fertility and laws of crop fertilization, the city realized balanced use of organic, inorganic, macronutrient, secondary-nutrient and micro-nutrient fertilizers, and continuously improved soil fertility through “scientific, economical and environmentally friendly” fertilization. From 2011 to 2013, Nan’an conducted soil testing and formulated fertilization in 2.13 million *mu* of farmland accumulatively across the city, including 1.2 million *mu* of rice, 210,000 *mu* of peanut, 320,000 *mu* of sweet potato, 100,000 *mu* of potato, 100,000 *mu* of citrus, 60,000 *mu* of tea leaves, and 140,000 *mu* of vegetables. Altogether 36,100 metric tons of formulated fertilizer was applied to 1.06 million *mu* of farmland. Soil testing and formulated fertilization can properly control the amount of fertilizer used, adjust the proportion of nutrients to be more rational and raise the utilization rate of fertilizer. The application of this technology cut fertilizer loss by 6498 metric tons, reduced environmental pollution and was significant for developing low-carbon agriculture.

5. **Stepping up eco-environmental protection in mines**

(1) Particularly enhancing environmental regulation of non-coal mines. The city sternly investigated and dealt with unlicensed and illegal mining and other violations that damaged the mine's geological environment, and resolutely shut down mines that were located in prohibited areas, didn't comply with mineral resource plans, industrial policies or environmental requirements, and had serious safety hazards. (2) Focusing on control of "quarries along roads or in scenic areas". In recent years, the city completed environmental projects in 12 such quarries including the Meihualing tunnel on Nan'an-Tong'an Road, and this year it focused on quarry control along Xiamei-Shijing (towns in Nan'an) Expressway and made great progress. (3) Prioritizing eco-environmental restoration and control of mines. The city formulated and implemented the *Plan for Eco-environmental Restoration and Control of Mines*, strictly pushed mine greening and environmental improvement step by step, and minimized the impact of mining on ecological landscape. In recent years, Nan'an completed greening in right abandoned mine areas including Mount Longfeng in Fuling, Meilin. This year, the city innovated in its work, applied eco-protection technologies to mines in landslide areas for the first time, and adopted "ecological bag" technology to address water and soil loss with Rongqiao mine area as a pilot site.

Chapter 18
Attaching Equal Importance to Economic Development and Environmental Protection—Haicheng

Located in the hinterland of Liaodong Peninsular, Haicheng covers 2732 km^2 with "50% mountains, 10% water and 40% farmland", has a permanent population of 1.3 million people, and has five development zones—Haicheng economic development zone, Teng'ao development zone, Liaoning magnesite new material industrial base, Haicheng agricultural and high-tech industrial zone, and Haicheng circular economy industrial park. It also has the 3A-rated Baiyunshan national tourist attraction, provincial-level Jiulongchuan natural reserve and Sanchahe wetland natural reserve. Haicheng ranks 10th among the top 100 small and medium-sized cities in China in terms of overall strength.

Since reform and opening up, Haicheng, leveraged on its resource and locational advantages and the daring spirit of reform and innovation, has achieved remarkable results in economic and social development, but the conflict between economic and social development and resource and environment is also conspicuous due to unscientific development philosophy and unregulated developing behaviors in the past. As a result, structural problems like extensive industrial layout, high pollution and energy consumption and low benefit were prominent, which damaged the ecological environment to some extent and curbed Haicheng's fast growth. Coordination between economic and social development and resource and environment has become a major issue that Haicheng has to address on the way of transformation and upgrade. To that end, the municipal CPC Committee and government went all out in recent years to adjust industrial structure, change the economic growth model, control pollution and protect ecological environment, and accelerated resource conservation, industrial clustering, concentration of enterprises and intensive urban development. Haicheng has taken on a new outlook on ecological development, especially the coordinated development between economy and society on one hand and resource and environment on the other.

© Social Sciences Academic Press and Springer Nature Singapore Pte Ltd. 2018

X. Li and X. Liu, *Green Development Model of China's Small and Medium-sized Cities*, Research Series on the Chinese Dream and China's Development Path,
https://doi.org/10.1007/978-981-13-0779-9_18

1 Determining the City's Strategic Layout with Scientific Planning and Functional Zoning

Making scientifically plans and strictly implementing them is the foundation for economic and social development and the essence of ecological progress. Centered on the ecological theme and aimed for economic growth, Haicheng municipal CPC Committee and government scientifically worked out the city's strategic and overall development plan, land use plan and ecological zoning plan. The city strictly implemented those plans and any revision could only be executed after being reviewed by the executive meeting of municipal government and standing committee of municipal CPC Committee and passed by the municipal People's Congress, thus ensuring the smooth implementation of ecological efforts.

(1) Working out strategic urban plan. The city hired personnel from Shanghai Tongji University to formulate the strategic urban development plan in light of Haicheng's economic, ecological and resource conditions, and determined the layout of "one body, two wings, mountain in the east and farmland in the west". "One body" refers to the area with An'shan-Haicheng Economic Belt and two development parks (Haicheng and Teng'ao) as the main body and the south-north Shenyang-Dalian Expressway and An'shan-Haicheng Road as the basis. Focused on urban construction, modern service industry and new industries, this area is where most residents are concentrated. "Two wings" refers to "mountain in the east and farmland in the west". The eastern mountainous area was divided into two functional zones. The zone with Jiewen, Gushan, Chagou and Wangshi towns as the main body was the water source area and ecological reserve of Haicheng, where industrial projects, especially polluting ones, were prohibited and forestry, orchard and tourism were encouraged. The zone with Pailou, Yingluo, Mafeng and Ximu towns as the main body focused on mineral product processing industry on the premise of resource and environmental protection. On the other hand, the western coastal zone with Wenxiang, Xisi and Gaotuo towns as the main body mainly developed modern agriculture focused on protected agriculture.

(2) Working out overall urban plan. Haicheng took protecting and building a sound ecological environment as the basis for survival and development and adopted the city development framework of "controlling the east, optimizing the south, boosting the west, expanding the north and relocating from the center". "Controlling the east" means development is controlled in the eastern part of Haicheng city proper that is close to mountainous and ecologically sensitive areas and designated for water source conservation for urban water supply and ecological protection. "Optimizing the south" means in the south of Haicheng River that is located in the upwind direction, the dominant wind direction of the city, industrial land use is controlled, tertiary and logistics industries are developed, and Haicheng River is turned into an inland river. "Boosting the west" means accelerating the Haicheng-Dongsi and Haicheng-Xiliu integration based on Haicheng development zone and Xiliu and Dongsi towns. "Expanding the north" means driving the city's northward expansion with industrial development centered on Tengda Avenue and Tenghai Avenue, and accelerating the

Haicheng-Nantai integration. "Relocating from the center" means given the concentrated population and industries in the old city area whose bearing capacity has reached the limit, Haicheng suppressed the second industry and developed the tertiary industry in this area, and relocated real estate development, residents and fine living elements to Haixi new city.

(3) Working out land use plan. In the old general plan for land use in Haicheng, farmlands were too widely scattered and mostly surrounding the city area, which seriously impeded urban development and ecological control. Meanwhile, land used for construction was too extensively distributed among 27 towns and districts, which didn't reflect the concept of economical and intensive land use. In view of this, Haicheng CPC Committee and government, on the principle that "land plan should accommodate ecology, farmland layout should accommodate long-term development, and quota and layout of construction land should guarantee key projects", implemented and completed a new round of revision of the general land use plan. First, the revised plan was aligned with urban construction, eco-environmental protection and the development of leading industries and scientifically arranged land for key industrial parks and projects across the city. Second, on the premise of not reducing the total area of basic farmland and not affecting the general eco-environment, basic farmland was moved to mountainous areas in the east and key agricultural areas in the western coastal areas, thus being far away from the city and municipal-level industrial parks. This guaranteed land for development while protecting the ecology. Third, construction land was mainly located in new city districts and new towns and leading municipal-level industrial parks to restrict development, protect the ecology and ensure concentrated and intensive land layout.

(4) Working out ecological zoning plan. According to the bearing capability of resource and environment, existing intensity of exploitation and development potential, Haicheng invited authoritative experts from the Institute of Biological Environment of Chinese Research Academy of Environmental Sciences to delimit the ecological zones. They divided land and space into five types of functional zones including that of optimized development, priority development, restricted development and prohibited development, and all approved projects were managed according to zones and categories and put in corresponding parks. Haicheng continuously beefed up the professional team of environmental approval, set up the evaluation center, and stressed the acceptance inspection of "three simultaneous". The environmental department worked closely with the development and reform committee and planning and land resources departments, environmental assessment was in the first round of project review by municipal planning committee, and the principle was established that projects that didn't comply with ecological zoning wouldn't be approved. No environment-polluting industrial projects were allowed in zones where further development is prohibited, like Gushan and Jiewen, and no environment-polluting rough machining projects were allowed in optimized development zones like Teng'ao and Tiexi. By insisting upon green development and guiding the rational deployment of productive forces, the city primarily created an industrial landscape featuring resource and energy conservation and environmental improvement.

2 Protecting and Using Natural Resources with Intensive Development and Economical Use

Economical and intensive utilization of resources is one of the key symbols of ecological progress. Haicheng CPC Committee and government made strenuous efforts to advocate the economical exploitation and intensive use of natural resources, especially mineral, land and water resources, and foster a sound production and living model.

The first is mineral resources. Magnesite is a precious non-renewable resource endowed by nature on Haicheng. Haicheng abounds in magnesite reserve, but resources, no matter how abundant, will be exhausted one day especially as problems such as unregulated and illegal mining and resource waste seriously threaten the healthy and sustained development of magnesite industry. In view of this, Haicheng CPC Committee and government intensified protection and utilization of magnesite resources from three angles—regulating mining, cracking down on illegal mining and promoting circular utilization. (1) Regulating exploitation. The city strengthened development and review of magnesite enterprises' mining plan, conducted dynamic supervision of their mining actions, and seriously punished those that didn't follow the design specifications and gave up low-grade mines for rich ones. In serious cases, their mining license might be revoked. Currently more than 95% of licensed mining enterprises in Haicheng exploit resources in accordance with standards. The city applied mining quota system, monitored mining enterprises in a dynamic way in strict accordance with the annual magnesite mining volume decided by provincial and municipal governments, and severely punished those exceeding the quota. The city also set up mineral product measuring department to inspect and measure magnesite-transporting vehicles. It charged mineral resource compensation fee for crude ore export, and urged mining enterprises to shift from selling mineral resources to selling processed products, thus effectively controlling the annual magnesite exploitation volume. The city allocated magnesite resources as a production factor, promoted integration of magnesite mines and pushed the resource to concentrate in deep processing enterprises more quickly. The number of magnesite enterprises in Haicheng has been reduced from 80 to 43. (2) Severely cracking down on illegal mining. The city adopted a range of measures to crack harder down on illegal magnesite mining, including local town/district taking respective responsibility, cross-departmental law enforcement and dynamic patrol by law-enforcing department. Haicheng destroyed and shut down 220 illegal mining pits accumulatively in recent years and confiscated thousands of mining tools, effectively curbed illegal mining and straightened out the mining order. At the moment, large-scale illegal mining is basically eradicated in Haicheng and magnesite resources are effectively protected. (3) Raising resource utilization ratio. Haicheng's mineral product processing industry stayed in the stage of primary processing in the past because of rich resources, traditional utilization concept and backward technology and process. In particular, some enterprises preferred rich mines to low-grade ones in pursuit for economic benefits. About 2 million metric tons of grade-3 and low-grade ores were exploited across the city every year, but less than 700,000 metric tons were used. A large amount of low-grade ores, tailings and mining wastes were abandoned, which was a serious waste of resources. To solve this problem, Haicheng government issued supportive policies in recent years to urge mining enterprises to adopt magnesite floatation technology, with a view to raising utilization ratio with new technology and process. Four enterprises have put into use their new magnesite floatation lines that float 3.78 million metric tons of magnesite a year, and a large group of flotation projects will come online in the future. (4) In the meantime, Haicheng worked hard to guide enterprises in technological innovation. For instance, Liaoning Huayu Magnesium Building Material Co., Ltd. used low-grade magnesite and tailings to produce fire-proof plates for tunnels and ships and new light wall plates; Haicheng Dadeguang Fire Door Material Co., Ltd. used the same materials to produce fire doors, fire-proof ventilation devices and isolation strips for buildings; and Xingshun Environmental Building Materials Co., Ltd. used magnesium tailings to produce new-type standard bricks. Other projects featuring energy conservation, environmental protection and resource recycling were also completed in succession. Especially, Houying Group invested RMB1.8 billion in a special magnesia project, which used low-grade coal to produce gas and used suspended kiln to calcinate low-grade magnesite into high-quality high-purity magnesium with 3.14 bulk density. By consuming 3 million metric tons of low-grade magnesite every year and selling byproduct SO_2 to sulfur soap plants, this project can recycle 480 metric tons of sulfur dioxide a year and reduce environmental pollution, making the fullest use of resource and energy.

The second is land resource. Land is the most important resource for economic development and the source of ecological progress and protection. Haicheng CPC Committee and government strictly controlled land and ensured economical and intensive use of resources. (1) Rigorously regulating transfer of state-owned land. The city set up the land reserve trade center that was responsible for the transfer of state-owned land, strictly implemented the bidding process and related party transaction in land transfer between enterprises and individuals was prohibited. The city carried out government expropriation of land, especially government-led demolition and open selling of clean land, which solved the drawbacks of the old approach of rough land transfer. Haicheng implemented strict policies on business attraction and investment invitation, made land a rare strategic resource and made it clear that there was no favorable policy on land transfer fee, thus preventing the loss of state-owned assets and problems ensuing from businesses based on zero land price. In recent years, Haicheng registered RMB10 billion of land transfer fee accumulatively, with a net yield of about 40% deducting the compensation for land expropriation and demolition. The net profits were all spent on urban and rural infrastructure, public facilities and environmental efforts in strict accordance with rules on how land transfer fee should be spent. As a result, urban and rural environment was largely improved. (2) Strictly controlling the purpose of land use. The municipal planning committee was responsible for approving construction projects and agricultural planning committee for approving agricultural projects. The purpose of construction land and plot ratio of the project was strictly controlled, and project land was linked with project investment and tax contribution to prevent enterprises from hoarding land.

The city launched a profound and long-term campaign to regulate "five markets" (mainly land market) and conducted "five special programs" mainly targeting illegal land use, whereby Haicheng rigorously investigated, dealt with and cracked down on illegal land use in urban and rural areas and brought land market to the track of standardized and healthy development. (3) Comprehensively implementing the "three relocations and four entries" campaign. On the basis of respecting people's wishes, expropriating land according to law and providing compensation in full, the city implemented the "three relocations and four entries" campaign in a standard way, namely "relocation of residents, enterprises and farmers, industry entering industrial parks, business entering towns, residents entering communities and agriculture entering facility areas". In recent years, Haicheng demolished and renovated more than 50 village communities and relocated about 90,000 people in 20,000 or so households as well as more than 200 enterprises accumulatively, involving 15km^2 land and clearing out 12 km^2 clean land. As a result, the city realized intensive land use, expanded space for industrial development and improved people's lives. (4) Revitalizing existing land resources. The city stepped up integration of type-3 land resources, including approved but unused land and abandoned brick plants, sorted them out by retrieving or expropriating them according to law, and reorganized 5 km^2 land in this way over recent years. For projects with low land use rate and poor profitability, the city applied strict tax levy and tightened environmental and safety supervision to enforce intensive land use. The city particularly initiated the reorganization of type-3 land in Pailou town and reorganized 5 km^2 abandoned mining land from closed mining pits that were unsuitable for greening, so as to put the land back to use again. (5) Linkingurban construction land increment with rural construction land decrement. To build new-type rural communities and raise the utilization ratio of rural homestead, the city linked urban construction land increment with rural construction land decrement. The main approach was land note. The city chose villages with low construction density, large area and high public enthusiasm as demolition area, took urban construction zone and industrial development zone as new construction area, and demolished the old area to provide construction land. In the meantime, re-cultivated land in demolition area was put under collective ownership and leased, and the rent was used to subsidize farmers because their living cost increased after they moved into apartment buildings. Linking land increment with decrement not only realized economical and intensive land use for urban and industrial development, but also improved production and living environment in the countryside and increased income for village-level organizations. This work is proceeding at a faster pace in Xisi's Xiangshui village right now. (6) Pushing agricultural land to the market. On the basis of verifying agricultural land right, the city set up the rural comprehensive property right trading center, and encouraged and guided farmers to transfer their agricultural land to new-type agricultural operators such as big industrial, commercial and agricultural operators, rural cooperatives, family farms and agricultural enterprises through the center. While promoting concentrated use of agricultural land, the city also achieved large-scale agricultural development and transformed the agricultural production model. At the moment, 100,000 *mu* of agricultural land has been transferred accumulatively, and we've cultivated a group of continuous and large-scale protected agricultural projects such as Wangtai greenhouse vegetables, strawberry and Gengzhuang garlic.

The third is water resource. Water is an important living factor that humankind lives on and an indispensable production factor for economic and social development. With 576 million cubic meters of water resources and per capita volume of 508 m^3, Haicheng is a city lacking in water. Especially with rapid economic development and rising population, water resource has become a new bottleneck that restricts Haicheng's economic development and affects people's lives. To address this problem, Haicheng CPC Committee and government took precautions and adopted a variety of measures to rigorously protect and fully utilize water resources. (1) Making full use of surface water. Haicheng has the annual precipitation of 700 mm and surface runoff of 320 million cubic meters. In the past, about 130 million cubic meters of water just ran away in vain every year due to weak awareness of water protection. To address that, Haicheng energetically built and repaired reservoirs, pit-ponds and rubber dams, maintained and reinforced 16 small and medium-sized reservoirs across the city, and built four rubber dams long the Haicheng River in light of riverside development. When all those reservoirs and dams store water, a 16 km-long and 3-million-square-meter water surface will take shape in the river section running through the city proper, which will result in effective use of surface runoff, conservation of underground water source and improvement of the city's ecological environment. The city is also building the Shimenling reservoir in Mafeng with the storage capacity of 127 million cubic meters, which, when completed, will meet Haicheng's demand for urban and industrial water and thoroughly guarantee urban water security for the next 20 years. (2) Making full use of groundwater. Due to rapid city expansion and excessive use of groundwater by urban and rural enterprises in recent years, the groundwater level in Haicheng has dropped significantly. To address that, Haicheng regulated the self-drilled wells of industrial and commercial enterprises, abolished all such wells that were unlicensed, and metered and charged licensed ones to control groundwater exploitation with tax. The city also strengthened the construction of artificial lakes and pit-ponds, and more than 1,000 of them of various sizes have been built in all towns and villages of the city, which are able to store flood in flood season, irrigate in dry season and conserve groundwater. The city also enhanced afforestation in water source areas on eastern mountains with the aim of planting a large number of high-quality trees and conserving water sources. (3) Exploring the use of reclaimed water. Haicheng built four sewage treatment plants in recent years, including one in the city proper and one in Niuzhuang, the former with the capacity of treating and generating 60,000 metric tons of reclaimed water per day and more than 20 million metric tons a year, which can be used for car wash, greening irrigation and business purpose like the production of corrugated paper. To promote full use of reclaimed water, Haicheng CPC Committee and government issued supportive policies and carried out administrative interventions, and guided car washing companies and other industries to use reclaimed water for car wash, so that wastewater was no longer a waste. (4) Enhancing people's water-saving awareness. In addition to stepping up publicity and coverage of water conservation, Haicheng CPC Committee and government studied the tiered pricing system for domestic water use and explored the use of market price mechanism to guide residents to economize on water. This guaranteed a reasonable price for residents' normal domestic water use and set several price levels for excess use. The more water was used, the higher the price. At present, more than 60% of Haicheng's industrial water was reused, efficiency factor of agricultural irrigation water was raised to 0.5, and recycling rate of reclaimed water was improved to 40%. Those measures helped Haicheng gather the resources for future sustainable development, carry out structural adjustment, change the growth model and promote economic transformation and upgrading.

Adjusting structure and transforming model are the inevitable trend of economic development and effective means of ecological progress. In recent years, Haicheng CPC Committee and government held fast to the balance line between ecological protection and economic development, refused to take the old path of competing in resources, worked hard to adjust the economic structure, corporate layout and industrial structure, and comprehensively elevated the economy-ecology balance.

(1) Adjusting economic structure. Following the philosophy of "steadily developing primary industry, consolidating and upgrading secondary industry and strongly developing tertiary industry", the city pushed the balanced, coordinated and sustainable development of the three industries and optimized the economic structure across the board. On one hand, the city steadily developed primary industry. Following the general agricultural layout of "orchard in the east, vegetable in the middle and rice in the west", Haicheng improved agricultural infrastructure and factor distribution, and focused on large-scale, protected, safe, brand-name and processing-oriented agriculture. The city invested RMB760 million accumulatively in recent years and completed about 200 irrigation and water conservancy projects including irrigation ditch renovation. The total agricultural output value remained around RMB7.6 billion and agricultural added value has increased steadily at the annual rate of 5% or so. On the other hand, the city consolidated and upgraded secondary industry. Haicheng invited businesses and investment and launched large projects, especially leading industries such as magnesite new materials, iron and steel, energy equipment manufacturing, textile, apparel, and bags and suitcases processing. In recent years, the city launched 595 new industrial projects above designated scale. There were 583 industrial enterprises above designated scale across the city at the end of 2013 and their industrial added value reached RMB40.1 billion. The city fostered three major industrial clusters with the sales income of over RMB10 billion each, namely magnesite processing, iron and steel and energy equipment, and textile, apparel, and bags and suitcases processing. In the meantime, Haicheng strongly developed tertiary industry. The city made developing service industry the focus of economic structural adjustment, and strengthened the service industry in such areas as specialized market clusters, business and logistics, real estate and cultural tourism. At the end of 2013, added value of tertiary industry across the city reached RMB39.85 billion. By expanding the service industry and reducing the proportion of industry, Haicheng optimized its economic structure from being dominated by industry to a model whereby secondary and tertiary industries press ahead side by side, with the proportion of the three industries being 5.2: 49.4: 45.4.

(2) Adjusting corporate layout. Industries and enterprises in Haicheng used to be scattered, resulting in low sharing rate of infrastructure, serious waste of production factors, lack of industrial chain and inability to form strong industrial competitiveness. To tackle this problem, Haicheng CPC Committee and government, in light of resource reserve and industrial foundation, planned and built a batch of municipal-level public industrial parks to serve as important carriers for industrial cluster development. Regarding agriculture, the city planned and built a 20 km^2 national agricultural science and technology park, which was focused on agricultural clusters covering ecological and organic fertilizer processing, agricultural equipment manufacturing and deep processing of agricultural produce. Regarding industry, the city planned and built a 30-km^2 energy equipment manufacturing park that was focused on energy and equipment manufacturing clusters. Based on the two specialized markets—Xiliu Clothing Market and Nantai Bags and Suitcases Market, the 7-km^2 processing park for the former and 9-km^2 processing park for the latter were focused on processing clusters. The 6-km^2 steel deep processing park undertook businesses from Ansteel Group and developed industrial clusters in that field. The 4-km^2 fine chemicals industry park was focused on coal tar deep processing products, dyestuff, pigment and pharmaceutical intermediates in the upstream, and oil paint, coating, printing ink and new chemical materials in the downstream. The 20-km^2 Liaoning (Haicheng) magnesite new material base was focused on clusters of magnesite new materials and high-end magnesium refractories. The 20-km^2 Yingluo circular economy science and technology park was focused on magnesite and soapstone deep processing and precision casting processing characterized by "energy conservation, emission reduction, eco-environmental protection, circular utilization and sustained development". Regarding service industry, the city planned and built a 40-km^2 concentration area of specialized markets represented by Xiliu Clothing Market and Nantai Bags and Suitcases Market, which was focused on developing differentiated and complementary industrial clusters. The 6.12-km^2 Teng'ao International Resort was a hotspring development complex integrating hotspring convalescence, recreation and vacation, business and residence, and entertainment. The city also planned the Baiyunshan Tourist Resort, where they built major scenic areas like Baiyunshan, Jiulongchuan and Hailongchuan, and strongly developed resort and tourism industry. Haicheng built the municipal public industrial park, for which the government invested in the infrastructure to avoid redundant construction and achieve concentrated projects and clustered industrial development. Haicheng CPC Committee and government especially put forth the "cross-region" economic policy, according to which all towns and districts that had no industrial parks or where new industrial projects were prohibited should launch projects in the public industrial park, and both regions (birthplace and destination of the project) should share local tax. At the moment, more than 90% of new projects across the city are located in the industrial park, laying a solid foundation for shifting from extensive to intensive development.

(3) Adjusting industrial structure. The city took new-type industrialization, service diversification and agricultural modernization as the main direction and worked hard to push for intensive industrial development. Regarding new-type industrialization, the city guided current pillar enterprises engaged in magnesium refractory and

iron and steel to carry out technological innovation and renovation and shift toward resource conservation, environmental friendliness and deep processing. For instance, primary steel processing in Haicheng has gradually shifted to equipment manufacturing, and a group of equipment manufacturers such as Xisi Oil Machinery, Ruifeng Oil Unit Train, Shenche Casting Industry and Zhengchang Wire rope have been put into operation in Haicheng equipment manufacturing park. In the meantime, chemical industry and textile, clothing and dyeing industry are also moving in the direction of fine chemicals and high-end products. To change the industrial landscape dominated by magnesium refractory industry, Haicheng, on the basis of traditional magnesium refractory, decided to prioritize light-body energy-saving magnesium materials such as magnesium alloy and finished products, new-type magnesium-based building materials, magnesium chemicals and other low-carbon and environmentally friendly chemical materials, so as to optimize the magnesite industrial structure with new business forms. At present, magnesium building material industry represented by Houying Thin Magnesium Plate, Huayu Thin Magnesium Plate and Dadeguang Fireproof Plate, magnesium metal and product industry represented by China Magnesium Industry Group's magnesium alloy product project, and magnesium chemical industry represented by Jinghua Mineral Industry's halogen-free flame retardant (HFFR) WPC new material and magnesium hydroxide flame retardant have strengthened continuously. The ratio of magnesium product deep processing has risen from about 30 to about 50% now, and new material industry is a brilliant highlight in Haicheng's magnesite industry development. Regarding service diversification, the city focused on modern specialized markets, real estate and modern business. Teng'ao International Resort is under construction, and famous Chinese real estate developers like Guangdong Country Garden and Qinhuangdao Yanyang have launched projects here. In particular, Xiliu Leather and Fur Shopping Mall was completed and began inviting business, Xiliu China Business Town was completed, and other projects such as Yiwu Xiliu Smallware, Nantai International Bags and Suitcases Market and North China Plumbing have picked up speed. They pushed Haicheng's traditional specialized markets to transform into modern ones featuring shopping mall style and cluster development. Regarding agricultural modernization, the city made great efforts to change the traditional agricultural development model that relied on natural conditions completely and turned to focus on protected agriculture, green and organic agriculture and agricultural produce deep processing. Haicheng has developed 550,000 *mu* of protected agriculture in recent years, fostered large-scale specialty agricultural projects like Wenxiang eggplant and Wangtai strawberry, and created several agricultural brands including Sanxing Jinwanjia Green Vegetables and Wangshi Tianying Organic Pear. Gengzhuang Garlic became a national Agro-product Geographical Indication, and coverage ratio of pollution-free agricultural produce, green food and organic food reached 95% across the city. Besides, by accelerating land transfer, the city bolstered a group of new-type agricultural operators including Sanxing Ecological Agriculture and Ruiya Vegetable Cooperative. Across the city, 172 enterprises are engaged in agricultural produce deep processing today and value-added ratio of this industry has reached 50%.

3 Creating a Livable and Ecological Environment by Respecting Nature and Taking Strong Measures

Ecological environment is precious wealth that Haicheng people live on and crucial guarantee for their healthy life. In recent years, Haicheng CPC Committee and government persistently made up for all environmental deficiencies and implemented four major projects—Green Mountain, Clear Water, Blue Sky and Clean Land—to comprehensively improve the eco-system and create a livable environment.

3.1 "Green Mountain" Project

Seizing the opportunity that Haicheng became the pilot city of Green Mountain project in Liaoning Province, it comprehensively launched the project that mainly included mine reclamation, small-scale wasteland cultivation, greening of traffic arteries and exits, and tree planting in towns, enterprises, industrial parks and villages. So far the city has completed 4,710 *mu* of mine reclamation, leveled mountains to create 1.25-km^2 land, cultivated 30,000 *mu* of wasteland through small-scale cultivation, planted trees in 400 villages and five industrial parks, and built 327 new round-village forest belts. As a result, forest coverage ratio in urban and rural areas reached 32.22%, urban greening ratio 37.3%, and per capita public greening area in the city 8.6 m^2. The successful implementation of pilot "Green Mountain" project turned mines that used to be covered by pits into natural ecological scenery of verdant trees and fresh air, and blazed out a new trail of eco-environmental protection and mine reclamation for Haicheng.

3.2 "Clear Water" Project

(1) Regulating water-polluting enterprises collectively. In recent years, Haicheng spent RMB490 million building four sewage treatment plants, either privately owned, stated owned or operated via BOT, which were located in the downtown area, Ganwang, Teng'ao and Niuzhuang respectively with the daily handling capacity of 125,000 metric tons. Haicheng therefore became the county-level city in Liaoning Province that had the most sewage treatment plants, largest sewage handling capacity and most flexible operation system. It also set up the first Public Security and Environment police station in northeast China, the first association of collective treatment of corporate sewage, and the state-owned Lvyuan Purified Water Co., Ltd. To address the chronic water pollution and consequent cross-region pollution dispute, Haicheng has taken strong measures to cope with wastewater pollution caused by five industries—printing and dyeing, washing, chemical industry, papermaking and butchering—since the end of 2009. While building sewage treatment plants, it com-

prehensively regulated 95 water-polluting enterprises across the city, shut down 21 of them, diverted wastewater from 53 to treatment plants, and held 11 legal representatives of enterprises that illegally discharged effluent in administrative detention. Thanks to these all-round efforts, water quality in Haicheng River, Jiefang River and Wudao River was notably improved and met the provincial requirement across the board. Among them, Haicheng River that was seriously polluted in the past has achieved level-4 water quality steadily, even recording level-3 quality in certain months. Fish and shrimps could once again be seen jumping in the river, and it is now exempted from inspection by the environmental protection department of Liaoning Province.

(2) Implementing the "beautiful river" campaign. The city launched the "construction and steady operation of sewage treatment plant" action. According to the provincial government's requirement for environmental improvement in "Da Hun Tai" (Daliao River, Hunhe River, Taizi River) river basin, Haicheng began to renovate and upgrade the two sewage treatment plants in Ganwang and the city proper last year, which, along with the one in Niuzhuang, were transferred to be operated and managed by Lvyuan Purified Water Co., Ltd. The three sewage treatment plants have now passed environmental acceptance inspection and realized steadily standard discharge. The city built the sewage pipeline network in Haixi New City and channeled its domestic sewage into the municipal sewage treatment plant for collective treatment. It carried out the "outlet closure" action whereby it shut down 12 plastic granule plants and closed all sewage outlets of substandard industrial enterprises along Haicheng River and Wudao River. The city developed the river monitoring and early warning mechanism and river cross-section examination method, designated 25 cross-sections to be monitored, regularly published the monitoring results, and incorporated all towns' and districts' ecological performance into the assessment system. It conducted overall riverway governance action, for which it worked out working plans, set up leading groups, specified duties and carried out multi-departmental collaboration. The city particularly tightened eco-protection of river systems, launched construction projects for water source conservation, water body purification, water ecology and waterscape, and planted 1.44 million *mu* of forests in the eastern mountainous area for water source conservation, which resulted in a forest coverage ratio of 35%. The city planned and built seven riverside belt-shaped parks along the urban section of Haicheng River, including Sanjiangyuan, Lishui Lanwan, Zuo'an Chengbang, Yanyang Huaxidi and Badong Haicheng, in order to reinforce water and soil conservation and effectively restore and rehabilitate the river's eco-system.

(3) Implementing the "water source guarantee" project. The city delimited water source protection areas, set up signs there and developed monitoring accounts for them. It inspected those areas, relocated 19 livestock farms from there and closed sewage outlets. The city set up warning signs to apply all-process monitoring of moving risk sources and prevent vehicles carrying toxic, hazardous and easily leaking articles from crossing the protection area. It improved the *Environmental Emergency Plan*, detailed emergency measures for water source protection areas, and built emergency warehouse so that materials could be used anytime in case of environmental pollution emergencies. It organized technical staff to set three monitoring spots in the

protection area for routine monitoring in order to know the water quality anytime and ensure the safety of drinking water. Sand mining was prohibited and embankment and revetment were built to conserve water sources and protect water well and river ecology.

3.3 "Blue Sky" Project

(1) Implementing collective heating. The city regulated coal-fired boilers in all established urban areas across the city. On the principle of "curing winter disease in summer", it adopted differentiated and targeted measures (e.g. concentrated network, adjusting fuel mix and replacing de-dusting facilities) on 211 coal-fired boilers of 174 entities in the city proper, including heating suppliers, hospitals and schools, service suppliers and production enterprises. Nine residential communities demolished 17 distributed heating boilers and joined the collective heating station, and 38 enterprises and public institutions including North Steel Pipe built 26 dedusters that reduced dust emission by 156 metric tons. Regarding heating layout, the city developed heating plans and designed collective heating pipe network for Haixi New City and Teng'ao New City, whereby Jufeng Heating and An'shan Pingsheng Property Management Co., Ltd. built the collective heating facilities and realized collective heating in downtown and industrial areas of Teng'ao New City. The city also incorporated Nantai and Xiliu in the collective heating plan and pipe construction for Haixi New City.

(2) Launching "Haicheng gasification" project. Haicheng actively urged residents and enterprises to shift from traditional energy like coal and heavy oil to clean energy like natural gas in recent years, and introduced China Resources Gas and Houying Gas of Liaohe Oilfield according to the requirement for "Haicheng gasification". Mainly providing gas for residential and commercial users in Haicheng's planned area, China Resources Gas has invested RMB200 million in building two gas stations and one gate terminal, laying 121 km gas pipeline and installing gas devices in 32,000 households. Mainly providing gas for commercial, residential and industrial users outside the planned area, Haicheng Houying Gas of Liaohe Oilfield has invested RMB200 million accumulatively in building 34.6 km gas pipeline. By 2017, more than 65% of the city will be able to use natural gas.

(3) Raising the bar for industrial furnaces and eliminating backward ones. The city launched the upgrade and renovation program for iron and steel mills, power plants, cement plants and coal-fired heating sources. It completed denitrification and de-dusting renovation of Hengsheng Casting's Unit 1 and 2 sinter machines and Hengye Heating's three 80-metric-ton boilers, and the denitrification project of No. 1 Cement Plant. The city carried out overall regulation of 116 magnesia producers in the city, demanded 95 of them to take corrective steps within a specified period, formulated and issued *Implementing Rules for Atmospheric Pollution Control* and *Regulating Measures for All Magnesia Furnaces in the City*, set time limit for corrections and followed on the implementation progress. The regulation campaign was

completed one year ahead of time. The city shut down 21 home-made calcinators, eliminated the rotary kiln of No. 1 Cement Plant, and shut down 15 magnesia producers located within 500 m radius on both sides of Dandong-Haicheng Expressway that had no environmental license. Following the work philosophy of "joint prevention and control and overall regulation", the city formulated *Working Plan for Dust Control in Eastern Mountainous Area* and established the 24-h monitoring mechanism targeting the five dust-emitting links of magnesia industry, namely mining, smashing, transport, stacking and calcination. It regulated more than 1,100 magnesia furnaces and shut down 96 home-made ones to clear out all backward capacity from the market. On the principle of "three relocations and four entries", the city encouraged enterprises to move to industrial parks, shut down 25 ones and relocated nine ones to the parks, standardized 137 construction sites and material stockyards covering 70,000 m^2, and hardened 34,000 m^2 operation field. As a result, Haicheng has reduced smoke and dust emission by nearly 6,000 metric tons (30%) accumulatively, completely changing the smoke-shrouded situation of mountainous area in the east.

(4) Controlling dust. The city carried out dust control project in eastern mine areas, restored vegetation in Zhangjiagou waste rock field and moved material stock into warehouses. The city hardened 79,000 m^2 of roads and material stockyards in enterprises located on both sides of Donggang-Panshan Line and Dandong-Haicheng Expressway in the eastern mountainous area, and covered materials stacked in 137 outdoor locations of 86 enterprises, totaling more than 70,000 m^2. The city strictly controlled dust in various construction sites and demanded them to standardize site management, and it applied greening and hardening approaches to leave no bare soil on the two sides of urban roads. It launched a special campaign to control dust at coal market whereby the city carried out 24-h monitoring of three main coal sale sites (west side of the train station, railway stockyard and both sides of Haicheng-Youyan Railway) and 29 coal sales companies, shut down 15 screening installations without valid de-dusting facilities, and demanded related enterprises to spray water regularly for dust control. The city also installed de-dusting facilities at Wanhai Energy's coal yard and Haicheng coal market.

3.4 "Clean Land" Project

(1) Carrying out continuous environmental improvement in the countryside. The city comprehensively completed this work in 65 villages of 5 towns (Jiewen, Teng'ao, Gushan, Chagou and Ximu), which benefited 112,200 people. The city invested RMB82.31 million in projects of drinking water source protection, domestic waste and sewage treatment, and livestock and poultry excrement disposal. It built 53 concentrated facilities for the protection of drinking water source and three collective sewage treatment facilities, laid 9,635 m pipeline, and built 3,630 distributed sewage treatment facilities and 1,087 pre-fabricated dustbins. The city handed out 22,166 family trash cans, provided 145 garbage trucks and trolleys, built 23 temporary

garbage dump sites and one domestic waste, livestock and poultry excrement recycling and disposal center, bought five excrement carts and built 597 livestock and poultry excrement collection tanks. Today more than 60% of rural waste is treated collectively, and the continuous environmental improvement raised the villagers' awareness of environmental protection and improved rural environment.

(2) Exploring recycling of livestock and poultry excrement. The city introduced the bio-fermentation technology from Guangxi Laiyuan Biotechnology Co., Ltd. for the project that used livestock and poultry excrement and straw as raw materials to produce organic fertilizer. This project could be located in concentrated breeding zone or livestock farm and turn livestock and poultry excrement and straw directly into organic fertilizer without the need of power or the generation of "waste water, waste gas and solid waste". It was a project of circular economy integrating environmental, social and economic benefits. Currently RMB10 million has been invested in Phase 1 and the demonstration project with the annual output of 10,000 metric tons is already in operation. With a planned investment of RMB25 million and annual output of 50,000 metric tons, Phase 2 is in the stage of land expropriation and equipment processing and the construction is expected to start in March next year. The city also organized departments of environmental protection, animal sanitation supervision and agricultural economy to develop the *Project Plan for Pollution Control and Overall Utilization of Livestock and Poultry Excrement and Waste Straw in Haicheng*. It planned to invest RMB800 million in three years to complete this project and achieve the goal of producing 1 million metric tons of organic nutrient soil. Besides, the city invested close to RMB1 million in a concentrated wastewater treatment facility in Bali town to treat wastewater discharged from Dongbali breeding zone in order to restrict direct discharge to the river and mitigate river pollution.

(3) Promoting garbage recycling. The city invested RMB32 million in a garbage recycling and disposal center in Teng'ao and disposed of domestic waste in the approach of "collection at village, transport through town and collective disposal by companies". It classified the collected garbage, used waste plastics to produce wood-plastic plates and the rest to produce organic fertilizer, thus realizing reduction, innocent treatment and recycling of garbage.

Going forward, Haicheng will firmly seize the rare opportunity of China strongly pushing ecological improvement, stick to scientific outlook on development and the concept of sustainable development, and strive to solve all environmental problems left from history. It will make down-to-earth efforts to push for ecological progress and make new and greater contributions to the ecological development of the province and the whole nation!

Chapter 19
Prospering the City Through Ecological Progress and Achieving Green Rise—Jurong

Jurong takes ecological environment as the most precious asset for development and the biggest potential for it to achieve leapfrog progress. Aiming to build a national ecological city and national exemplary city for environmental protection, Jurong stepped up ecological efforts by placing equal importance on protection and development. Ecology is its most precious asset for development, without which Jurong's competitiveness would be largely compromised. Therefore, the city strongly advocated the idea of "prosperity through ecological progress and green rise". On the one hand, it exploited ecological resources scientifically. It integrated ecological protection with scientific development, made good commercial use of ecological resources by developing modern high-efficiency agriculture and leisure tourism, and turned its ecological advantages into development ones and resources into products and brands. In recent years, Jurong's countryside tourism and leisure tourism flourished and led to the "win-win results" that the city became more popular and farmers became better-off. On the other hand, it enhanced eco-environmental protection. Ecological development requires not only "soft" development but also "hard" protection. By strictly implementing environmental requirements, environmental impact assessment and "three simultaneous" system, Jurong disapproved 10 projects that didn't comply with national industrial policies and dissuaded 54 ones in the past two years, and execution rate of environmental impact assessment and "three simultaneous" reached 100%. In 2013, several health care and old age care projects as well as headquarters projects landed in Jurong for its ecological environment, such as Kangyuan Chinese health care park and Country Garden's east China headquarters. Jurong is establishing its ecological brand of "close to ecology, next to the city".

1 Prospering the City Through Ecological Progress

Optimizing ecological space and fostering ecological security. Jurong continuously strengthened the implementation and management of ecological zoning to promote

© Social Sciences Academic Press and Springer Nature Singapore Pte Ltd. 2018

X. Li and X. Liu, *Green Development Model of China's Small and Medium-sized Cities*, Research Series on the Chinese Dream and China's Development Path,
https://doi.org/10.1007/978-981-13-0779-9_19

coordinated development of local economy and environment. The city scientifically optimized the ecological spatial layout according to requirements for main functional zones, actively pushed Phase 2 of Jurong River Scenic Belt project, and carried out the 236-*mu* eco-plaza project at the cross-section of Ersheng Road and Dongchang South Road. Regarding ecological restoration, they conducted the lakeside landscape project by Chishan Lake, returned fishing area to the lake, fortified its dyke and dredged it, and returned fishing area to wetland landscape at Baishuidang. They restored abandoned pits at the water source area of Beishan reservoir and controlled dust discharge from Yongsheng Quarry to earnestly restore the ecological forest at the reservoir and create a demonstration area for ecological tourism.

Consolidating the basis and building an ecological living environment. The city intensified overall improvement of water environment, continuously improved water quality in the Taihu Lake basin, stepped up prevention and control of water pollution in the Yangtze River, and tightened regulation and supervision of sewage outlet to the river. They made greater efforts to regulate inland rivers in the city, including the Gaoyang River governance project, dredging and desludging of old Jurong River, renovation of the upper reaches of Yuqing River and desludging of Beishan reservoir. They reinforced protection of water source area, launched a special project targeting the 23 enterprises along the irrigation channel, and implemented the in-depth running water treatment project at No. 2 Waterworks, muddy water pipeline project from Beishan reservoir to No. 2 Waterworks, and emergency waterworks project. The city continued environmental improvement work in the countryside and the renovation of old and dilapidated communities. They promoted environmental infrastructure construction, and completed the Huangmei Sewage Treatment Plant with the daily capacity of 20,000 metric tons, the sewage header pipe and lifting pump station in the southern new city, and the 9.5 km pipeline and pump station from Biancheng Prison and the sewage plant. The city implemented the Blue Sky project to improve air quality, improved the regulatory mechanism of vehicle exhaust pollution and strengthened management of vehicle environmental inspection, and stepped up prevention and control of industrial dust pollution and supervision of construction dust. They intensified the project of overall straw utilization and improved the long-term mechanism for prohibiting straw burning, strengthened prevention and control of cooking fume pollution, and accelerated regulation of ecologically fragile areas such as key mining areas and areas of water and soil loss to promote ecological governance and restoration in the region. They enhanced enterprises' environmental responsibility, studied the application of corporate liability insurance for environmental pollution, and pushed environmental improvement projects. The city sped up the construction of municipal environmental emergency center, bettered the system of environmental risk management and emergency aid, and enhanced the city's capability of dealing with environmental safety emergencies. They reinforced comprehensive environmental improvement in urban and rural areas, improved urban greenbelt construction and worked harder to purify stinky riverways in the city. They made active efforts to build a provincial garden city in Jurong, took a series of steps to comprehensively raise the greening quality, and strived to create a living environment of harmony between modernity and ecology and between man and nature.

They also stressed environmental protection in rural areas and pushed the creation of ecological villages.

Stepping up publicity for a special cultural system. Targeting the general public, the city organized publicity events aimed to improve the level of civility of citizens and the moral and ethical standards of the whole society, and make people more aware of ecological protection. They took steps to publicize eco-environmental information with the aim to mobilize all social forces to participate in environmental protection. They established an effective mechanism for the public to participate in ecological efforts, expanded and protected their eco-environmental rights and interests, and made them an important force of Jurong's ecological development. They guided and regulated the development of private environmental organizations so that they can play an important role in advancing environmental protection and ecological improvement.

2 Developing Ecological Economy

Taking developing ecological economy as a key measure for promoting green development, Jurong accelerated industrial transformation and upgrade, and worked hard to forge a green and low-carbon industrial structure. They focused on accelerating the establishment of an industrial system featuring low energy consumption, low pollution and high benefits, and pushed economic growth to shift from being factor-driven to innovation-driven and from extensive to intensive growth, so as to make dual breakthroughs in economic aggregate and development quality.

Focusing on transformation and upgrade and making breakthroughs in creating industrial specialties. Adhering to the main task of transforming the economic development model, the city optimized the industrial development path from a "post-industrialization" perspective and worked faster to make industries more specialized, efficient, resource-light and green. They facilitated the whole agricultural industrial chain. Aiming to build a national demonstration zone for modern agriculture and leveraged on the advantageous industries such as organic rice, tea leaf and seasonable fruits, they promoted the extension of industrial chain at both ends by means of large-scale layout, standardized production, industrialized operation and park-based operation. As a result, they created a complete industrial chain ranging from "farmland to dining table", made agriculture a "promising" industry and farming a decent profession. The city improved the agricultural technical service system, created a mechanism to link technical progress with agricultural benefits, encouraged more technological workers to base their papers on the farmland and provide practical technology for farmers, and solved the "last mile" problem in the promotion and application of agricultural technologies. They made solid efforts to make Jurong's agricultural produce better and safer in order to make them more competitive and ensure food safety for the people. The city made rational industrial layout. According to the requirement for "concentrated and intensive" industrial development, it developed and reviewed plans for various industrial parks, and strived to have manufacturing projects with the investment of more than RMB3 billion, service projects of more than RMB2 billion and modern agricultural projects of more than RMB100 million all in the parks. The city put a lot of effort into creating three specialized parks with the output value of more than RMB5 billion, with the one of green building materials and new road materials becoming a provincial industrial base. In the development zone, they completed the infrastructure construction for the western industrial park and made it a provincial demonstration base for new-type industrialization. Aiming to achieve the sales target of RMB100 billion, Xiashu portside industrial zone proactively aligned with Longtan International New Port City. With green building materials, equipment manufacturing and power as main industries, the industrial zone expanded the scale, fostered strong industrial clusters, and made Jurong one of the "top three industrial towns" of Zhenjiang, a main force for industrialization and the No. 1 growth engine of Zhenjiang. Jurong worked on the special advantages in modern service industry. Adapting to the trend of "slow travel", it stepped up resource integration and development to establish a service industry development system characterized by "pan-tourism" and focused on modern recreational industries and production service industry. They strongly developed the "six-garden economy", namely "flower garden, tea garden, vegetable garden, fruit garden, happy garden and home garden" in the region of Nanjing and the Yangtze River Delta. Striving to create a batch of high-quality projects, they enriched ten agricultural parks including Yanteng Farm, Flower Expo Park and Tea Expo Park, started construction of Phase 1 of Ersheng Lake National Agricultural Park and the sky tower of "Green Beauty" vertical farm, and planned and built the capital-intensive "Heaven of Flowers". Jurong upgraded countryside tourism and steadily regulated land along greenways to make sure the city is as picturesque as European countryside for its beautiful views everywhere. They launched the planning and development of Mount Jiulong, actively built an "ecological green valley", and chose eligible villages such as Panchong and Lita to create a group of demonstration villages for countryside tourism. They worked hard on key scenic areas—Mount Maoshan was licensed as a national 5A-rated scenic area and Chishan Lake became a national wetland park. The city pushed the combination of real estate with health care and recreation and energetically developed recreational resorts and high-quality real estate projects for old age care, in an effort to create a "second home" for urbanites in the Yangtze River Delta and a "new home" for Nanjing residents. Jurong moved faster on such projects as provincial innovation and entrepreneurship base for young talents and Keyi Culture & Art Park, stressed logistics development and fostered new highlights in modern service industry. They upheld innovation-driven development, established the industry-college-research institute mechanism with enterprises as the main player, guided enterprises to invest more in technological upgrade, and supported them in working with colleges and research institutes for technical breakthroughs. R&D investment accounted for 1.9% of total social investment. The city accelerated the construction of innovation carriers. The provincial high-tech entrepreneurship service center was delivered for use, and a new provincial science and technology incubator was built. Jurong established and improved the technology-based financing mechanism, explored IPR pledge loan, encouraged technological enterprises to go public for financing, and channeled investment to concentrate on technology-intensive enterprises. The city profoundly implemented the "blessed land for talents" program in order to attract more high-caliber talents and high-end intelligent results to serve Jurong's development, and strived to bring in 5 talents from China's "Recruitment Program of Global Experts".

Focusing on project construction and making breakthroughs in reinforcing development momentum. The city improved the level of professionalism inattracting business, planned this work with vision, an open mind and strategic positioning, stressed the three links of scientific regional layout, systematic industrial planning and professional team of business attraction, and introduced a number of good projects with integration advantages, core technologies and great market prospects. The city followed closely on prospective projects and guaranteed services for major ones, making sure prospective projects could be signed early, signed projects could be launched fast, and existing projects wouldn't be lost. It divided the responsibility for project implementation clearly, launched a program to tackle difficulties in key industrial projects, strengthened the project association and joint promotion system, strictly implemented relevant measures and forged a "responsibility chain" to guarantee the completion and start of operation of a group of projects. For major projects with the investment of RMB10 billion, the city carried out a contact and responsibility system and realized seamless connection, all-process service and all-out support. It cultivated and enlarged the real economy and attached equal importance to cultivating big enterprises and groups and bolstering small and medium-sized enterprises, trying to enable enterprises of all sizes to "flourish with specific characteristics and through competition". It earnestly implemented the policy on fostering large-scale enterprises, studied and formulated supportive measures to help small and micro enterprises to grow more quickly, and worked faster to create a spate of "champions" in specific industries that were excellent, specialized and strong despite their small size. It is the city's goal to have 600 reportable enterprises (those whose taxable income exceeds a certain number according to standards set by local statistical department) and 50 enterprises with annual sales volume of more than RMB100 million, including two of more than RMB5 billion.

Bibliography

Agenda 21, translated by State Environmental Protection Administration. 1993. Beijing: China Environmental Science Press.

An Example of Environmental Education Legislation in New South Wales. *Environmental Education.*

Bai, Lei. 2006. Green Urbanism in Europe—A Look at China's Urban Development from the Perspective of 'Green Urbanism: Learning from European Cities'. *Urban Problems* 7.

Bai, Yan, Qingchao Wei, and Qingyun Qiu. 2006. On Urban Traffic Development Based on Green Traffic. *Journal of Beijing Jiaotong University (Social Sciences Edition)* 2.

Bao, Hongmei. 2007. Overview of Chinese and Foreign Studies on Environmental Education. *Journal of Inner Mongolia Normal University (Philosophy and Social Sciences Edition)* 36 (1): 54–58.

Bao, Shuangye. 2014. On Coordinated Development Between New-type Urbanization and Ecological Progress. *Qiu Shi* 8.

Cao, Wei, Shenglu Zhou, and Shaohua Wu. 2012. Progress on Studies of Smart Urban Growth and Land Utilization. *Urban Problems* 12 (2012).

Decision of the Central Committee of the Communist Party of China on Some Major Issues Concerning Comprehensively Continuing the Reform. Adopted at the Third Plenary Session of the 18th Central Committee of the Communist Party of China on November 12, 2013.

Du, Liang. 2011. A Brief Introduction to Green Education Overseas—Ideas and Practices. *Journal of Educational Studies* 7: 6.

Editing Committee of Green Education Campaign in Middle and Primary Schools of China. 2008. *Ten Years of Green Education in China* (Introduction). Beijing: People's Education Press.

Filho, W.L., and K. O'Loan. 1996. *Teacher Education for the Environment: European Perspectives.* New York: The Parthenon Publishing Inc.

Goodson, Ivor F. 2001. *The Birth of Environmental Education.* Translated by He Xiaoxing and Zhong Xin. Shanghai: East China Normal University Press.

Gruenewal, David A. 2004. A Foucauldian Analysis of Environmental Education Toward the Socioecological Challenge of the Earth Charter. *Curriculum Inquiry* 34 (1): 71–107.

Gu, Ruizhen, Jingjing Wu, and Sha Luo. Xi Jinping: Building a Beautiful China with Ecological Progress—The 7th Discussion on How to Fully Understand and Implement the Essentials of Xi Jinping's Keynote Speeches.

Gu, Shuzhong, Yongjun Hu, Hong Zhou. 2013. Scientific Connotations and Basic Path of Promote Ecological Progress. *Resources Science* 1.

Gu, Shengzu, and Chao Zheng. 2013. Strategic Thoughts on Enhancing the Function of Small and Medium-sized Cities in Population Gathering. *Modern Urban Research* 5.

Guan, Hailing, and Hongfang Jiang. 2014. Methods of Overall Evaluation for Urban Ecological Development Level. *Statistics & Decision* 15 (2014).

© Social Sciences Academic Press and Springer Nature Singapore Pte Ltd. 2018
X. Li and X. Liu, *An Analysis of Green Growth and Development of Small and Medium-sized Cities*, Research Series on the Chinese Dream and China's Development Path, https://doi.org/10.1007/978-981-13-0779-9

Hu, Jintao. 2007. Hold High the Great Banner of Socialism with Chinese Characteristics and Strive for New Victories in Building a Moderately Prosperous Society in All Respects. *Report to the 17th National Congress of the Communist Party of China*, October 15, 2007.

Hu, Angang. 2010. Global Climate Change and Green Development in China. *Journal of the Party School of the CPC Central Committee*, 4.

Hu, Angang. 2010. Building Green Beijing with Innovations; Practicing and Achieving Green Development Model. *Qian Xian* 1.

Hu, Jintao. 2012. Firmly March on the Path of Socialism with Chinese Characteristics and Strive to Complete the Building of a Moderately Prosperous Society in All Respects. *Report to the 18th National Congress of the Communist Party of China*, November 8, 2012.

Hua, Shuhua. 2007. Implementation of Environmental Education Overseas. *Journal of Educational Development* 8.

Li, Xuefeng. 2012. International Lessons on Urban Development in Ecological Age and China's Vision. *Shanghai Urban Management* 5.

Liu, Qi. 2008. Moving Faster to Build Cultural, Tech-driven and Green Beijing. *Qiushi* 23.

Liu, Bomin. 2011. Transformation from Grey City to Green City. *City Planning Review* 3 (2011).

Liu, Jianhua. 2014. Thoughts on Construction of New-type Rural Community in the Context of New-type Urbanization. *Tribune of Social Sciences* 8.

Long, Hualou. 2003. Transformation of Regional Land Utilization and Land Regulation. *Progress in Geography* 2.

Marx, Karl, and Frederick Engels. 1972. *Selected Works of Karl Marx and Frederick Engels*, vol. 3. Beijing: People's Press.

Marx, Karl, and Frederick Engels. 1972. *Complete Works of Karl Marx and Frederick Engels*, vol. 25. Beijing: People's Press.

Ren, Zhiyuan. 2010. On Development Trend of Large, Medium-sized, and Small Cities in China. *Urban Development Studies* 9.

Shan, Zhuoran, and Yaping Huang. 2013. A New Type of Urbanization: Concept, Connotations, Goals, Contents, Plans, Strategies and Misconceptions. *Urban Planning Forum* 2.

Shen, Qingji. 2013. On New-type Urbanization Based on Ecological Progress. *Urban Planning Forum* 1.

Sun, Xinzhang, Lanying Wang, et al. 2013. Promoting Ecological Development with Global Vision. *China Population, Resources and Environment* 7.

System Theory of Green Universities in China. *Journal of Taiyuan Normal University (Social Sciences Edition).*

UNCED. 1992. Agenda 21: Programme of Action for Sustainable Development. Rio Declaration on Environment and Development. New York: United Nations.

UNESCO. 2005. UNESCO and Sustainable Development. France: UNESCO.

Wang, Baozhong, Shuqing An, Fuqiang Song, Ping He, Zhijun Zhang and Mingyang Li. 2005. Green Space Theories, Practices and Lessons in the US. *Human Geography* 5.

Wang, Rui, and Jirui Yang. 2006. Guiding Urban Land Regulation with Scientific Outlook on Development. *Economist* 4.

Wang, Yuanchou, and Min Wang. 2009. Environmental Education Legislation in Australia, 11.

Wen, Hui. 2010. Sun City: Zero Emission Community in Holland. *Metallurgical Enterprise Culture*, 3 (2010).

Yang, Wanren. 2007. Environmental Education in Sweden and Its Implications. *Ningxia Education* 4.

Ye, Jun. 2006. Ecological Progress on Green Education, vol. 5, 5.

Yu, Huang. 2003. International Development of Environmental Education and Green Schools in China. *Comparative Education Review* 1: 23–27.

Yu, Qingchen. 2011. Green Education in China—Ideas and Actions. *Journal of Educational Studies* 7: 6.

Zhang, Junlian, Xianwen Li, Qing Liu, et al. 2003. Study of Land Regulation Model in Foreign Cities. *China Land Sciences* 1.

Zhang, Xueguang. 2000. International Environmental Education and Sustainable Future—Overview of International Conference on Environmental Education in Australia. *Comparative Education Review* 2: 27–30.
Zhao, Fang. 2012. Urban Green Traffic Development and Innovations in Carbon Finance Mechanism. *Environmental Protection* 9.
Zhao, Shanjun. 2008. *Environmental Education and Its Legislation in Japan*, 4–30. Thesis Paper for Master's Degree at Ocean University of China.

MIX
Papier aus verantwortungsvollen Quellen
Paper from responsible sources
FSC® C105338

If you have any concerns about our products,
you can contact us on
ProductSafety@springernature.com

In case Publisher is established outside the EU,
the EU authorized representative is:
Springer Nature Customer Service Center GmbH
Europaplatz 3, 69115 Heidelberg, Germany

Printed by Libri Plureos GmbH
in Hamburg, Germany